To

....

From

....

Date

....

He makes me to lie down in green pastures;
He leads me beside the still waters.

Psalm 23:2 (NKJV)

Beside Still Waters

Daily Devotional

D. James Kennedy and Jerry Newcombe

Design and composition by Koechel Peterson & Associates, Minneapolis MN.

ISBN: 978-1-929626-78-6

Printed in China

Truth in Action Ministries
P.O. Box 1
Fort Lauderdale, FL 33302
1-800-988-7884
letters@tiam.org
www.TruthInAction.org

Beside
Still Waters

Daily Devotional

Dr. D. James Kennedy
Dr. Jerry Newcombe

TRUTH
IN *Action*
MINISTRIES

The late Dr. D. James Kennedy (1930-2007) was a fountain of wisdom. For 48 years, he served as the senior pastor of Coral Ridge Presbyterian Church in Fort Lauderdale. Many of his sermons became classics, which are still broadcast on TV, radio, and the Internet.

One of his classic messages was "Beside the Still Waters," which invited us, in the hurried and worried state that is modern life, to spend time alone with God each day. In it, Dr. Kennedy urged us to rest and be revived daily by feeding on His Word—by sitting at the feet of Jesus like Mary.

We have aimed to distill much of the wisdom of Dr. Kennedy in daily doses in this daily devotional. Since the sincere wish for all God's people is that we would know Him better, a key component to the knowledge of God is spending time with Him daily in His Word and in prayer.

The format of this book is very simple. Each day has a Bible verse, a short meditation, and a journaling question. It is our prayer that you will seek His face as you read these Scriptures and commentaries, and add your own thoughts—while letting the Holy Spirit lead you.

Soli Deo Gloria

—Dr. Jerry Newcombe

Dr. Jerry Newcombe is the senior producer and host of the television program,
Truth That Transforms with Dr. D. James Kennedy (*formerly* The Coral Ridge Hour).
He has written or co-written 21 books, including 15 co-authored with Dr. Kennedy.

A Special Thank You

This book would not exist in the present form without the incredible help of Kirsti Newcombe. She helped edit everything, making it user-friendly, and she helped write many of the "questions to ponder," if not most of them. Her help was invaluable.

In memory of
Donald E. Van Curler
1931-2010

Longtime Boardmember, Supporter,
and Benefactor of Coral Ridge Ministries
(now Truth in Action Ministries).

Friend of D. James Kennedy
and Jerry Newcombe

JANUARY 1 ═══

Godly Goals

Commit your works to the Lord,
and your thoughts will be established.
Proverbs 16:3

Many people make New Years' resolutions. We see a new beginning and a new chance to make something better of our lives. Our God is a God of second chances, and with His help and in His strength, we will succeed.

We need to set godly goals. We need to lay them out before God in prayer, importunate prayer, prevailing prayer, persistent prayer. We need to obey God with lives that are yielded up to Him, to His will. We will not be successful in doing these things if we are disobedient to God. That is why we cannot expect to have victory in our private lives or our church if we are living in disobedience.

Are we faithful in God's work and are we faithful to our spouse and family? Are we faithful in giving? Are we keeping His commandments and do we live lives of honesty and integrity? When we live godly lives, we will have godly goals.

Question to ponder: What are the five most important goals and plans that you have for this coming year?

....

....

....

....

....

....

....

....

Get Lost

*If we say that we have no sin, we deceive
ourselves, and the truth is not in us.*
1 John 1:8

This is salvation—"And this is life eternal, that they might know thee the only true God, and Jesus Christ, whom thou hast sent" (John 17:3). We are justified by knowing Christ—knowing Him who is the Son of God, the Savior of men; knowing Him who took our sins upon Himself and died in our place. It is through knowledge and trust in Christ, our Savior that we are justified

Christ shows us in the parable of the Prodigal Son that very frequently the respectable and the religious are often the farthest from the kingdom of God. One minister said years ago, "The problem in America is not getting people saved. They all think that they are saved already. The problem is getting them lost." How true that is.

Have you ever been lost? If not, you are not saved. Jesus came to seek and save the lost. The first requirement to being saved is to be lost.

For 24 years I lived without the slightest shadow ever crossing my mind that I was separated from God and on my way to perdition. Not until I came to that realization did the door of God's mercy open to me.

Question to ponder: What does it mean that a person knows he is lost?

JANUARY 3 ⟹   *Salvation by Faith*

*...Even we have believed in Christ Jesus, that we might be
justified by faith in Christ and not by the works of the law;
for by the works of the law no flesh shall be justified.*
Galatians 2:16

When we consider God's laws, we know that it is impossible to
keep them. That is precisely why Jesus came and endured death for us. If we
could make ourselves acceptable to God, His death would not be necessary.
His work on the Cross was perfect, complete, and finished.

I recall reading once of a master wood craftsman who spent months
constructing a beautiful coffee table for his friend. He wrapped it in a soft
cloth, brought it to his friend, unveiled it, and said, "Voila. There it is—the
long anticipated gift."

Though it was indeed a thing of consummate beauty, his friend said,
"Oh, I ... I think it is just magnificent, but I simply couldn't accept it as a gift.
You have done all the work. I must do my part." With that, he picked up a
piece of sandpaper, with the intent of sanding the top of the table. The master
craftsman grasped his wrist and said, "Stop that. You'll ruin it. It is finished."

So it is with the great redemption wrought by Christ. It is done. "It is
finished." It is perfect. We can add nothing. We can contribute nothing.

Question to ponder: Are you sure that you have accepted
Christ's finished work on the Cross on your behalf?

Joy in the Lord

Rejoice in the Lord always. Again I will say, rejoice!
Philippians 4:6

The secret of rejoicing always is found in the words: "in the Lord"—a secret many people never discover. They are, instead, looking for happiness. In this country we are guaranteed the *"pursuit of happiness."* Unfortunately, there are very few people that find it, though many pursue it diligently. The reason is that happiness is determined by happenings. The word "happening" comes from the same root as happenstance.

Happiness is determined by happenings and happenings fluctuate constantly—ever changing and shifting about us. Joy is determined by Jesus, who is the wellspring of joy, the source of all joy.

"At thy right hand there are pleasures [joy] forevermore" (Psalm 16:11). Rejoice in your circumstances? No. Rejoice in the Lord Jesus Christ. That is the secret of rejoicing, of singing, and making melody in your heart to the Lord.

Jesus said that the best reason for rejoicing is that our names are written in the Book of Life (Luke 10:20). That is something we can count on as a source of joy.

Question to ponder: Are you pursuing true joy or mere happiness?

JANUARY 5 ══

The Antidote to Sin

The Son of Man has come to seek
and to save that which was lost.
Luke 19:10

Suppose a man out in the Florida Everglades is struck by the fangs of a water moccasin and its deadly venom is pumped into his blood. Staggering in agony, he collapses and he soon will be breathing his last. Yet at Holy Cross Hospital in Fort Lauderdale there is a locked cabinet, which contains within it the antidote for that and many other poisons. There are no doubt some orderlies or doctors who have the key to that cabinet.

Now any rational, reasonable person will understand immediately that it is the fault of the orderly that that man has died. Not so, you say . . . and properly so. It is not his fault. He had nothing to do with it. The reason that man is dying has nothing to do with the antidote, the anti-venom there in the hospital or the doctors or the orderlies who have the key. The reason that he is dying is because of the venom of the poisonous snake.

Christ came to save us, not to condemn us. For as His Word says: We were condemned already. We are condemned for our sins because of the venom of that ancient serpent that caused mankind to fall into sin and causes us to manifest that deadly poison in so many vile ways in our lives. That is the reason we are dying. We need to unlock the Gospel and get it out to the highways and byways, so that sinners may be redeemed.

Question to ponder: Do you think there's any more you can do in your life to help the lost hear the good news of Christ?

╫ ....

....

....

....

A Year Under God's Protection

He who dwells in the secret place of the Most High
shall abide under the shadow of the Almighty.
Psalm 91:1

We live in a time when fear seems to be stalking the land, even the world. It is a time of crisis, we are told—certainly a time when dangers are very real. I thought, therefore, that we would start the year by turning to one of the most comforting and assuaging passages of Scripture: the ninety-first Psalm.

There is a wonderful promise in Psalm 91. "He that dwelleth in the secret place of the most High shall abide under the shadow of the Almighty." The Hebrew word for "shadow" here originally meant "shade," or "shadow," then it came to mean a "covering," and then it came to mean a "protection."

Those who dwell in the secret place of the most High shall dwell under the protection of the Almighty, and there is nothing that can hinder them, even as the Israelites, when they came forth out of Egypt, had the pillar of fire by night and the pillar of cloud by day. They had God on their right hand and God on their left; God in the forward and God in the rearward. They were guarded by omnipotence and guided by omniscience. There was none that could overwhelm them. They dwelt in the protection of the Almighty.

Question to ponder: As you start a new year, how do you picture God's protection over you?

....

....

....

....

....

....

....

Quiet Time

Be still, and know that I am God; I will be exalted
among the nations, I will be exalted in the earth!
Psalm 46:10

In our busy age, despite all the conveniences of modern luxuries, many professing Christians find it difficult to set aside time alone with God. But the Lord commands us to be still and know that He is God.

Peter told Jesus he would never deny Him, but, of course, when the testing came, he failed. Not only was Peter self-confident and proud, he also followed from afar.

We absolutely need our quiet time with God. We need the time of prayer. We need a time every day of reading His Word. At the outset of this new year, what a good thing that you are choosing to have a quiet time. I hope this is part of an on-going habit with you. But if not, please make it such.

Consuming God's Word through spending time with Him is like eating food. What happens if you don't eat? We become weak physically. What happens to our spirits if we neglect to "eat" God's Word? We become weak spiritually.

It is absolutely essential for Christian growth in our lives to spend time in God's Word and in prayer. We are told to have our lives transformed by the renewing of our minds. As we do that, He begins to conform us to the image of Christ. Spending time alone with Him is a major key in the process.

Question to ponder: When you set aside time to be alone with the Lord, what role does prayer play and how can your quiet time be more effective?

....

....

....

....

Beside the Still Waters

But one thing is needed, and Mary has chosen that good part, which will not be taken away from her.
Luke 10:42

Many people are offended when they read the story of Mary and Martha in the Scripture. I would venture to say that if a hundred people read that passage, they would say that Martha, who is very busy tending to the guests and fixing the food after the traumatic event of Lazarus' death, was certainly the hero of the plot. "Do nothing" Mary, who is sitting at the feet of Jesus listening to Him, was certainly the lesser of the two. Whereas Jesus said of Mary that she had chosen the better part.

This is a lesson that type A personalities need to learn. We need to hear afresh: "Be still and know that I am God" (Psalm 46:10). We need to know that sitting and listening to the Word of Christ may be more important than the activity everyone else may be applauding. We need to learn how to change our thinking about what is really important in life.

All our stress and busyness should be put at the feet of Jesus. When we learn to spend time there every day, to be still and hear from Him, then we will know that it is the better choice. It is the "good part." There, at the feet of Christ, we will find peace, refreshment, and renewal. At the start of this New Year, why not resolve to spend time daily at the feet of Jesus? He invites us to come and sit "beside the still waters."

Question to ponder: Are you taking enough time to be still and be with Jesus?

JANUARY 9 ═══   *Being Restored*

He restores my soul.
Psalm 23:3

It is in the quietness of God's presence that we can find an antidote to the hurried stress of our lives. Sitting there, dwelling with God, we will find body, mind, and spirit renewed.

God said to Elijah, who had just been through a very stressful experience with King Ahab: "... hide thyself by the brook Cherith..." (1 Kings 17:3). That was God's prescription for a very over-stressed prophet. "Hide thyself by the brook Cherith" ... "He leadeth me beside the still waters."

Someone said that he liked to take one-minute vacations to go in his mind to some pleasant place and there to wait. Actually, we need to spend twenty or thirty minutes at a time, taking time to pray, to meditate, to read God's Word, and to let Him restore our soul. You will notice right after these pleasant meadows, these quiet waters, the words: "He restoreth my soul" (Psalm 23:3). If we are to know the peace of God and the joy of God, that is where we will find it.

Question to ponder: Are there any obstacles in your life to spending time alone with God?

....

....

....

....

....

....

....

....

Overlooking Something

But God said to him, "Fool! This night your soul will be required of you; then whose will those things be which you have provided?"
Luke 12:20

Time management experts tell us that we should always be setting goals. I think it was Steve Covey who said, "Begin with the end in mind," and work backwards. That is, think about your death or the obituary you would like to see written about you, and work backwards from that to the present, and so live your life as to try to reach that end. Begin with the end in mind.

That is good advice from a worldly point of view, and yet the error is that death is not the end. Those who see nothing beyond the "obit" column have a very shortsighted view of life, to say the least. They are overlooking something—death. The last word about our life in this world will not be written in the newspaper, but in the Lamb's Book of Life and in the judgment books of God. A review of the last chapters of the book of Revelation puts all of life into sharp focus and helps get our priorities right.

How thankful I am to know Jesus, who forgives my sins and has put my name in His book of life.

Question to ponder: Is death the end or the beginning? How so?

JANUARY 11 ≡ *Doing the Impossible*

For with God, nothing will be impossible.
Luke 1:37

My friend, let me instruct you in protocol. When you are having a conversation with God, there are some words you just do not use. One of them is "impossible;" another one is "incredible." Those words are not even in God's dictionary.

The Queen in Lewis Carroll's *Alice in Wonderland* proclaimed that she could think of at least six impossible things before breakfast. She is not exactly a hero, but it is a great exercise to think of the impossible. Sometimes a lofty thought comes to mind; for example, "I think I would like to build a school." Right at its heel comes the thought, "That's impossible—you can't do that." Usually, that is the end of our impossible thought. But we serve a God with whom nothing is impossible.

Now, at the beginning of a new year, imagine some great goal or project you would like to see happen. Bearing in mind, it should be primarily for God's glory and others' good. Place that goal before the Lord and see what happens.

Question to ponder: Do you have an "impossible" dream?

Justice and Mercy

*Blessed be the LORD God...who has
not forsaken His mercy and His truth.*
Genesis 24:27

Suppose the president decides to pardon a criminal in prison. Do you suppose that the people in America are going to rise up in righteous indignation and *demand* that he open the doors of every prison in the country and turn loose several millions of criminals on the populace of America? Of course not.

You see the Bible makes it very clear about God—and what is true for Him is also true for us—every one of us must be just. We must not act unjustly. But when it comes to mercy or grace, God says that nobody has any claim upon that. He says, "I will have mercy on whom I will have mercy" (Romans 9:15). If it were something that was earned or deserved by everyone, then that wouldn't be mercy; it would be deserved, and it would be justice.

No one has a claim on mercy. We all have a claim on justice, but it is not true that God must give anyone an opportunity for mercy.

Question to ponder: How does it make you feel knowing that God has chosen to give you His mercy?

....

....

....

....

....

....

....

....

JANUARY **13** ═══ *Better Than Silver or Gold*

Happy is the man who finds wisdom, and the man who
gains understanding; for her proceeds are better than
the profits of silver, and her gain than fine gold.
Proverbs 3:13-14

What is the consequence of foolishness, of lack of wisdom, of spiritual ignorance? One thing Proverbs makes very clear is that the result of that ignorance is pain. It is not simply that your IQ is a little less or that you do not graduate *summa cum laude.* It is pain—real, wrenching, oftentimes long continued pain. It is often death with an arrow through the liver, as the foolish bird walks right into the trap. All this, my friends, because one does not seek the wisdom of God.

In Jesus Christ we find that Wisdom has become incarnate. We read that Jesus Christ has been made by God unto us as wisdom, and He has become our wisdom. Fear of the Lord can grow into a complete love and adoration of God, who now has come to live in our midst. If we live by God's wisdom, we will tend to find a good and protected life—not trouble-free, but indeed good.

Question to ponder: How does the wisdom of God make a difference in your life?

....

....

....

....

....

....

....

....

An Everlasting Kingdom ≡ JANUARY 14

Therefore whoever hears these sayings of Mine, and does them, I will liken him to a wise man who built his house on the rock.
Matthew 7:24

Our faith is built upon a solid rock that neither pagan nor demon can overthrow. Yes, there have been small clouds that have come and obscured the sun for a moment. "Julian was such a cloud" said Athanasius, the great defender of the Trinity. (He was referring to Julian the Apostate who attempted to return the Roman Empire back to paganism in 361 A.D., away from the Christian freedom that Julian's uncle, Constantine, had given the Church. Julian's reign lasted only two years.) But the cloud as he said, "is a little cloud, it passes away."

So Julian passed away and all of the critics of Christ pass away, but the sun continues to shine in its brightness in the sky, and so it is with Christ. The critics come, and the critics go, but the brightness of Christ continues to grow apace throughout the world until at last the whole world shall be filled with His glory.

Our foundation is sure. All of Christianity has a strong and solid foundation that will never crumble. Kingdoms rise and fall, but God's kingdom will stand. It is built upon the words of Christ. We can trust that even though heaven and earth will pass away, His words will never pass away.

Question to ponder: The hymn says, "On Christ the solid rock I stand; all other ground is sinking sand." How has God put your feet on the Rock?

....

....

....

....

JANUARY 15 — *Christ Above All*

> *Nor is there salvation in any other, for there is no other name*
> *under heaven given among men by which we must be saved.*
> Acts 4:12

Christ, like no other religious founder, based His entire teaching upon Himself. Every preacher is told, "Do not preach yourself." We have this treasure in earthen vessels; we're the earthen vessels. We are not to preach ourselves, but we are to preach Christ. But interestingly, Christ preached Himself. "I am the true vine" (John 15:1). "I am the door" (10:7). "I am the way, the truth, and the life" (14:6). "I"—Jesus Christ preached Himself. You would think that He was egotistical, and yet He was the humblest of all men. Jesus built His religion upon Himself.

The Mohammedans do not do that. They don't even like to be called Mohammedans, nor do they like the religion to be called Mohammedanism. They want to be called Muslims; their faith is Islam. But we delight to call ourselves Christians, and this is Christianity because it is based upon Christ.

Christ is the only perfect person who ever was—absolutely unique in every way, the utterly, totally sinless One, the greatest person who ever lived and those who have looked at Christ have seen One in whom there is not the least stain of sin, and they have in reflection seen themselves. Every honest person will find that the closer he draws to God, the more clearly he sees his own sinfulness and his own defilement. Jesus is the only Savior.

Question to ponder: In the presence of our holy, sinless Savior, what do you see in yourself?

Seated With Christ

> *...Jesus Christ, who has gone into heaven and is at the right hand of God, angels and authorities and powers having been made subject to Him.*
> 1 Peter 3:21-22

Jesus Christ now sits at the place of honor and favor, not only for Himself, but also for us, because He is our surety, our representative, and our head. Headship means not only dominion, but also union with the body. We are His body and He is our head. If He sits at the right hand of God the Father, we do also. The raising and elevation of Christ is not only for Him, but it is the raising and elevation and acceptance of all believers in Him. For the Scripture says that God "hath raised us up together, and made us sit together in heavenly places in Christ Jesus" (Ephesians 2:6).

Even now, you and I are positioned in Christ in the heavenly places at the place of honor and favor. Even now, in Christ we are seated at the right hand of God the Father Almighty in the position of honor. That is what it means when we confess that He "sitteth on the right hand of God" (Colossians 3:1).

To be one with Christ is an incredible doctrine. That we should be crucified with Him or suffer with Him perhaps is easier to understand, but that we should be lifted up to a position of honor and power with Christ— that is exalting and humbling.

Question to ponder: What difference does it make that I am "seated with Christ"?

JANUARY 17 ═══ *The Whole World Has Flunked*

For all have sinned and fall short of the glory of God.
Romans 3:23

There are so many who live on pure presumption, as I myself did for years. I presumed that I was so good that I would enter into God's kingdom. I did not realize that I was calling God a liar, for He says, "There is none good but one" (Matthew 19:17). I presumed that because I kept the commandments, I would enter into that kingdom. I did not know that Christ said, "Moses gave you the commandments and none of you has kept them." I thought I was as good as many, or even better, and I did not know that the Bible said we "are together become unprofitable" (Romans 3:12). This meant that the whole world has flunked and that I needed the Savior. I was trying to reach the Kingdom through the back door by my own good deeds and good works.

Finally, when I heard the old, old story of Jesus for the first time and understood it, the rock of my heart was riven. I found myself upon my face on the floor, weeping tears of repentance for my sins, and receiving Him into my heart as the risen and blessed Redeemer and King. My life was changed and I came to know—even as a thief beside Him on the Cross came to know—that I would be with Him in Paradise.

Question to ponder: When did you realize you were a sinner in dire need of a Savior?

....

....

....

....

....

....

Be Courageous

*Have I not commanded you? Be strong and of good
courage; do not be afraid, nor be dismayed, for the
LORD your God is with you wherever you go.*
Joshua 1:9

Courage and fearlessness are, and ever have been, the hallmarks of true believers. In the New Testament the Jews took note of the disciples that they had been with Jesus when they saw their "boldness," their intrepidity, their courage, their fearlessness. Those, who but a few weeks before had fled before the wagging finger of a little servant girl, now stood before the Sanhedrin and dressed them down.

What made Joshua bold, and what changed the disciples? It was the promise of the Lord that He would be with them. It was seeing and experiencing the mighty deeds of God. Most of all, it was the Holy Spirit empowering them and equipping them to be His servants. The reason we can be fearless in serving the Lord is the profound knowledge that He Himself is with us and that He has promised to never leave us and never forsake us.

The great missionary David Livingstone courageously went where no man had gone before him in order to proclaim Christ to those living in darkness. He said, "Shall I tell you what sustained me in the midst of all of these toils and hardships and incredible loneliness? It was a promise, the promise of a gentleman of the most sacred honor; it was this promise, 'Lo, I am with you always, even unto the end of the world'" (Matthew 28:20).

Question to ponder: How are you called by the Lord to be bold for Him?

JANUARY **19** ═══

Deliverance

> *Who will deliver me from this body of death?*
> *I thank God—through Jesus Christ our Lord!*
> Romans 8:24-25

What is salvation? It is essentially the deliverance from sin. In our society today, that would seem rather irrelevant because we have gotten rid of sin. Several years ago, a famed psychiatrist authored a book entitled *Whatever Became of Sin?* It has evaporated. Bring up the subject of sin on some talk show and people would look in stark horror at you.

Sin, of course, is any disobedience to God. Salvation is deliverance from disobedience to God. You cannot have a salvation which becomes a license to disobey God; yet there are those who hold that position today.

The great English pastor, Charles Spurgeon, put it this way: "The amazing thing is not that everybody is not saved. The amazing thing is that *anybody* is saved."

Think of heaven as a place where there is not even the possibility of so much as a sinful thought. That is total deliverance from sin. In our lives here on earth God frees us from sin by forgiving us, but He also frees us from committing sins because we walk with Him.

Question to ponder: Can you think of a time when the Lord kept you from sinning?

╫ ....

....

....

....

....

....

....

Flee Temptation

Flee also youthful lusts; but pursue righteousness, faith, love, peace with those who call on the Lord out of a pure heart.
2 Timothy 2:22

We live in a world that is constantly bombarding us with all manner of sinful thoughts and actions so that our consciences become continually more and more desensitized. This is what the world does; this is what Hollywood does. It continually desensitizes us until we come to accept things that at one time we would never accept at all.

"Is thy servant a dog, that he should do this great thing?" (2 King 8:13) says one character in the Old Testament. He was appalled when someone suggested such a great sin. Yet time went by and guess what; he did it.

What a time of desensitization we have been living through. It is tragic. I hope that our consciences are startled awake by the Holy Spirit, even as a cattle prod would cause a cow to jump and run, and we might realize how sinful sin is.

If you're tempted, then flee. Be like Joseph when Potiphar's wife tried to seduce him. Run from the temptation and don't look back. Ben Franklin once put it this way, "Tis easier to suppress the first desire, than to satisfy all that follow it."

Question to ponder: Is there any situation tempting you that you need to cut yourself off from?

....

....

....

....

....

....

JANUARY 21 — *The Biblical Secret to Mental Health*

The things which you learned and received and heard and
saw in me, these do, and the God of peace will be with you.
Philippians 4:9

The Bible says, "Finally, brethren, whatsoever things are true, whatsoever things are honest, whatsoever things are just, whatsoever things are pure, whatsoever things are lovely, whatsoever things are of good report; if there be any virtue, and if there be any praise, think on these things" (Philippians 4:8).

Here we find the biblical secret of mental health. Actually, it is a secret not only of mental health but also of a happy life, of a positive attitude, of a winsome personality, of advancement in life, of acceptance by others. Certainly these are things that every one of us desires. You can be sure that losers and loners do none of these things that are revealed in this tremendous chapter of the New Testament. That is precisely why they are losers and loners. People who are ever-failures in life are such because they ignore, to their own detriment, these great teachings from the Word of God.

It takes discipline to train the mind, just as it takes discipline to train the body. But it pays us back well when we focus on positive things. In the big picture, for the Christian our thinking should be positive because the overall reality is positive. Our past is forgiven, our present is abundant life in Christ, and our future is eternal life with Jesus in heaven.

Question to ponder: Do you find you tend to think positively or negatively?

....

....

....

....

....

Right to Life

> *For You formed my inward parts;*
> *You covered me in my mother's womb.*
> Psalm 139:13

One of the great evils in our time is abortion, and it is done in the name of "choice." The only "choice" the abortionists ever give anybody is "Tuesday or Friday? When do you want to have the abortion?" Any of you who may be pro-choice, I just want to say to you this: "You ought to get down on your knees and thank God that your mother wasn't pro-choice."

It is interesting that abortions for incest, rape, and the life of the mother constitute less than 2% of the total number of abortions in this country, and yet they constitute 98% of the rhetoric of the pro-abortionists.

Thankfully, many Christians are providing alternatives to abortion. There are now more crisis pregnancy centers than abortion clinics. Many are seeing abortion for what it is and are repenting of having anything to do with it. And there is mercy and grace from the Lord for those who repent and call on Jesus.

Question to ponder: What can you do to help those who are struggling with a crisis pregnancy or the pain of a past abortion?

....

....

....

....

....

....

....

JANUARY 23 ≡≡≡≡

Consistently Pro-Life

*Whoever sheds man's blood, by man his blood shall
be shed; for in the image of God He made man.*
Genesis 9:6

I believe the Bible teaches capital punishment and that our crime problem would plummet if justice were faithfully and swiftly carried out.

One time after speaking on the matter of abortion someone said to me, "Do you believe in the sanctity of life?"

I said, "Yes, I do."

"Then I assume you are against capital punishment."

"No, I'm not."

"Why not? You're not being consistent."

"No sir. You are not being consistent. I believe in the sanctity of life and it is simply because man was made in the image of God that God declared, 'Whoso sheddeth man's blood, by man shall his blood be shed.' And we know that the nature of the punishment fits the heinousness of the crime."

Is it not strange that those who speak most loudly in favor of abortion and infanticide and euthanasia are the people who are usually most opposed to capital punishment? They are willing to kill the innocent, but they are not willing to kill the guilty. That is inconsistency. As someone said, "It is interesting that today we kill our babies and baby our killers."

Question to ponder: What are your thoughts on capital punishment?

⑃· ....

....

....

....

....

Teaching Diligently

And these words which I command you today shall be in your heart. You shall teach them diligently to your children, and shall talk of them when you sit in your house, when you walk by the way, when you lie down, and when you rise up.
Deuteronomy 6:6-7

The Bible says, "Train up a child in the way he should go: and when he is old, he will not depart from it" (Proverbs 22:6). I think it needs to be made very clear what God is talking about here.

Someone said, "I can't understand it. What did I do wrong? My son is involved in dope, sin, adultery, and rebellion. I can't understand it. I trained him up in the way he should go. I sent him to Sunday school every week."

It's great to send your children to Sunday school, but if that's all you did, it wouldn't be enough. The Old Testament makes it abundantly plain that parents have a duty to train their children in the home daily.

However, if you did all you could to teach and guide, pray for and pray with your child, and that child is a prodigal, take heart. God Himself is portrayed by Jesus in Luke 15 as the Father of the Prodigal Son. Do what He did, watch, wait, pray, and remember that the end of the story is yet to be told.

If you still have a chance, use every opportunity, when you walk and talk, day and night, to teach and, above all, to live out God's Word before your children.

Question to ponder: What can you do in your family situation to strengthen your family's relation to the Lord?

....

....

....

....

Avoiding Church

*Not forsaking the assembling of ourselves together, as
is the manner of some, but exhorting one another, and
so much the more as you see the Day approaching.*
Hebrews 10:25

Many people offer a multitude of reasons as to why they don't go to church. But they tend to gloss over the real reason. They don't want to go.

I talked to a man one time who told me all the reasons why he didn't go to church: he'd rather stay home and read the funny paper, he had to work . . . he had all sorts of excuses. I said, "Would you like for me to tell you the real reason you don't go to church?"

He was startled, but he said, "Yes."

I said, "All right. This is the *real* reason why you don't go to church: Very simply, it is because you have never been born again."

Many people think you don't have to go church to be a Christian. But if Christ is truly in you, you will want to go to church. Corporate worship is for our benefit. We need each other in the Body of Christ. As logs in a fire need to stay together to burn, so a log by itself will see its fire go out. We are a body of believers, and none of us can function alone.

Question to ponder: Is there more you could do with your own church experience to get more out of it?

Winners and Losers

A bruised reed He will not break,
and a smoking flax He will not quench.
Isaiah 42:3

Are you a winner or a loser? It's obvious which is preferable. But I'm certain there are some who feel they are born losers. Maybe they didn't do well in school; they embarrassed themselves and perhaps their parents. They haven't done well in the workplace, having perhaps been fired from numerous jobs. Even their home life has not worked out so well. It seems like they just can't do anything right. They have two left feet. They are ambidextrous, but neither one of their hands works well.

And yet, my friend, take heart. God did not make you to be a loser. He created you to be a winner, and that is what He is able to make you into. God made us for His purpose and when we feel discouraged and sad about our lives, we can be reassured that He is the perfecter of our lives, our faith, our past, and our future.

Sometimes we feel weak and powerless. Sometimes we feel worn out and as burned out as a smoldering wick. It is in our weakness that we can find His love and in our need that we find our God to be all sufficient. Let God bind your broken heart and watch Him make you whole again.

Question to ponder: What are the broken pieces in your life? Hand them over to the Lord today.

....

....

....

....

....

....

JANUARY 27 *Cast Your Burden on the Lord*

*Come to Me, all you who labor and are
heavy laden, and I will give you rest.*
Matthew 11:28

Jesus is inviting us to come to Him with our burdens, to take our troubles to the foot of the cross and lay them down.

One verse I particularly like is found in I Peter 5:7 where he says: "Casting all your care upon him; for he careth for you." The Greek verb used here for casting shows a person with a great burden on his back, coming to Christ and rolling that burden off into the arms of Jesus.

What burden is right now weighing you down, tensing your muscles, robbing you of your serenity? Cast all your care upon Him.

It seems so simple to take it all to Jesus. It is simple, but it is not easy. We tend to take our problems to the Lord, then five minutes later we go back and pick them up to carry them again. If we shall learn to leave them there at the foot of the cross, we must learn to trust Him. Instead of picking our burden back up, we must say, "I have given this burden to the Lord. It is in His capable hands, and I can leave them there." That is how we find rest.

Question to ponder: What are the burdens you are carrying today? Take them to the foot of the cross and leave them there.

A New Nature

*Therefore, if anyone is in Christ, he is a
new creation; old things have passed away;
behold, all things have become new.*
2 Corinthians 5:17

Can the leopard change its spots? Can the Ethiopian change his skin? Of course not. No more than human beings can change their nature; but that is precisely what Christ does. He doesn't merely change our outward behavior; He changes our nature. He comes within us and plants therein a new man and a new nature—a new creation created by God—a new you.

In Christ, we now desire things we didn't desire before. Christ did that to me. God placed a screwdriver in my "wanter" and turned it upside down, and to my utter amazement, I now wanted things I had never wanted before.

Charles Spurgeon said that if you were to take a hog out of the mud and the mire, out of the trough and the herd, and by some magic wand transform him into a prince sitting upon a throne, he would not be changed as much as when God Almighty by His grace transforms a depraved sinner into a prince of the Royal Realm. He is now a child of the King of kings, living in a dominion that has neither end nor limit of extent.

Question to ponder: How can your new nature be nourished today?

The Fear of God

The fear of the LORD is the beginning of wisdom,
and the knowledge of the Holy One is understanding.
Proverbs 9:10

We hardly ever hear any more that so-and-so is "a God-fearing person." What has happened to "the fear of God" in our land, much less in many of our churches? Jesus said that we should fear God. We should fear God, not for fear of punishment (Jesus has taken our punishment), but for fear of disappointing Him. We may be forgiven, yet still bear the scars for our sins. We should fear the results of sin in our lives.

If you had a father who loved you, you can remember that at times he chastened you. And if your Father in Heaven has received you, He has also chastened you. I can add my testimony to that of thousands of others who have lived in past centuries and say that the chastening of the Lord is not pleasant. I have experienced it as you have. Indeed, I can say: "I fear the rod of my Father." But that is a wholesome fear.

In a world that has come to the place where it despises authority and rebels against parents and schools, state and police, and everything else, it is well that we be reminded that it is good for us to have a reverential awe and fear of the great and holy God who has made us. This fear is elicited when we contemplate sin and not when we contemplate our Father, for there His love also draws us.

Question to ponder: The love and the fear of God—what is the relationship between the two?

....

....

....

....

The Bride of Christ

*Blessed are those who are called to
the marriage supper of the Lamb!*
Revelation 19:9

Did you ever consider the fact that marriage is a major theme of the Bible? One theologian noted that the Bible opens with a marriage, and it closes with one. Jesus is the bridegroom who left heaven to seek out a bride. When we become believers in Him, we become part of the bride of Christ.

Marriage was God's idea in the first place. Marriage is above all a picture of Christ and His bride, the Church. Perhaps this is why Satan aims his big guns at marriage, to tear it down any way he can.

In the Old Testament it was a great disgrace for a wife to be barren. Many a wife lamented and wept over her barrenness. We are the bride of Jesus Christ. He is our bridegroom. It is even more disgraceful to be *spiritually* barren, and yet how many Christians weep over their barrenness?

It is a great honor for a Christian to have spiritual children, as well as physical children—our spiritual children being those we have led to Christ. It is a great privilege as Christ's bride to invite others also to participate in the marriage supper of the Lamb. True Christian marriages proclaim God's plan to the world and benefit all who partake in it.

Question to ponder: What can we do to strengthen our marriages so they truly proclaim God's plan to the world?

....

....

....

....

....

JANUARY **31** ═══ *The Blessing of Children*

> *Behold, children are a heritage from the LORD,*
> *the fruit of the womb is a reward.*
> Psalm 127:3

If there is one thing which is made abundantly clear, both in the Old and New Testaments, it is that children are a gift from God. They are loaned to us for a little while and we, as parents, are responsible for giving them a godly education. We are to rear them in the nurture and admonition of the Lord—that line upon line, precept upon precept, His truth is to be taught to them.

In our society, children are not always looked upon as a blessing. But God's Word is clear. The psalmist goes on to say, "Happy is the man that has his quiver full of them." To have children is a wonderful gift and a great opportunity to be a part of God's creative process.

If you have children, thank Him for them daily and ask constantly for His help to raise them. Jesus promised to lead gently those sheep who have lambs.

Question to ponder: Take some time to reflect upon the gift of children and pray for your own children or for a child who is special to you. How can you bless him or her today?

....

....

....

....

....

....

....

The Greatest Promise

*And we know that **all things** work together for good to those who love God, to those who are the called according to His purpose.*
Romans 8:28

This is one of the greatest texts in all Scripture: "All things work together for good to them who love God." No other text covers as much territory; no other text offers any more than that; no other text conveys such hope and such comfort as that. Unfortunately, for many people, no other text seems more difficult to believe. In face of all of the problems that we know in this life, some would say it cannot possibly be true.

Paul never said that everything was good. Indeed, there are many things in this world which are anything but good—terrible diseases, drastic accidents, wars, hurricanes and earthquakes are certainly anything but good. They are ghastly and horrible things. And yet God has made it plain in this text that whatever event—however grim, however ghastly, however calamitous it may be in itself—as soon as it touches your life the hand of the Almighty will reach down and take it captive and hold it ransom. And God will not let it go until it yields up its treasure to your soul. That is the promise of the Almighty.

Question to ponder: Are there some difficult circumstances in your life right now? Does it change your perspective to know God will bring good out of them?

....

....

....

....

....

FEBRUARY 2 — *A Hostile or a Friendly Universe?*

And we know that all things work together
for good *to those who love God, to those who*
are the called according to His purpose.
Romans 8:28

We live in what appears to be a very hostile universe. Just a few thousand feet beneath us is molten lava waiting to consume us. A few thousand feet above us there are deadly cosmic rays that would slay us in a moment. The entire universe is governed by the basic law of entropy, which is determined to crush us in the final extinction of all things. This world is filled with war and pestilence and famine, sickness, disease, decay, and death. How can we say that all things are working together for good?

God is the One who is supernaturally working all things together for our good. They don't just happen naturally. But God, the great Almighty alchemist, is taking whatever ingredients that come into our life, and working them for our good. All things, whatever they may be.

Question to ponder: Is your universe hostile or friendly? How about in the light of Romans 8:28?

....

....

....

....

....

....

....

....

God's Synergy

*And we know that all things **work together** for good to those who love God, to those who are the called according to His purpose.*
Romans 8:28

A physician may prescribe some medicine for us. Previously, when we would take the prescription to a pharmacist, he would gather the various chemicals from his shelves and with mortar and pestle he'd begin to mix them together. Now the interesting thing is that not infrequently there might be found among those various ingredients things which, of themselves, would be quite deleterious to your health, if not in fact, fatal. For example, arsenic is found in many medicines and yet if you were to take it by itself it would kill you. But when all the ingredients in the prescription are mixed together, they provide something that is beneficial to your health and produces healing. So it is in our lives.

The Great Physician is at work in our lives, causing all things to work together for good for those who know Him and are called by Him. The root Greek word for "working all things together" is *synergeo,* from which we get the word synergy. Romans 8:28 speaks of God's synergy.

Question to ponder: Can you think of a recent example in your life where God worked all things together for your good?

⁂ ....

....

....

....

....

....

FEBRUARY 4

Don't Miss the Ending

Being confident of this very thing, that He who has begun a good work in you will complete it until the day of Jesus Christ.
Philippians 1:6

Once a man went to see a play in three acts. He came back and recommended it to a friend and said, "It was a marvelous play. You will just love it. It is so uplifting and exhilarating. You will be greatly encouraged." So his friend went to see it.

The next day the man saw his friend and said, "Well, how did you like it?" "How did I like it? I hated it. I thought it was just terrible. How could you possibly have thought that a play like that was good? Why, the child was kidnapped, the father lost his job, and the mother was in the hospital. I was terribly depressed. How could you possibly have thought that a play like that was good?" The man said, "But that's not the way it ended." Then his friend said, "Oh, I don't know how it ended. I got so depressed I left after the second act."

Well, my friends, there is a final act to life. We pass through a curtain that leads us to the final act of the drama of God's redemption. Without our belief in that we could not believe that all things will ultimately work together for our good. If you're a Christian, God is at work in your life. Paul promises that He who began a good work in us will complete it until the day of Christ Jesus. This good news puts everything in our lives in perspective and gives us great hope for those who are now fallen away from the truth.

Question to ponder: Do you remember some of the things God did when He began the good work in your life?

The Big Lie

By the word of the LORD the heavens were made,
and all the host of them by the breath of His mouth.
Psalm 33:6

Evolution simply says that the whole universe is made up of nothing but matter; that matter, time, and chance—the trinity of materialism—have brought all things into existence and, therefore, there is no God. A great multitude of people believe this because it is what they have been taught. The results of this teaching have been devastating.

The root of the problem of most of the great ills that have afflicted society and still afflict it today is the teaching of evolution. It has been called "The Big Lie." It has deceived hundreds of millions of people and has probably brought about more deaths than any other view in the history of the world.

For example, Adolf Hitler and the Nazis were committed Darwinists. They were trying to speed up evolution by creating a master race. They exterminated millions of "undesirables" because they viewed them as genetically inferior—this included Jews (the largest sub-group of victims of the Holocaust), Gypsies, Slavs, and others. The Holocaust was "Darwinism on steroids."

But God has revealed Himself in His creation and in His Word. What a difference a worldview can make in society.

Question to ponder: What would be the value of human life if evolution were true?

FEBRUARY 6 ═══   *A Godless Universe?*

For He spoke, and it was done;
He commanded, and it stood fast.
Psalm 33:9

Whether God created the universe or not makes all the difference in the world. It is not true that all scientists believe in evolution. The
teaching of the "godless universe" has ramifications beyond the world of
science.

One scientist who is a Christian observes, "Parents can work hard to
educate their children to be patriots and morally upright citizens. But four
years of college of the kind I experienced—where I was surrounded by a
culture of drugs, sexual libertinism, political radicalism and little home-
work—can destroy the efforts of the best parents in America."

If that doesn't do it, he says a couple of years of graduate school are
almost certain to destroy any remaining vestige of belief in God, moral absolutes, morality, Americanism, patriotism, or any other of our values. That,
my friends, is the consequence of the teaching of evolution in our public
schools and universities and colleges—like the one this scientist attended. It
has made them a mortal danger to the lives and souls of young people and
brought tragic consequences.

Question to ponder: How does a godless
outlook affect morals?

A Real Live Saint

To all the saints in Jesus Christ who are in Philippi....
Philippians 1:1

While visiting recently with a couple who did not know Christ, we talked about what a Christian was and I said, "Have you ever met a real live saint?" They assured me they hadn't.

"Well," I said, "how would you like to meet one?"

They asked, "Do you know one?"

I said, "Yes, I do. In fact, there is one right here today." I reached out my hand and said, "Meet Saint James, for I am a Saint. Every Christian is a saint, set aside, sanctified unto God, as kings and princes unto God our Father."

This sainthood is achieved not by our own righteousness, but by the righteousness of Christ alone. Therefore, a saint is a forgiven sinner. God makes us saints by His Holy Spirit, forming us into His image. A saint is a person who is set apart for God's use, a person who is being sanctified. A saint is a person who belongs to Jesus Christ, and that is who we are.

Question to ponder: Could you live differently before the watching world today, knowing that you are indeed a saint?

FEBRUARY 8 ═══

The Salt of the Earth

You are the salt of the earth; but if the salt loses its flavor, how shall it be seasoned? It is then good for nothing but to be thrown out and trampled underfoot by men.
Matthew 5:13

Unfortunately, a lot of people don't want to get out of their "salt-shakers." They are very comfortable. Why some of them even have stained glass walls. These people don't want to get in contact with the "meat," because maybe it is already beginning to get rotten and corrupted. They don't want to get their hands on it, and so they avoid it. They are not functioning as salt.

Salt has a number of qualities. It stings. If you get salt in a wound, you will know it is there. Salt also heals. We are to be the healing work of Christ in the world, and that does sting. Sometimes people don't like the thought of causing that uncomfortable feeling, and so they don't get involved with that healing work of Christ.

Another thing salt does is to bring out the flavor in many dishes. That is what Christians should do. Salt also, of course, preserves. We, as Christians, are called to preserve that which is best in our culture. We are called to be salt, to go out and bring out the best in others.

Question to ponder: Can you think of a recent time where you or some other believer has acted as salt in our decaying culture?

....

....

....

....

....

Justified ≡ FEBRUARY 9

Knowing that a man is not justified by the
works of the law but by faith in Jesus Christ.
Galatians 2:16

If God had called us to climb Mt. Everest in order that we might have eternal life, there would be millions lined up to try it. But He calls us to no such arduous task as that, but to a simple trust in Christ as our Savior. To do that, we must realize that we are unworthy and undeserving. We do not merit eternal life, and it is, therefore, a humbling experience to receive Christ. We must acknowledge our sin; we must acknowledge our unworthiness; we must acknowledge our guilt, and cast ourselves upon Him and His mercy.

When we realize that the law, and all the works of keeping the law, won't make us right with God, we are ready to have our own self-righteousness smashed. As we come to Jesus Christ, we can be justified—made right with God. This is justification—that God out of His mercy forgives us our sins, clothes us in the righteousness of Christ and looks at us through Him, as if we had never sinned.

Question to ponder: Picture yourself clean and beautiful before God in Christ Jesus. What is your response?

....

....

....

....

....

....

....

FEBRUARY 10 ===

Holiness and Happiness

*Just as He chose us in Him before the foundation
of the world, that we should be holy and without
blame before Him in love.*
Ephesians 1:4

I know a friend who just went through major surgery and then, after
he was home and thought all was well, a massive infection was found. The
doctors had to go back in and cleanse that out. That is like sanctification.
Sanctification deals with corruption. A beautiful apple, when cut in half,
reveals one dark spot. It is obviously rotten, and the spot must be cut out.
God is purifying us in this life through sanctification.

The holiness of God is imparted to us by faith as we trust in Him, and
His holiness is infused into us gradually in sanctification, as we become
more and more pure. We need to pray that the impartation of the holiness
of Christ might be ours. We need to pray that God would make us holy
people. You can be sure that as you become holier, you will become happier
in your life. We will never be completely holy before we reach heaven, but
the furthest we can come is the longing to be more holy. The strange fact is
that the more holy we are, the less we will be concerned with our own holiness and more concerned with the welfare of others.

Question to ponder: How is it that the more focused
we are on others, the happier we find ourselves?

....
....
....
....
....
....

Serving Self or Serving Others? — FEBRUARY 11

So He said, "Truly I say to you that this poor widow has put in more than all; for all these out of their abundance have put in offerings for God but she out of her poverty put in all the livelihood that she had."
Luke 21:3-4

Psychologist Abraham Maslow claimed that those who demonstrate the greatest amount of self-love and have the highest self-esteem exercise dominance. In any relationship—a husband and a wife, two friends, or business partners—if one of them has a higher opinion of himself or herself than the other, the one with the highest amount of self-love will dominate. There will often be arrogance. There will be exploitive aspects involved. It does not necessarily follow that the dominant one will love the other.

Which one is able to help other people more? A man who spends all day long in a gym working out with weights, developing huge muscles, standing before the tanning machines, admiring his biceps, or a person who is poor and weak and frail and unmuscular?

I am not sure the answer is clear. It may be that a strong person is more capable of helping people. It may be that Arnold Schwarzenegger is more capable of helping people than Mother Teresa was. However, it doesn't at all follow logically that he *has* helped more people than she has. Many of the world's greatest people have been people who have not been strong, muscular, and healthy at all, but they have sought to do for the Lord the best they could. The key is to serve others, including the widow and orphan, whenever we can.

Question to ponder: Are you taking the opportunities you get to serve the Lord and others?

FEBRUARY 12 ⸺

Refined by Fire

*...That the genuineness of your faith, being much
more precious than gold that perishes, though it is
tested by fire, may be found to praise, honor, and
glory at the revelation of Jesus Christ.*
1 Peter 1:7

One of America's greatest presidents was born on this day. Although
he entered the White House as a non-believer, by the time of Gettysburg,
there is strong evidence he had met the Savior (especially when seeking
solace after the death of his beloved son).

Jesus was on the mind of Lincoln when he died. You history buffs will
remember that 1865 was the year that the Civil War ended. In that same
year, on Good Friday, Abraham Lincoln, sixteenth President of these United
States, died. He was sitting in a box in Ford's Theater, not listening to the
play, but talking to his wife. He uttered his last words. "Mary, now that the
war is over, [it was just over that day] what I would like to do more than
anything in the world is to take you on a trip to the Near East. We could go
to Palestine. We could go to Galilee where He walked. We could go to Bethlehem, and then we could go up to Jeru-."

BANG. The shot rang out that was also heard around the world and
ended the life of Abraham Lincoln. The last phrase, not quite completed,
from his lips was, "We could go to Jeru[salem]." He never did...in this life.

He became a great president because he was tested by fire. Great and
hard-earned wisdom was found in him, as he let the refining work of God's
Spirit ultimately mold his life.

Question to ponder: When God's refining fire
touches your life, what is your response?

⫘ ....

....

....

The Source of Love

Beloved, if God so loved us,
we also ought to love one another.
1 John 4:11

God is the source of all love in this world. More than that, He is love. Whenever people love each other in word or in deed, wherever people learn to put others first, there God is present. There is the Spirit of Jesus.

No man ever loved like Jesus. He brought the far-off God nigh through the channel of the Father's love, "Foxes have holes, and birds of the air have nests; but the Son of man hath not where to lay his head." He went about doing good; He demonstrated love; He healed the wounded; He raised the dead; He healed the sick. He did all things well.

It is because Jesus came that we know what love is. As we celebrate love, we should show appreciation for those nearest to us. Let us thank God, the source of love. Love was His idea in the first place.

Question to ponder: How can we be imitators of Christ in our love and service to others?

FEBRUARY 14 ═══   *The Superiority of Love*

Love never fails.
1 Corinthians 13:8

It's hard to believe, but arranged marriages, for example, those in India, have often fared much better than marriages in the West based on romantic notions of love.

What these people have learned, that we often have forgotten or have been deceived about, is that love is not some exotic bird that comes flapping down with its wings and sets our hearts aflutter and then disappears just as mysteriously. But love, as I Corinthians 13 tells us, is a way of treating other people. There is not an emotion in that whole chapter—but there is instruction about how to deal with people. "Love is patient and kind; love does not envy or boast; it is not arrogant or rude. It does not insist on its own way" (13:4-5, ESV).

Those who truly love have learned that when people treat other people the right way, that feeling we call "love" will develop. We may have that feeling in great abundance before we are married. However, if we treat our spouse in some contrary manner, we will find, before long, that the mysterious bird has flapped his wings and flown away. Then we say, "Alas, what can we do? There is naught left but the divorce court, because, you see, I don't love him anymore," or "I don't love her anymore. It's not there any longer. It is gone. It's dead."

That is all "a bunch of baloney." We have been fed a lie, and we have believed it. We have based our whole society on the romanticist concept of love and in so doing, we have rejected the biblical teaching about the subject.

Question to ponder: What can you do to strengthen the commitment you have toward your spouse?

....

....

....

Change Me, Lord

*If it is possible, as much as depends
on you, live peaceably with all men.*
Romans 12:18

We see many conflicts taking place in marriages today. Some households are like mini-battlefields.

It takes two to tangle, as well as to tango, though, so we can forget about blaming our spouse. That never does anything but change things for the worse. I think of the innocent young thing who came into the pastor's office. She was weeping and telling of how miserable and horrible and mean her husband was. Then she said, wiping a tear from her eye, "And he wasn't that way when I married him."

The pastor said, "Oh; then you changed him for the worse."

Do you know what unhappy couples try to do? They want to change their spouse, so they spend their whole lives alternating between various methods of doing so. They try yelling and it doesn't work, so then they try silence, and that doesn't work. So, then they try pouting and that doesn't work. Then they try threats and that doesn't work. So they conclude therefore, "It's impossible. Nothing works."

But God wants us to forgive and to patiently learn love. He wants us to work through these conflicts. Marriage was His idea, and it is ultimately a picture of the relationship between Christ and His bride, the Church.

Question to ponder: If you're having problems getting along with someone (perhaps even your spouse), what can *you* do to make things better?

....

....

....

....

FEBRUARY 16 — *Gimme, Gimme, Gimme*

Give us this day our daily bread.
Matthew 6:11

It's often easy to make our prayers just one "gimme, gimme" after another. Give me good health. Give me a new car. Give me a new house. Give me a new spouse. Give me more money.

Some people spend much of their time simply making demands of God as if He were their personal genie.

It is not wrong to ask God for what we need. The prayer to "Give us this day our daily bread" encourages us to bring our supplications to Him. But there should be a balance in our prayers. Praise, thanksgiving, adoration, and gratitude will help put our needs into perspective. Pray with confidence to our Father who has promised to provide everything we need. At the same time, remember who He is, and remember the needs of other people as well. In Nehemiah, he commands the Jews, "Go your way, eat the fat, drink the sweet, and send portions to those for whom nothing is prepared" (8:10).

Question to ponder: How can we seek God's face rather than His hand?

I'm Not Complaining

Now when the people complained, it displeased the Lord.
Numbers 11:1

We have a whole marketing industry that is based on discontent. From class warfare to envy and petty jealousy, the goal is to make people unhappy with what they have. It is so easy for us to complain, because there is always a "snake in paradise." As long as we live in this world, there will be trouble and imperfections, from bugs that ruin your picnic to life-threatening disease.

God hates the discontented spirit, the murmurers. The Old Testament describes all the marvelous things God did for the Israelites when they came out of Egypt on their way to the Holy Land. But soon we read, "They murmured against Moses." They murmured. They were always murmuring. God was sorely displeased with them and He sent fiery serpents upon them because they were rebelling against His providence. This is a picture of what discontentment is.

Now this doesn't mean that we may not strive to improve our circumstances, but we are to recognize the providence of God and His promise to provide for all of our needs out of His riches in glory. We are to be content in all our circumstances and in whatever state we are in. Paul said, "I know how both to be abased and I know how to abound . . . both to be full and to be hungry" (Philippians 4:12).

Question to ponder: How can gratitude and trust overcome our natural tendency to complain?

....

....

....

....

....

FEBRUARY 18 ≡ *The God of All Comfort*

"Comfort, yes, comfort My people!" says your God.
Isaiah 40:1

The great preacher Dr. R. W. Dale said, "People need consolation. They really need it and not merely long for it." Another gentleman, Bill Elliot, says, "Christianity is a religion of comfort. Our God is not only 'the God of all grace,' He is also 'the God of all comfort.'"

From the cradle, where a crying baby is picked up by loving arms, to the deathbed, where a cool hand is stroking a wrinkled cheek, comfort is crucial. Life is never easy and we all need comfort from each other. But we also need comfort from God. He is the one who saves our tears in His bottle and ultimately will wipe away every tear from our eyes. He knows how we are made, and He remembers that we are dust. We have a loving and kind God whose eyes are always on His own.

When people tell us, "Everything will be OK," those are nice words. But when God says, "Weep no more," it is because He has made all things new. When Jesus saw the people, he had compassion on them, for they were like sheep without a shepherd (Mark 6:34). He sacrificed Himself so that all could be well with our souls. What a difference it makes in our lives to receive God's comfort.

Question to ponder: To whom can you show compassion and comfort today?

⊩⊩ ....

....

....

....

....

....

On Things Above

And my God shall supply all your need
according to His riches in glory by Christ Jesus.
Philippians 4:19

What does it mean to be content? According to Webster's it means: "Having the desires limited to that which one has; not disquieted or disturbed by desire, even though not every wish is gratified."

There are two words that come from the same root; they are spelled exactly the same way. However, they mean altogether different things, and they are pronounced differently merely because of the accent. Con*tent* is exactly the same word as *con*tent. The only difference is in the accent.

I think there is a story there. You see, being contented means to have the desires limited to that which one *has*—limited to that which is *contained* rather than always desiring those things that are not in the container, those things that you don't have. Unfortunately, most of us lean toward the latter.

We would all like to live contented lives. How do we do that? By fixing our hearts on things above. Is Christ our delight, our joy, our satisfaction, our contentment, and our rest? Rest and contentment are only found in Christ Jesus, because He knows our needs and He has promised to give us all that we need (Philippians 4:19).

Question to ponder: Today, how can you set your heart on things above?

....

....

....

....

....

....

FEBRUARY 20 — *"The Sin No One Supposedly Commits"*

And He said to them, "Take heed and beware
of covetousness, for one's life does not consist in
the abundance of the things he possesses."
Luke 12:15

What is covetousness? It is the inordinate desire for the things of the world. The Bible tells us that we must, indeed, try to provide the things needed by our family. In fact, the Scripture says that if any man provide not for his own household, he is worse than an infidel and has denied the faith. The Scripture also tells us to go to the ant that gathers in the summer to provide for the winter. But covetousness goes beyond providing for the needs of our family. It is the attitude of being provident run amok, gone loose. It is seeking to gather more unto one's self.

Covetousness has been called the sin that no one commits. One confessor declared that in fifty years of hearing the confessions of people, no one had ever confessed to committing this sin. A minister declared that in decades of leading prayer meetings, where many sins were confessed, this sin was never heard on anyone's lips.

The lust for more and more is ever present, and we must constantly guard against it. When you find yourself lusting after things that God has not given you, confess it as a sin, and at the same time, bring your earnest needs and supplications before Him.

Question to ponder: How can you guard your heart today against covetousness?

All Truth is God's Truth

Where were you when I laid the foundation of the earth?
Job 38:4

A well-known Florida state legislator once introduced a bill stating that creation should be taught in our public schools as one of the possible theories concerning the origin of man along with evolution. I was very interested at the outcries that appeared in the letters to the editor sections after that happened. One writer fulminated, "Why don't we just teach fairy tales, if we are going to teach creation?" Indeed, are they not just the same? Does not every rational person know that the Bible and the Genesis account are just fairy tales? Aren't irrational and uneducated people the only ones who could possibly believe such obscurantist explanations?

I am absolutely confident that were I to have the privilege of confronting any of these people with the request to name a number of the scientific evidences that are set forth by creationists and then to state why they disbelieve them, that none of them would be able to name even one. My friends, *this* is total obscurantism. "I have made up my mind... don't confuse me with the facts...I am in the dark and I want to stay there."

The Bible says that men love darkness rather than the light because their deeds are evil; neither do they come to the light lest their deeds be reproved.

As Christians we need never fear the truth, and any honest scientific truth that is discovered is God's truth.

Question to ponder: What does it matter that God is the Creator of all things seen and unseen?

....

....

....

....

....

FEBRUARY 22 — *The Faith of Washington*

Therefore be imitators of God as dear children.
Ephesians 5:1

It has been said that we live in a time when there is a dearth of real heroes. A recent survey showed that the heroes for American youth included many sleazy celebrities. Surely, there is a need for some godly heroes in our day, and I think that George Washington fills the bill in a remarkable way. He led our troops to victory in the Revolutionary War; he superintended the writing of the Constitution; he was unanimously elected first President of the United States.

But what made him so great? It was his Christian character.

George Washington said to the Delaware Indian chiefs, "You do well to wish to learn our arts and ways of life, and above all, the religion of Jesus Christ."

In 1783, Washington sent out a letter to the governors of the states saying that we can never hope to be a happy nation, unless we imitate Jesus Christ: "I now make it my earnest prayer, that God would have you, and the State over which you preside, in his holy protection…that he would most graciously be pleased to dispose us all, to do Justice, to love mercy, and to demean ourselves with that Charity, humility and pacific temper of mind, which were the Characteristics of the Divine Author of our blessed Religion, and without an humble imitation of whose example in these things, we can never hope to be a happy Nation."

Question to ponder: How would we be a happier nation if we were to imitate Jesus, the "Divine Author of our blessed Religion"?

....

....

....

The Cultural Mandate ⟹ FEBRUARY 23

Then God blessed them, and God said to them,
"Be fruitful and multiply; fill the earth and subdue it;
have dominion over the fish of the sea, over the birds of the
air, and over every living thing that moves on the earth."
Genesis 1:28

God has given us the Cultural Mandate. "This is my Father's world… I rest me in the thought," says a familiar hymn. Yet, I am afraid that we have abandoned this world to the unbelievers, to the ungodly, to the Christ-haters. And when we see how unbelief has affected every phase of this life, we see that they have taken the world and made it into something ghastly,

Some people think that God is Lord only over our spiritual lives—but He is Lord of all. We as His people should spread His grace, His gifts, and His influence into every area of life as best as we can.

We need to fulfill the Cultural Mandate to subdue the earth and have dominion over it. We need to see Christians going into every sphere of life to have an influence upon this world for Christ, to bring His teachings and principles to bear in every phase of life. We should live so that our culture might have the face of Jesus Christ indelibly imprinted upon it. That is what needs to be done. That is our task.

Question to ponder: What can you do to expand Christ's influence?

....

....

....

....

....

FEBRUARY 24 — *Your Sins Will Find You Out*

And Joshua said, "Why have you troubled us?
The Lord will trouble you this day."
Joshua 7:25

The Bible reminds us: Be sure your sins will find you out. Yet how often we seem quite sure that they won't. I am sure Achan must have felt that in the midst of three million people God would never notice what he was doing. And yet God ordered that the tribes be brought one by one, and it fell on Judah, and then the lot fell upon his great grandfather and then his grandfather and finally upon him. And so, as described in Joshua 7, Achan not only brought defeat upon the army of God, but he brought death upon himself. He, and his wife, and his children, and his cattle were all brought into the valley of Achor (the valley of sorrow and trouble), and there they were stoned until they were all dead. Then their corpses were burnt with fire and covered over with stones.

And so, as this account shows us, our sins always affect others and bring trouble upon people beyond ourselves.

Question to ponder: Is there any sin in your life that only you and God know about? What do you plan to do about it?

....

....

....

....

....

....

....

The High Cost of Unbelief

Then, when desire has conceived, it gives birth to sin;
and sin, when it is full-grown, brings forth death.
James 1:15

Did you ever think about the high cost of unbelief in our society? Just think about what sin has done to our young people today.

Drugs, alcohol, and hard rock music—with its prevalent themes of sex, suicide, drugs, and devil worship—are all having a catastrophic affect upon the thinking, morals, and behavior of young people today. Our schools, with their secular, humanistic bent toward removing references to God and absolute morals from curriculum, contribute mightily to the powerful influences that send young people on the road to the "far country."

My friends, weigh the difference that faith makes. I hope that when you consider the cost of secularism and humanism and unbelief, you will say, "Enough. We have had enough of this. This is an alien, godless view and we want no more of it foisted on our children. We don't want them or us to have to pay the consequences now and in the years to come." If we think it is bad now, what will happen when the millions of young people who are indoctrinated with these views in our schools reach maturity and get to the graduate school of unbelief?

Question to ponder: Has unbelief ever cost you something precious in your life?

FEBRUARY 26 — What Do We Add to Our Salvation?

*...Being justified freely by His grace through
the redemption that is in Christ Jesus.*
Romans 3:24

Today there are so many people who don't even begin to understand the rudiments of Christianity and who suppose that salvation is something they earn by their own good works. They are utterly far afield. They don't know that salvation is an unearned gift—unmerited, undeserved, and unworked for. It is a gift given purely by the grace and goodness of God.

I have asked many people, "What do you think we contribute to our own salvation?" Do you know? If you don't know, you should. Do we contribute some good works? We have none to offer for every one of our works is stained by sin. Do we contribute some faith that we work up ourselves? We have none.

What do we contribute? Only one thing. Our contribution to our salvation is just one thing. We contribute the sins that Jesus took upon Himself and for which He died.

Question to ponder: Although Jesus paid it all, there is still one thing we can yet do—thank Him continuously. What is your response to such a great salvation?

Boasting in God's Presence?

...Not of works, lest anyone should boast.
Ephesians 2:9

Many people mistakenly think they can work their way to heaven by being good. Centuries ago, a simple farmer from England indirectly laid this myth to rest. He was an old and very godly plowman and was acquainted with a young English curate who had recently started a ministry in England. Though the plowman had no education, he had been educated by the Spirit of God and the Word of God. One day, in one of their many conversations, while they were talking about the greatest hindrance to spiritual attainment and growth, the curate said that he believed the greatest hindrance to spiritual attainment was the unwillingness to surrender one's sinful self.

Sounds reasonable, but the plowman said, "No, I think not. I think the greatest hindrance to the advancement in the spiritual faith is the unwillingness to surrender one's righteous self."

It is a long way from, "I am proud to stand before God and tell how I have lived my life for the betterment of mankind," to "God have mercy upon me, a sinner."

Question to ponder: Have you surrendered all your self-righteousness to the Lord?

FEBRUARY 28 ═══ *A Negative Example*

*Now all these things happened to them as examples,
and they were written for our admonition, upon whom
the ends of the ages have come.*
1 Corinthians 10:11

Samson's life was a great tragedy, but we learn much from a life such as his that had great potential, but went awry. In a certain way, he was a picture of Christ—a very, very imperfect picture. Christ also had His birth announced by angels. He also was consecrated unto God. He also had a great calling. His calling was also to deliver the people of God, not from the tyranny of the Philistines, but from the tyranny of all evil.

Yet Christ never violated His vows. He never compromised His consecration. He lived a spotless sinless life all of His days. Then one day in the temple of the devil—upon a Cross with outstretched arms—Christ, the greater one than Samson, pressed upon the columns that upheld the very kingdom of evil, and with a mighty push, they went down. Christ did what He came to do. He destroyed the works of Satan.

Question to ponder: Is there more you can do to live up to your Christ-given potential?

....

....

....

....

....

....

....

A Gift Every Four Years === FEBRUARY 29 •LEAP YEAR

...I will sing aloud of Your mercy in the morning.
Psalm 59:16

Time is a funny thing—either we have too little of it or too much of it. This year we get an extra day, a gift to do with it what we want. Twenty-four shining hours. We were made for eternity; therefore, we are never fully at home in time. Every new day is a gift, and the rays of eternity light it up and show us what is important.

Some of you have planned to serve Christ. You have determined that you would do great things for the Lord. Oh yes, you have planned to be a witness for Him, but you have been so busy. You have no intention to come before Him without one soul with which to greet Him. You do not desire to come into His presence empty-handed.

When we look at all the urgent things we need to do today, we should ask ourselves, "Are these things really important? In light of eternity, will they matter? What will matter a thousand years from now?"

While we go about our duties, let us not get caught up in what has been called "the tyranny of the urgent" and miss that which is important. Today, ask God for one beautiful opportunity to do something of eternal value for Him.

Question to ponder: How will you use the gift of an extra day?

....

....

....

....

....

....

....

MARCH 1 — Five Prayers That Will Change Your Life

...I give myself to prayer.
Psalm 109:4

All Christians need to learn how to abide in prayer. I am sure most of you have your stated times of prayer in the morning and at night, before your meals and after. The Bible says that we are to pray always. In all times, in all things, we are to pray. We should constantly be in touch with God. We are to walk with Him and talk with Him. Our last thoughts at night and our first thoughts in the morning will be of Him, as we learn to be always in prayer and thus to be dwelling in the secret place of the most High.

In the next few days, we will go through five prayers that can change our lives. Here they are:

Slay me (i.e., my old nature).

Cleanse me.

Fill me (with Your Holy Spirit).

Lead me.

Use me.

Try and pray these every day, and you'll begin to notice changes.

Question to ponder: Have you given yourself over to prayer?

....

....

....

....

....

....

....

....

Slay Me

I know that nothing good lives in me, that is, in my sinful nature. For I have the desire to do what is good, but I cannot carry it out.
Romans 7:18 (NIV)

As long as we live here on earth, we will have two natures—one foul, the other blest. The old nature is irreparably evil and corrupt. The only thing that can be done with it is to destroy it. It must be crucified with Christ, and a new nature must replace the old. While the old nature diminishes, the new nature grows.

Remember, the old nature can't be improved; it has to be removed. It can't be mended, therefore it must be ended. Only Christ can do that. He does it by the continual supply of His grace. Having come to live in our hearts, He continually supplies His grace, so that we can grow in that grace. It is all done by Christ; it is all done by the work of His Holy Spirit in our hearts.

When we ask God to slay us, it is not a prayer of destruction, but rather a prayer of reconstruction. We are asking the Lord to slay our sinful nature and to put to death all that is opposed to Him and all that hinders our new nature and steals our peace. It is because of our trust in God's goodness that we can pray this prayer, "Slay me."

Question to ponder: Are you reluctant to pray this prayer?

....

....

....

....

....

....

MARCH 3 ═══   *Cleanse Me*

Purge me with hyssop, and I shall be clean;
Wash me, and I shall be whiter than snow.
Psalm 51:7

We must come and ask God to cleanse us in every part of our being. Many people forget that even their memory is tainted by its intimate connection with the old self. All manner of sin has been brought into the sanctuary of the mind. Our memory needs to be cleansed. Have you ever asked God to cleanse your memory from all of the evil stored there? Our affections need to be cleansed and purified. Our wills need to be cleansed.

We need to realize that only through the blood of Christ is there cleansing for sin. "What can wash away my sin? Nothing but the blood of Jesus."

If we are going to come into the presence of God and expect Him to hear and answer our prayers, we dare not come into His presence besmirched and befouled and tainted with our sins.

"Cleanse me, O God!" That means, of course, that we are going to confess our sins and repent of them as well as ask to be cleansed from them.

Question to ponder: Why is daily cleansing necessary?

Fill Me

Then they laid hands on them,
and they received the Holy Spirit.
Acts 8:17

When we are first born into God's Kingdom, we receive the Holy Spirit. Then we are sanctified by the continued renewing and refilling of the Holy Spirit.

The Christian life is a supernatural life. The spiritual man was dead, and only as the Holy Spirit, the giver of life, comes and quickens our lives will there be the slightest stirring in the garden of our soul. Unless the Spirit, which comes each spring to this barren earth and causes the blade and the flower to burst forth across the earth—unless that same Spirit of life comes into our souls, there will be deadness, spiritual lethargy, and spiritual apathy. Without Him, there will be no life. We need to pray that the Spirit would fill us and enliven us—that He would bring us to spiritual life and joy that only God can give, that He would empower us to live for Him, to overcome temptation, and to serve Him throughout our lives.

It is the work of God's Spirit to sanctify us in this way. Then we may be able to bring forth good works. It is the Holy Spirit who daily teaches us, convicts us of sin, and calls us to a closer walk with Christ.

Question to ponder: What do you see of the work of the Spirit in your life?

....

....

....

....

....

....

....

MARCH 5 ≡

Lead Me

*You hold me by my right hand. You will guide me
with Your counsel, and afterward receive me to glory.*
Psalm 73:23-24

The Bible says that as many as are led by the Spirit of God are the children of God, the sons of God. The Holy Spirit would lead us by the hand into a great adventure day by day, but too often we have our own plans. We make up our own agenda. We do not submit to the Spirit of God, nor do we ask that He veto any or all of our plans.

He has a perfect and better plan for our lives—a better plan for this day than you have. As you pray for guidance, you will find that as the Spirit of God guides and leads your life, you will live a life more exciting and adventurous than you ever dreamed the Christian life could be. Truly, it will be a day of discovery.

Let us be sensitive to God's leading, lay all our dreams and plans in His hands, and see His purpose and plans unfold in our lives.

Question to ponder: Can you think of a time you obeyed God's leading and benefited greatly from it?

···
···
···
···
···
···
···

Use Me

If anyone serves Me, let him follow Me;
and where I am, there My servant will be also.
If anyone serves Me, him My Father will honor.
John 12:26

The final prayer of the five prayers is that God would use us. We should pray, "Dear Lord, use me this day for Your glory. I want to be used by You today to serve You." This is why God has made us—to fulfill His perfect plan.

Offer yourself each morning to God, to Jesus Christ as Master and Lord of your life, and you will be amazed at what will happen, at the opportunities for service you will have that will make the end of your day a glorious thing. As you lie down at night, you will know that God has used you, that your life has had eternal significance. People will be brought into your presence who have deep needs, those who have need of Jesus Christ, and you will have the pleasure of pointing them to the Savior.

Your life will begin to bud and blossom and bring forth fruit abundantly to the glory of Jesus Christ, if you are available to Him. And if you sincerely pray, "O God, use me today," He will.

So recapping these five prayers that will change your life:

Slay my old nature.

Cleanse me.

Fill me with Your Holy Spirit.

Lead me.

Use me.

Question to ponder: Has God used you to be a channel of His grace to someone in need of the Savior? What was it like?

....

....

....

....

The End of the World

*As it was in the days of Noah, so it will
be at the coming of the Son of Man.*
Matthew 24:37 (NIV)

We are told in Scripture that just as there was a deluge of wrath in the days of Noah, so there is a deluge of wrath coming at the end of time as well. The Lord is going to destroy the world, though not again by water, for He has promised "while the earth remaineth, seedtime and harvest, and cold and heat, and summer and winter, and day and night shall not cease" (Genesis 8:22).

But there is a day coming when the earth will no longer remain; when God will at last drop the curtain upon the great drama of the ages and will bring to a resounding conclusion the story of mankind—not with water, but with fire, "When the elements shall melt with a fervent heat" (2 Peter 3:10). The Lord will destroy the world with fire.

There are many who believe that day is near. We do not know the day or the hour when it shall be, but certainly the cup of iniquity in the modern world is filled almost to full, if not overflowing. When it is, there will come another deluge of wrath.

Then every eye shall see Him, both the living and the dead, the sheep and the goats, the saved and the lost. We shall all see Him in that great day, which shall dawn like any other day. People will be going about their business, most of them completely absorbed in the things of this world, most of them giving no thought to the things of Jesus Christ or to His gracious offer of salvation to those who will trust in Him.

Question to ponder: What other parallels can you think of between our time and the time of Noah?

Not Ashamed of the Gospel

For whoever is ashamed of Me and My words in this adulterous and sinful generation, of him the Son of Man also will be ashamed when He comes in the glory of His Father with the holy angels.
Mark 8:38

One of my favorite stories illustrates the courage it takes to obey God and never be ashamed of Him. This story is about a senior high school football player who was a star quarterback. He was also a dedicated Christian. Every day he attended a little Bible study after school, so he took his Bible to school and carried it right on top of all of his other books.

Of course some of the other guys on the football team mocked him and laughed at him. One day after football practice, after the team had finished showering and dressing and were about to leave the room, this young quarterback started to pick up his books with the Bible right on top of them. One of the other football players looked at him and said, "Don't you feel like a sissy carrying that Bible around with you all the time?"

The young man looked at his teammate and then he looked down at his Bible. He picked it up and hit the fellow right in the gut with it. "Here," he said. "You carry it around for a week. See how much of a sissy it takes."

Paul declared that he was not ashamed of the Gospel of Jesus Christ. Nor should we be.

Question to ponder: Is there any context where you are tempted to hide the fact that you're a Christian?

....

....

....

....

....

MARCH 9

Meaning in Life

*For we are His workmanship, created in Christ
Jesus for good works, which God prepared
beforehand that we should walk in them.*
Ephesians 2:10

All of our philosophies have degenerated into irrationalism as man has discovered that apart from revelation he cannot find meaning or significance in life.

If you want to find significance and purpose and meaning in life, whether you are a man or a woman, there is only one place to find it. I don't care what siren songs are sung and what lies are told, the only place you will find significance and meaning in life is right in the center of God's will for you. Outside of that, no matter how appealing the lie may appear, you will finally find that it will turn to ashes in your mouth.

Aldous Huxley, the renowned agnostic evolutionist of the twentieth century, said he believed in the meaninglessness of the world. Huxley said he and his contemporaries objected to the idea that the universe has meaning, i.e., that there is a God, because this idea interfered with their sexual freedom.

If life has no purpose, it has no meaning and consequently, it has no significance. No wonder that today suicide is the second major cause of death among young people. Suicide becomes a tempting option when life has no meaning.

But life does have purpose—we were created to glorify God and to enjoy Him forever.

Question to ponder: Since we are His workmanship, what good works do you think He may want you to do today?

....

....

....

....

The Problem Solver

...Casting all your care upon Him, for He cares for you.
1 Peter 5:7

Ours has, very properly, been called the "Age of Anxiety." It seems that worry, tension, and fear are endemic in modern society. We had thought that by conquering the forces of nature and bending them to the will of man, we would deliver ourselves from our problems and enter into a golden age.

Unfortunately, it did not quite work out that way. Rather, like Dr. Frankenstein, we have produced a monster. He hoped that the creature he made would be a helpful one. But, you may recall, it went wild, terrorized his life, and finally brought him to a horrible and untimely end.

Do you have a problem today? Well, I have a problem solver. Do you have a big problem today? Well, I've got a problem shrinker, and it never ever fails. I don't care what your problem is. You may be worrying about what you are going to do. Is that merger in your business going to work out? What about that balloon payment you have on your mortgage? What is going to happen in your marriage? How will you get your kids through college? Will he ever call me again for a date?

I don't care how big your problem is, try this problem solver: Jesus Christ, the One who conquered life's only real problem—the problem of *death.*

Question to ponder: What do you perceive as your biggest problem right now?

MARCH 11

Do Not Judge

But if you bite and devour one another,
beware lest you be consumed by one another!
Galatians 5:15

One of the commandments God has given us is found in the Sermon on the Mount and it should be familiar to most of you: "Judge not, that ye be not judged. For with what judgment ye judge, ye shall be judged: and with what measure ye mete, it shall be measured to you again" (Matthew 7: 1, 2). Most of us, I suppose, have heard that, but many of us have not heeded it, and that to our own hurt and detriment.

Christ said that we are not to be fault-finders for we will be judged. One New Testament scholar has said that not only does this mean that if we judge others we will receive judgment from them upon our lives here— and that is true—but also, in the final Judgment of God the One who is the Judge of all of the earth will judge us at that time for trying to take His place as the Judge of all the earth. God's judgment is absolutely perfect and righteous. Ours is frequently anything but that.

We should look for ways to encourage and build others up, not to tear them down. God doesn't want us to be fault-finding busy-bodies. Self-righteousness is miles apart from real righteousness.

Question to ponder: Are there any areas in your life where you could be less judgmental?

In Whom Do We Trust?

*Some trust in chariots, and some in horses; But we
will remember the name of the LORD our God.*
Psalm 20:7

Our trust should be in the Lord and not in the tools or weapons at
hand. Joshua learned this lesson.

God told Joshua, "Have not I commanded thee? Be strong and of a
good courage; be not afraid, neither be thou dismayed: for the Lord thy
God is with thee withersoever thou goest" (Joshua 1:9). The Lord told
Joshua that he was to be strong and very courageous. To face the giants?
No. Strong and very courageous "to observe to do everything I have commanded you, and this is so important that you are to meditate upon it day
and night" (paraphrase of Joshua 1:7-8).

God didn't say, "When the Hittites come out, you want to use the
spear, so you should have your spears. They should all be seven feet long,
sharpened to a point. When you are facing, however, the Canaanites or the
Philistines, the sword is more effective." He didn't tell Joshua how to deal
with those problems at all.

Why? Because God was going to deal with them. "No man shall be
able to stand before you," Joshua was told. He put his faith in the Lord; he
obeyed Him. And the rest is history.

Question to ponder: What tool in your hands are you possibly
tempted to trust in, as opposed to trusting in the Lord?

....

....

....

....

....

═══

Pride vs. Humility

*I will halt the arrogance of the proud, and
will lay low the haughtiness of the terrible.*
Isaiah 13:11

God opposes the proud, but gives grace to the humble.

I trust you remember the story of the publican (i.e., tax-collector) and the Pharisee. Publicans were low caste Israelites who collected taxes from other Israelites for the Romans. They were hated by the people. It seemed on this particular day a Pharisee—Pharisees were religious rulers who judged Israel—and a publican both went into the temple at the same time to pray. One went in the front and the other one went in the back door.

The Pharisee self-righteously thanked God that he was not like that sinner, the publican. Whereas, the publican, we are told, "would not lift up so much as his eyes unto heaven, but smote upon his breast, saying, God be merciful to me a sinner" (Luke 18:13). He prayed to God; the Pharisee did not.

The publican didn't say, "God, be merciful to me, *a* sinner," but "God, be propitiated unto me, *the* sinner." In his mind, he was the only one. And we read that the publican—not the Pharisee—went down to his house justified.

No one will receive salvation from God until he realizes he is a sinner, needing His grace. There is no place for arrogance in the Kingdom of God.

Question to ponder: Why is it so hard to be humble?

The Justice of God

For He made Him who knew no sin to be sin for us,
that we might become the righteousness of God in Him.
2 Corinthians 5:21

The judgment of God is to come upon this world. Mankind has been convicted and condemned. There is only one place of escape, and that is Calvary. There is the fire of God's retributive justice. His wrath for sin fell upon His own dear Son Who took upon Himself our guilt and endured the capital punishment we deserved, suffering the wrath of God in our stead.

When I was in seminary in Atlanta, I preached in a jail to some men in a harsh cage who were there for various crimes. I had preached for no more than a minute when a great big burly fellow stepped up to the bars and said, "Preacher, you just go tell that God of yours that all I want from Him is what I deserve." I looked at him and said: "Sir, if you got what you deserve, the floor would open up beneath you this instant and you would plunge into Hell, because that's what you deserve. I'm not saying that because you're behind those bars and I'm in front of them, because if I got what I deserve, that's exactly where I would go too." All of the saints down through the centuries have said the same thing.

We all need God's mercy. Thankfully, He is a merciful God.

Question to ponder: Why is it that in our natural state, we all deserve God's displeasure?

MARCH 15 — *Justification and Sanctification*

*Therefore, having been justified by faith, we have
[a] peace with God through our Lord Jesus Christ.*
Romans 5:1

One of my seminary professors said, "Gentlemen, justification and sanctification must always be distinguished, but they can never be separated." There is no man who is justified, pardoned by God, who is not in the process of being sanctified. If you are not being made holy, you are not justified. You are not saved. You are not a Christian and you are not going to Heaven.

Justification is an act; it happens instantaneously the moment we trust in Christ. It is perfect. It is complete. It is forever. Fifty years later, we are no more justified than we are in the first moment after we trust in Christ. The perfect righteousness of Jesus Christ never changes. It is finished. It is complete. It is done.

Justification deals with the guilt we have incurred because of our sin. It is a judicial, legal term. It is something a judge does. Sanctification is the work of a physician cleansing us from the corruption in our life.

It has been said that justification by faith alone is the article of a standing or falling church, of a standing or falling nation, of a standing or falling soul. Sanctification is the lifelong process of becoming more like Christ.

Question to ponder: Can you see God's work of sanctification in your life? Are you more like Jesus than you were five years ago?

....

....

....

....

....

Heirs of God

"This is the heritage of the servants of the LORD,
and their righteousness is from Me," says the LORD.
Isaiah 54:17

What would an inheritance from God Almighty involve? We are told that it involves all things, whether in this life or the life to come. We have been delivered from death, and we have been given eternal life. In life we have all things. We have been promised by God that He will meet all of our needs in this world, that He will work all things together for our good, and one day He will take us to be with Him in Paradise. There is probably no one who has even the slightest conception of the wonders that God has provided for us— for those who love Him. Truly, it has not "entered into the heart of man, the things which God hath prepared for them that love him" (I Corinthians 2:9).

What must Paradise be like? We know the wonder of this world, the myriad of exciting things that God has given us here. What will it be like there, when there is no more pain, when there is no more sorrow? On earth there are many people who are in pain. There are those who suffer sorrow and heartache over loved ones; there are those who are depressed with problems; there are those who are separated from those whom they love. But then there will be no more separation; there will be no more sickness; there will be no more heartache; there will be no more loss; there will be no more pain; there will be no more death—for the former things will have passed away. That is part of the inheritance God has prepared for those who are His.

Question to ponder: What do you think of your inheritance?

....

....

....

....

MARCH 17 ══ *The Breastplate of St. Patrick*

For to me, to live is Christ, and to die is gain.
Philippians 1:21

On this day, many people will sadly get drunk, supposedly to honor the memory of St. Patrick. But in fact they dishonor his memory. This man was a great Christian missionary from England to Ireland. He brought the Gospel to the Emerald Isle and saw virtually the whole country converted under his ministry.

St. Patrick was fearless and bold, and Christ was the source of his strength. He prayed something ("the breastplate of St. Patrick") that we can all pray:

> I bind to myself this day
> The Power of His Incarnation,
> The Power of His Crucifixion,
> The Power of His Resurrection
> With His Ascension.
> Christ be with me, Christ within me,
> Christ behind me, Christ before me,
> Christ beside me, Christ to win me,
> Christ to comfort and restore me,
> Christ beneath me, Christ above me,
> Christ in quiet, Christ in danger,
> Christ in the hearts of all that love me,
> Christ in the mouth of friend and stranger.

Christ is life. Christ is all in all. "For me to live is Christ." That is the real meaning of St. Patrick's Day.

Question to ponder: What does it mean that Christ is all around us?

Learning from the Mature

However, we speak wisdom among those who are mature, yet not the wisdom of this age, nor of the rulers of this age, who are coming to nothing.
1 Corinthians 2:6

We need to hear from the mature saints—those who have searched the strength of their spiritual lives. We need to hear how they escaped the snare of the fowler, by what subtleties they have been beguiled, how they have taken the hill, what footwear they have found best for the enterprise, and how they have comforted their hearts after they dug the grave by the side of the way.

What about those who have grown old in Christ? What delicacies does the Lord have for the aged pilgrims along the way? Have they seen any particular and wonderful star in the evening sky? Have they seen the glimmering of that city made of gold? Is it already drawing their hearts? Do they yearn to be with those whom they have loved, those who have gone before? How much could we learn from those who have suffered many things and endured the battle for many years for Christ?

Question to ponder: Is there a mature saint you can seek out for counsel? If not, why not pray for one?

MARCH 19 === *Life—a Tragedy or a Triumph?*

Do not let your hearts be troubled.
Trust in God; trust also in me.
John 14:1 (NIV)

Will my life count for something? This question has perplexed the minds of thinking men and women from time immemorial: What will be the outcome of my life? Men have wondered whether their lives would end in triumph or tragedy.

Life is a probation; it is also an education and a school. The tragedy is that the vast majority of people in America, as well as in other lands, don't even know the one central lesson God is trying to teach them in the school they are attending—the school of life.

The lesson is this: God says "Trust Me." Throughout the Scriptures, from one end to another, God is teaching people the great lesson of faith— to trust Him amidst all of the vicissitudes of life.

Every class is the same in every subject we go through—Trust 101. Some of us do not go any further, and others have learned to trust Him in virtually all things.

Question to ponder: A life of triumph is a life of trust. How can you better trust Him today?

....

....

....

....

....

....

....

The Purpose of Life

*I have glorified You on the earth. I have finished
the work which You have given Me to do.*
Jesus in His high priestly prayer, John 17:4

In 19th century England, after years of hard work, a young man rejoiced after having graduated from Oxford University. Well placed from a family that was well positioned, he had the privilege of meeting with the prime minister, William Gladstone, perhaps the greatest and godliest of all England's prime ministers.

The young man told Gladstone how he intended to attend law school and become a lawyer.

"Very good, young man. And what then?"

"Then, sir, I hope to practice law here in England for a number of years."

"That's fine; and what then?"

"Well, sir, I hope then to stand for Parliament. It is my devout wish that I may be elected to Parliament."

"That's just fine, young man. What then?"

"Sir, I hope to serve my country to the best of my ability in Parliament."

"Very good, young man. What then?"

"Well, sir, I suppose one day I will retire."

"Yes, and what then?"

"Well, I ah, suppose I'll die."

"That's right . . . and what then?"

The young man seemed completely befuddled and said, "Well, sir, I really hadn't thought that far into the future."

Gladstone, fixing him with his eyes, said, "Young man, you are a fool. Go home and think life through."

I wonder how many relatives that young man has sitting in our midst today—people who are guilty of the folly of shortsightedness and have never really thought life through.

Question to ponder: What is your purpose for living? How can you glorify God today?

MARCH 21 ====

Beautiful Savior

Nor is there salvation in any other, for there is no other name under heaven given among men by which we must be saved.
Acts 4:12

There are many today who would say that there are innumerable doors that lead to spiritual safety. My friend, there is but *one.* There was but one door into the ark of Noah; there is but one door into the ark of Christ, and that is the door of faith—the faith of the Cross. The door of the ark of Christ is cruciform: it is shaped like a Cross. He is the one and only place of safety in this world, our only sanctuary from the stormy blast that God has said will come upon the world. Other religions have teachers. Only Christianity has a Savior.

Because He is the only savior, His name is so precious to His saints. The name is whispered over a cradle and to the dying. The name of Jesus is praised by millions in worship. His name gives comfort and peace. It stills the storms around us and conquers our fears within. It is the most beautiful name in the world.

Question to ponder: Why do you love the name of Jesus?

....

....

....

....

....

....

....

....

Jesus Calms the Storms ═══ MARCH 22

And they feared exceedingly, and said to one another,
"Who can this be, that even the wind and the sea obey Him!"
Mark 4:41

We see something of the Deity of Christ and His uniqueness in the fact that He never bothered to trouble Himself to explain His frequently ambiguous conduct. For example, Jesus was asleep in the back of a boat in the midst of a great storm. Waves were breaking over the sides of the boat and the disciples were paralyzed with fear. They cried, "Teacher, do You not care that we are perishing?" (Mark 4:38).

"Well, I'm sorry fellows. If you had only awakened me earlier, I would have tried to help, but you see, it's been such a long day and I was so tired. I just had to get some rest."

No. He didn't say anything like that. He simply said, "Peace, be still." The waves ceased and the wind stopped. That is not the way any other man lives his life.

Jesus can calm the storms of our lives; the wind and the waves still obey His voice. He still calms storms.

Question to ponder: What storm are you possibly experiencing in your life that you need to take to Jesus to calm?

╟╟ ....

....

....

....

....

....

....

MARCH 23

The Humble Christ

*Blessed are the poor in spirit, for
theirs is the kingdom of heaven.*
Matthew 5:3

To be poor in spirit is to recognize that you are spiritually needy. It is to see that in ourselves we are poor and in need of a savior.

Christ came—not with pomp and circumstance, not with royal splendor, not with power, not with armies, but into a family with a great lineage, however, one that had fallen into poverty. He grew up in the home of a carpenter. He grew up in a city that was a byword: "Can anything good come out of Nazareth?" (John 1:46 NKJV).

He grew up with no education, and yet He was the wisest person who ever lived. He grew up, astonishingly, with no background. He exited that town, which was nothing, walked up on a hill, and there delivered the greatest discourse on human ethics the world has ever heard—the Sermon on the Mount. It has never been equaled and certainly never excelled.

The humble carpenter spread His blessings all over the world and taught us that humility is a virtue.

Question to ponder: What is the relationship between having spiritual riches and being poor in spirit?

....

....

....

....

....

....

....

Joy in the Morning

Weeping may endure for a night,
but joy comes in the morning.
Psalm 30:5

Sorrow, sadness, and weeping are all part of this life. None of us are untouched by the troubles of the world. But it is temporary, whereas joy, for the Christian, is everlasting.

One time at a speaking engagement in Indianapolis, a man came up to me and said, "I was down in Ft. Lauderdale on vacation, and I met a lady in your church who shared with me those good tidings of great joy." She had told him the Gospel and he had accepted Christ. He continued: "You certainly cannot know, you cannot imagine the indescribable joy I have known for the last year since I came to know Christ. I never would have believed it."

It is never recorded once that Jesus ever laughed, and yet the night before He went to the agony of the Cross, He said, "These things have I spoken unto you, that my joy might remain in you" (John 15:11). He came from the source of all joy—from Heaven—and He came to bring that joy to us. He took all of our sorrows and our griefs upon Himself, and thus, though He never laughed that we know of, He did weep. And He wept, so that we might be glad.

Question to ponder: What difference does it make that sadness is temporary?

....
....
....
....
....
....

MARCH 25

Logic Incarnate

Beware lest anyone cheat you through philosophy and empty deceit, according to the tradition of men, according to the basic principles of the world, and not according to Christ.
Colossians 2:8

Jesus is the Eternal Word of God. "In the beginning was the Word, and the Word was with God, and the Word was God" (John 1:1). *Logos* is the Greek word translated "Word." The *Logos,* the wisdom of God, or it can aptly be translated "logic" from logos—the logic of God. In the beginning, there was Logic and the Logic was with God and Logic was God and Logic became flesh.

Many people think that Christianity is not rational—not reasonable. However, it is the very essence of reason. Well did the demon Wormwood warn his understudy Screwtape in C.S. Lewis' fictional work, *The Screwtape Letters,* not to employ argument to bring his charge safely home to his father below. "The trouble about argument," Screwtape explained, "is that it moves the whole struggle on to the Enemy's own ground." Indeed it does, for Christ is Logic incarnated.

Paul said that through the preaching of the "foolishness of the cross" we are saved. Men may think the message to be foolish. But it is the power of God unto salvation.

Question to ponder: God who made the mind and the intellect is all wise. Is there logic and wisdom with the devil?

....

....

....

....

....

The Loneliness of Jesus

*But if we walk in the light as He is in the light, we
have fellowship with one another, and the blood
of Jesus Christ His Son cleanses us from all sin.*
1 John 1:7

Millions are lonely today. Yet Jesus experienced a gut-wrenching type
of loneliness. Christ Jesus was alone for a time, so that we don't ever have to be.

For the first time in eternity, when Jesus suffered on the Cross, the
fellowship He had with His Father was broken. And thus He did not know
the comfort of His Father. For Him the heavens were turned to brass and
there was none to help. Abandoned by man, abandoned by His nation,
abandoned by His Church, abandoned by His disciples, abandoned by His
Father, He was alone. This will be true of all who do not trust in Him; they
will someday be alone forever in Hell—which is not a big cocktail party as
some wags suppose it to be. It is unmitigated loneliness.

Because of what He underwent, we need not ever experience loneliness. I think we desperately need to have our attention drawn to true and rich
Christian fellowship, as seen, for example, in the early Church. That is especially the case in these days when people are becoming increasingly depersonalized, when they are only numbers, when they pass by thousands in the vast
cities of our countries and yet seldom enter into any sort of communion. How
many there are in the midst of the teeming masses of this land who are suffering the yearnings and heartache of loneliness. We need that sense of community, that fellowship of the saints the New Testament so often speaks of.

Jesus always calls us into fellowship—with Him, and with His church.

Question to ponder: Are you experiencing good Christian
fellowship on a regular basis? If not, whom could you
contact to seek it more often?

MARCH 27 — *Silence of the Lamb of God*

*Then Pilate said to Him, "Do You not hear how many
things they testify against You?" But He answered him
not one word, so that the governor marveled greatly.*
Matthew 27:13-14

Jesus was silent, we are told. He "opened not His mouth" before His accusers. Scripture states, ". . .he opened not his mouth: he is brought as a lamb to the slaughter" (Isaiah 53:7).

Why was Christ silent before His accusers? He easily could have defended Himself. They could not prove anything against Him. He, indeed, confessed that He was the Son of God when questioned—and this is what brought about His crucifixion.

There was no deceit, there were no lies in His mouth. He was absolutely without sin. Why didn't He say something?

The reason, my friends, and you should never forget this, is that He *was guilty*. He was the most guilty man the world has ever seen, for all of *our* guilt was imputed to Him, and He became *sin* for us, the Bible says. It was your guilt and mine, all of ours, that was upon Him. For our guilt He endured the agony of His crucifixion. He bore our griefs and carried our sorrows. Our guilt was imputed to Him and He became sin for us.

Question to ponder: What must it have been like for the Creator of the Universe to stand before His creatures as they condemned Him to death?

Holiness in an Unholy World — MARCH 28

...It is written, "Be holy, for I am holy."
1 Peter 1:16

There is no doubt that this world is becoming increasingly unholy. I told a group of young people recently that I was born in a different country than the one we now live in. Of course, geographically it was part of America, but it was a different world then, as some of you who are older can clearly attest. Our nation is truly, as one writer has said, going down the gutter into an ocean of slime.

On time a young lady approached me and said she would like to ask me to do her a favor. I said, "I would be happy to, if I can. What is it?"

"Well, I am really almost afraid to ask," she said.

"Go ahead."

"Would you pray for me that I may become a holy person?"

I have tried to think back, and I really can't recall anyone else in what was at that point thirty years of ministry asking me to pray that particular request. It should be the cry of all our hearts: "Lord, make me holy."

Question to ponder: Are there any areas of your life that may possibly hold you back from holiness?

....

....

....

....

....

....

....

....

══ *Holiness Equals Wholeness*

For just as you presented your members as slaves of unclean-ness, and of lawlessness leading to more lawlessness, so now present your members as slaves of righteousness for holiness.
Romans 6:19

How important is holiness? In Hebrews 12:14, we are told to seek after holiness "without which no man shall see the Lord." That is pretty straightforward. You can't miss it. He declares unequivocally that we are to pursue after holiness, "without which no man shall see the Lord." No man who is not holy is going to live in Heaven with an all-holy God.

It is ironic that the closer we get to the light, the more clearly we see our sins. Imagine a filthy man. He has been wallowing around in the dirt and the slime. He is also blind. Imagine, at the same time, two things slowly happening: he is very gradually, over a period of days, gaining his sight and he is very slowly being cleansed. Those are the objective facts, but what does he perceive? When he was blind, he didn't see the dirt at all, but now that he is beginning to see, the more he becomes aware of his dirt, the more vile he becomes in his own eyes.

You will never be truly happy if you are not holy, because holiness leads to wholeness—wholeness of mind, spirit, heart, and body. And, of course, it is the *Holy* Spirit who works this wonder in our lives.

Question to ponder: How important is holiness to you in your life?

....

....

....

....

....

....

Only One Sacrifice

*...Who does not need daily, as those high priests, to offer
up sacrifices, first for His own sins and then for the people's,
for this He did once for all when He offered up Himself.*
Hebrews 7:27

There were priests in the Old Testament, but now Christ, our great High Priest has come. He completed the work that they could only begin.

With a priest and an altar you have something else: you have a sacrifice. For hundreds of years, at God's instruction, the ancient Hebrew priests offered sacrifices with many specific guidelines. There were daily sacrifices and specific annual offerings. They may have "forgiven" sins temporarily, but never permanently.

All of these sacrifices foreshadowed the once and for all sacrifice of Jesus Christ on the Cross. What He did is the basis for all forgiveness. His blood was much more precious than that of bulls and goats.

Read Hebrews 9-11 and you will notice that one word appears over and over and over again. It's a word that I recommend you underline. It is "once" or "one." By *one* sacrifice Christ has forever reconciled us to God. There was only *one* sacrifice, and it took place upon the Cross 2,000 years ago. On that finished sacrifice all of our hopes are founded.

Question to ponder: What does it mean that our High Priest offered Himself up "once for all"?

MARCH 31 — The Cup of Wrath

"Father, if it is Your will, remove this cup from Me."
Luke 22:42

When Jesus was praying in the Garden of Gethsemane on the night of His betrayal, He realized how horrible was the cup that He was about to drink from—the cup of God's wrath. This is why He prayed that the cup be passed from Him, if possible. It was not possible, so He submitted to drink it.

Earlier that night, Jesus had said, "For the prince of this world [Satan] cometh and he hath nothing in me" (John 14:30). Satan only has a claim upon those who are guilty of sin and are under the curse. But Christ was the Sinless One, and so Satan had nothing in Him and could not hurt Him at all.

Nevertheless, when Jesus hung upon the Cross, He became the very quintessence of sin. He was the most delectable morsel for that lion that goes about roaring, seeking whom he may devour. And so the very demons of hell, with cackling sound, leaped upon Him and tore at His soul as He endured demonic rage.

Jesus saw all of that in the cup, and His soul recoiled against it. This was one of the last temptations of Christ, and our Savior met it magnificently. "Nevertheless not my will, but thine, be done" (Luke 22:42).

Question to ponder: What you think of the cup of God's Wrath, how do you picture it?

Fools

Who is wise and understanding among you?
Let him show by good conduct that his works
are done in the meekness of wisdom.
James 3:13

What's the difference between wisdom and folly? Between the wise person and the fool?

"The fool," Proverbs tells us, *"despises wisdom and instruction."* I trust there is no one reading who despises wisdom and instruction, but I daresay there are varying degrees of avidness in our quest after wisdom and instruction. There are some who will tolerate a little bit of wisdom if it is fed to them like pablum in bite-size mouthfuls. But what about those who are willing to spend hours digging and studying on their own? Ah, at this point the ranks thin out.

How much time have we spent this week searching and digging for wisdom and instruction from the Word of God? Remember who it is that despises and ignores it—the fool. Let us strive to learn more and apply more of God's wisdom as revealed in the Scriptures.

Question to ponder: Have you ever been foolish in a way that had major consequences?

APRIL **2** ═══ *The Mystery of the Cross*

But we speak the wisdom of God in a mystery, the hidden
wisdom which God ordained before the ages for our glory.
1 Corinthians 2:7

Jesus Christ and Him crucified is the center of Christianity. The very heart of the mystery of Christian redemption is this: That He who is the spotless, sinless Son of God, become sin for us on the Cross. He who knew no sin became sin. Christ bore our sins in His own body on the tree—that is the essence of the Christian mystery.

In His Passion, Jesus suffered not only physically, but spiritually. Now, for the first time in His life, for the first time in history, for the first time in eternity, in some mysterious, inexplicable way, the very tri-unity of God is wrenched apart and Christ is abandoned by His Father. He would cry, "My God, my God, why hast thou forsaken me?" (Mark 15:34). He is more alone than any person in all the history of the world has ever been—abandoned by God whose pure eyes could not look upon sin, even when that sin is in His beloved Son. For Jesus Christ became on that day, on that Cross, "sin."

The mystery of the atonement is that the death of the Son of God made it possible for ordinary people to receive forgiveness and to become right with God. We can never understand it. We can only stand in awe of it and with thankful hearts believe it.

Question to ponder: What does imputed righteousness mean?

....

....

....

....

....

....

The Horror of the Cross ═══ APRIL 3

> *...Looking unto Jesus, the author and finisher of our faith, who for the joy that was set before Him endured the cross, despising the shame, and has sat down at the right hand of the throne of God.*
> Hebrews 12:2

After having been skewered to the cross, lifted up naked before all the world to see, Jesus endured the shame and the horror and the agony and the pain of the worst kind of human suffering. For three interminable hours He hung there, until at last there came high noon.

Then, in the peak of the heat of that day, suddenly the sun's light failed, and a great darkness descended at noon, and a blackness covered the earth. In that darkness, unseen by mortal eyes, there came a hand down from Heaven and extended before His face that cup containing the sin of the world. It was placed to His lips, and willingly Jesus drank it down to the very dregs, and the Scriptures tell us that Jesus Christ, the Holy One of God, became sin for us.

The physical sufferings of Christ were so horrendous that we can hardly contemplate them at all. But it was the spiritual suffering that killed Him. Every sin and sorrow was laid on Him—everything from a harsh word to murder, betrayal and hatred, He carried it all.

As the hymn puts it, "What Thou my Lord has suffered was all for sinners gain. Mine, mine was the transgression, but Thine the deadly pain."

Question to ponder: How can we respond to the greatest expression of love in the universe?

⸎ ....

....

....

....

....

APRIL 4

The Blessings of the Cross

He who did not spare His own Son, but delivered Him up for us all, how shall He not with Him also freely give us all things?
Romans 8:32

The Cross is the source of our blessings. It is that Cross through which all of God's riches will flow into our lives—pardon, forgiveness, provision, adoption into the family of God, and care for all of our needs. Because of the Cross, one day we will be taken to be with Him in Paradise forever. That means we must let go of all supposed goodness of our own, acknowledge ourselves to be dead in sins, and trust in the divine Son, who came that we might have all things.

Jesus loved us even unto the Cross. He took upon Himself our guilt, our sin, and the punishment that it deserves. He paid the price entirely. He offers us forgiveness. By His grace, unmerited and free, He offers us the gift of life abundant and eternal, freely bestowed to those that will place their trust in Him. Those who will cease to trust in any supposed goodness of their own and rest their hopes upon Christ and His atoning work may know now the blessings of His heaven.

It is because of the Cross that we have all the riches of God in this life, and eternal life, which continues in heaven with our Savior. Jesus secured all this for us by His death on the Cross and His resurrection from the dead.

Question to ponder: What is the greatest blessing of the Cross in your life?

Christ is Risen Indeed

But now Christ is risen from the dead, and has
become the firstfruits of those who have fallen asleep.
1 Corinthians 15:20

My friends, the evidence for the resurrection of Jesus Christ, the evidence for the revelation of God in the Scripture is overwhelming. One of greatest authorities in the history of evidences who ever lived was Dr. Simon Greenleaf (1783-1853) of Harvard Law School. He examined the evidence for the Resurrection and demonstrated in his classic book, *The Testimony of the Evangelists,* that it would hold up in any court of law. Irrational blind faith? Hardly.

On that Sunday morning, unseen by human eyes, there descended the omnipotent and supernatural hand of God, right through that stone, and touched the body of the Beloved Son, and Jesus arose from the dead, quickened by the immeasurable and illimitable power of God Almighty.

This is the greatest fact of history. Jesus changed all history when He came out of that tomb, victorious over the grave. Because He lives, we shall also live.

Question to ponder: How is the resurrection the bedrock of Christianity?

....

....

....

....

....

....

....

....

APRIL 6 ═══ *Righteousness by Faith Alone*

But the father said to his servants,
"Bring out the best robe and put it on him."
Luke 15:22

Are you clothed in the new white robe of right¬eousness that only Christ can give? That is the gift He came to bring. He came to take away all of our foul smelling sin, to go outside the city wall to the dung heap of Jerusalem and there to lay Himself down on the Cross to die for us. He took away our uncleanness when He rose on that Sabbath morn and He clothes in white righteousness all who will come to Him in faith, acknowledging their uncleanness, acknowledging their sin and unworthiness, and saying, "O Christ, O Divine Redeemer, clothe me in Thy white righteousness that I may faultless stand before Thy throne, clothed in Thy righteousness alone."

Righteousness comes through faith in Christ, the righteousness which is of God, by faith. God is our righteousness. What is that robe of righteousness made of? It is made from the perfect life of Christ—His active obedience, and, secondly, from His passive obedience—His passion, when He suffered and agonized and died upon the cross.

Question to ponder: Does it change your view of sin to think of it as dirt on your white robe of righteousness?

. . . .

. . . .

. . . .

. . . .

. . . .

. . . .

The Sacrifice of the Cross ≡ APRIL 7

*...But now, once at the end of the ages, He has
appeared to put away sin by the sacrifice of Himself.*
Hebrews 9:26

In the cross of Christ we so clearly see one of the paradoxes of Christianity. For Christ is both High Priest and Sacrifice.

It is interesting that in both the tabernacle in the wilderness and again in the temple of Solomon, one could find beautiful furniture. There was the table for shewbread; the altar of incense; the great seven-pronged candelabra. Within the Holy of Holies, was the ark of the covenant with the glorious gold-covered cherubim.

Nowhere, however, in either the tabernacle or the temple was any chair, bench, or pew to be found because the work of the priests was never done. Day after day the priests offered sacrifices for sin—sacrifices that had to be repeated continually—for it was not possible for the blood of bulls or the blood of goats to take away sin.

Yet Jesus of Nazareth offered one sacrifice for sins forever and then He sat down. His work was over. Not enough people understand that Christianity is not about "doing," it is about "done." Jesus declared "It is finished." It is done. It is paid. It is accomplished. The atonement for our sins was paid in full—we cannot add to it.

The final evening sacrifice has been offered—perfect and complete, the fulfillment of the whole Old Testament sacrificial system. This is the sacrifice which is pleasing and acceptable to the Lord.

Question to ponder: Why was Jesus the only One that could be a pleasing and acceptable sacrifice to the Lord?

APRIL 8

Archaeology and Jesus

But He answered and said to them, "I tell you that if these should keep silent, the stones would immediately cry out."
Luke 19:40

Some critics falsely state that there's no archaeological evidence related to Jesus. That's wrong on many fronts. Included among recent archaeological finds is a large stone that was part of a building built by Pontius Pilate in honor of Tiberius Caesar, and on that stone is inscribed, "Pontius Pilatus, Procurator of Judea." I've been there, I've seen it, and I've read it.

In 1990 an ossuary (a first century bone box) was discovered, containing the bones of one Joseph, the son of Caiaphas. Caiaphas was a surname, and Joseph Caiaphas was the high priest who concocted the whole scheme to crucify Jesus after the priests were upset over Jesus raising Lazarus from the dead. They didn't know what to do. It was cunning Caiaphas who said, "Ye know nothing at all, Nor consider that it is expedient for us, that one man should die for the people, and that the whole nation perish not" (John 11:49-50). It was expedient, he said, that Jesus should die—the death of expediency. It was Caiaphas who examined Him there in the Sanhedrin. It was Caiaphas who led the mob over to Pilate's palace. It was Caiaphas who turned Jesus over to Pilate and demanded His crucifixion.

So there you have archeological evidence for Caiaphas, the high priest of the Jews, who condemned Jesus, and for Pontius Pilate, the procurator of Judea, who unwillingly and reluctantly was finally forced to cave in and deliver Jesus up for crucifixion.

As has been said, the very stones cry out to the truth of Christ.

Question to ponder: How do you view archaeological finds—do they strengthen your faith?

With God All Things Are Possible ⟹ APRIL 9

With men this is impossible, but
with God all things are possible.
Matthew 19:26

The impossible is happening. Christ is risen and death is defeated. We shall live again. This is the declaration of Easter. The Great I AM has made all things new.

In fact, with God, all things are possible, and nothing is incredible. Why should it be thought incredible that God should raise the dead? God, who created us out of the dust of the earth, can bring us back in an instant. The God who swirled the galaxies into the sky can raise the dead. Not only is this the teaching of the Scripture, but the pledge that we will live again after death is made certain by the fact of the resurrection of Jesus Christ from the dead. "I am He that liveth, and was dead; and behold, I am alive for evermore" (Revelation 1:18). The resurrection of Christ from the dead is what we celebrate each Easter Sunday. It is a celebration of the fact that with God, all things are possible.

Question to ponder: Eternal life, never to die, the true "fountain of youth"—are these not all here on Easter morning?

....

....

....

....

....

....

....

APRIL 10 — *Blind Faith or Faith Based on Evidence?*

He also presented Himself alive after His suffering by many infallible proofs, being seen by them during forty days and speaking of the things pertaining to the kingdom of God.
Acts 1:3

Often people are heard to say, "Oh, you Christians just believe in blind faith." The truth of the matter is that Christians do not believe in blind faith. The Bible never calls us to a blind faith. Blind faith is faith without evidence; the Bible calls us to faith in evidence. Our text says that by many infallible proofs Jesus Christ showed Himself alive from the dead. Christianity is the only historical and evidential religion in the history of the world. It is built upon evidence so overwhelming that I have never met a person who has rejected Christianity after having examined the evidence. However, I have met many that have never examined it at all.

Evidence. Evidence. Evidence. I am not the least bit afraid of any person who wants to challenge me on the evidence. It is blind unbelief which refuses even to examine the evidence, refuses even to look at it, and that bothers me. Have you ever heard anyone refer to "blind unbelief"?

We are commanded to love God with all our minds, and that certainly includes using our intellect to examine evidence and work out answers to difficult questions. The God who made our minds surely wants us to use them. Christianity is based on facts of history, not on "blind faith."

Question to ponder: What were some of the proofs that Jesus gave His disciples to convince them that He was risen from the dead?

The Skeptics and the Resurrection

*Now if Christ is preached that He has been
raised from the dead, how do some among you
say that there is no resurrection of the dead?*
1 Corinthians 15:12

Look at the resurrection, my friends, from the eyes of the unbeliever. I want to tell you that the resurrection is a highly unlikely thing. In fact, it is incredible when you really stop to think about it. It is so incredible that David Hume, the famous Scottish philosopher and skeptic, said that the universal experience of mankind declared that when people die they are dead, and the dead stay that way. Oh, yes, there are those who are clinically dead for a few minutes, but it has never been seen, he said, in the experience of mankind that those who have been dead for days or weeks or years or centuries have ever popped up out of the sod and walked again.

So the universal experience of mankind is against that ever happening. Of course, Hume forgot to include the only really significant experience in his statement. Jesus Christ transformed the world when He walked out of the tomb on the first Easter morning. He answered that question, "Shall man live again?" in the affirmative, once and for all.

Question to ponder: Have you encountered skepticism toward the resurrection? If so, how did you counter it?

....
....
....
....
....
....
....

A Mother's Legacy

...When I call to remembrance the genuine faith that is in you, which dwelt first in your grandmother Lois and your mother Eunice, and I am persuaded is in you also.
2 Timothy 1:5

A Christian heritage is the best gift a mother can give her child. Ladies, I hope you will not believe the siren song of the radical feminists who would deprive you of the greatest significance and joy in the world—the joy of motherhood.

Former First Lady Barbara Bush was invited in 1990 to give the commencement address at Wellesley College. Hundreds of angry coeds protested. They were outraged that a woman who had never done anything but rear a family would be invited to speak at Wellesley, where in those sacred halls of higher learning, for a generation or more, women had been told that rearing a family and staying at home was an abominable thing to do. But, she was, nevertheless, allowed to come and to speak. At the end of her speech she said something that I think needs repeating. She said: "At the end of your life, you will never regret not having passed one more test, not winning one more verdict or not closing one more deal. You will regret time not spent with a husband, a friend, a child or a parent."

I think that note needs to be rung again and again—that ultimately in life, the things that really count are the relationships we have—first with God, and then with our spouse, our parents, and our children.

Question to ponder: What is the heritage you are leaving through your relationships?

....

....

....

....

....

Toying With Sin

So when the woman saw that the tree was good for food,
that it was pleasant to the eyes, and a tree desirable to
make one wise, she took of its fruit and ate.
Genesis 3:6

It is amazing to me that so many professing Christians can toy with sin and think they won't get stung.

When I was thirteen or so I was at a Boy Scout camp in Michigan. Snakes and turtles and all kinds of other lovely creatures had been cleaned out of a huge pen. The serpents were put into a huge box about five feet high, with a hole in the top. One of my friends caught a snake that had escaped. He held it by the tail and the neck, but tried to put the serpent in the hole in the box headfirst. The tail of the serpent wrapped around his wrist and when he pulled his arm back, he pulled the serpent out of the box. The snake's head went down near the ground, and slowly came up. A number of people stood there frozen in terror. Finally that serpent hissed and bit my friend's hand probably twenty times with his fangs.

I've never forgotten that event. I think that toying with sin is a snake that you don't want to pick up by the head or the tail. Sometimes, the effects of dallying with sin can be gradual and deceptively fun; other times they can be like that serpent—swift and deadly. Either way, sin is not to be toyed with.

Question to ponder: What is the lure of sin—why does it seem attractive to us?

APRIL 14

Honesty is the Best Policy

Let him who stole steal no longer, but rather let him labor, working with his hands what is good, that he may have something to give him who has need.
Ephesians 4:28

"Thou shalt not steal," says the eighth commandment, yet I'm afraid that old Diogenes, walking around with his lamp looking for an honest man, might have a difficult time finding one in America today. If he walked up to you and held up his lamp in your face, would he find an honest man? an honest woman? an honest boy or girl?

Once a man parked a car on his front lawn with a sign: "For Sale." Someone stopped to inquire about it, and the teenage son answered the knock on the door. The man made a very generous offer. The son was excited, because there were some things he wanted, and the family was hard pressed for money at the time.

He called his dad excitedly. His father came out and the man told him about his offer. The father said, "Well, you see, there are some problems with this car—some problems that are going to take rather expensive fixing"—and he enumerated exactly what they were. The man thanked him and decided, in the light of that information, he would not buy the car. The owner obviously was the loser in that situation—or was he? His son never forgot that lesson. Years later he could still say, "My father is an honest man." Can your son say that about you?

Question to ponder: Can you think of any time where you have been less than honest? What can you do to make it right?

Theft by Any Other Name — APRIL 15

*Render to Caesar the things that are Caesar's,
and to God the things that are God's.*
Mark 12:17

"A kleptomaniac," said Henry Morgan, "is a person who helps himself because he can't help himself"—or so they claim. It seems like a lot of people today seem to "not be able to help themselves" to all sorts of things.

Consider some ways of breaking the eighth commandment, "thou shalt not steal":

> Failure to pay taxes or over-taxation on the part of an over-reaching government; Shoplifting; Slum lording; Cheating for grades [in school]; Welfare for the able-bodied; Wasting time at work; Shoddy auto and house repairs; Looting in disasters; Ripping pages from library books; Switching price markers at supermarkets; Price manipulation; Marrying or divorcing for money; False advertising claims; Bribing public officials; Fraudulent stock market trades; Kickbacks on contracts; Profit skimming; Vandalism; Passing unqualified students; Fake insurance claims; "Borrowing" and not returning, and so on.

Paul says let him who steals steal no more, but instead work with his hands to provide for himself, his family, and others. May God grant us grace not to steal in any way.

Question to ponder: In our dishonest society, how can we develop a right view of our own and others' property?

Humanistic Religion

Let God be true but every man a liar.
Romans 3:4

The humanistic religion, which is the foundation of our recent legal revolution, is based upon evolutionary theory. It holds that man has evolved from inanimate matter and exists in a universe without God and is therefore responsible for developing his own laws, which are not in any way answerable to a supreme being. As a result our laws have become more man-centered and godless.

It is interesting that for almost 2,000 years, much of civilization (including laws) was theocentric (God-centered), but in the last several decades there has been a great shift taking place, and now the law is becoming anthropocentric (man-centered). Anthropology is replacing theology as the principle focus of attention. Self-image has become an overriding concern on the part of numerous writers. We are told that the most important thing is to develop a positive self-image. We are told that unless we love ourselves, we cannot love others; that self-love is an indispensable prerequisite to useful living (even Christian living) in this world.

Humanism is just another way of talking about atheism. There was a time, years ago, when it was not politic to be an atheist, and so, instead of that, they switched to humanism. Atheism says "down with God"; humanism says "up with man"—but the end is the same.

But God will not be mocked forever. He will arise in due time and judge all.

Question to ponder: Do you think you have any godless humanistic tendencies in your own thinking?

Christt the King

The LORD has established His throne in heaven, And His kingdom rules over all.
Psalm 103:19

Jesus is the Lord of heaven and earth. He is not just the future ruler, but His reign began (though not in its fullness) with His death and resurrection. His kingdom is ever expanding over the hearts and minds of men. He is the conquering King.

When Jesus began the battle, the Captain of the well-fought fight was minus an army, yet every enemy He slew was revived and enlisted into the army of the King. As the King travels across the world, the army behind Him grows, becoming so vast a horde that no man can number it. We see that all the soldiers of the conquering King are but those who were first conquered by Him. These are they who shall come into the great city above wearing crowns on their heads and holding prizes for valor in their arms. They shall come to the very throne of God to lay their spoils at His feet.

Christ is the Great Conqueror. He has succeeded gloriously in all that He has done. He has conquered not only men and empires, but He has conquered even Satan and the world of demons.

Question to ponder: What difference does it make today that Jesus our Savior is also the King of kings?

....

....

....

....

....

....

....

APRIL 18 ≡

Justice and Mercy

*The LORD is longsuffering and abundant in
mercy, forgiving iniquity and transgression....*
Numbers 14:18

We want justice. We want everything to be fair. God is a just God, and we tend to know deep down what is right. In God's justice, He will by no means clear the guilty. Because He is a just God, He must punish evil. We have all fallen short and what we need is not justice, but mercy. So Christianity is beyond fair. God does not treat us as we deserve. He is a God of mercy. Justice would not be good for us.

Christianity is *not* just. Christ didn't come to bring us justice; He came to save us from justice. If any one of gets justice, we would be condemned. That is what we deserve. "For all have sinned, and come short of the glory of God" (Romans 3:23).

There are some in our midst who think that they have nothing to worry about on judgment day. No, they don't need Christ, thank you very much. "Religion is just a crutch for the weak," they say. They don't recognize the magnitude of their sins before a holy God. They will be in for a great shock when they stand before the Lord.

But if you know Jesus personally, you recognize that without His shed blood at Calvary, you would have no hope. You would only be staring God's justice in the face, with no hope for mercy.

Praise be to God for sending us Jesus Christ and for forgiving our sins and extending mercy to us.

Question to ponder: God's mercy is new every morning. And His justice never sleeps. Reflect on the relationship between justice and mercy.

Claims of Christ

*Then Jesus spoke to them again, saying, "I am
the light of the world. He who follows Me shall
not walk in darkness, but have the light of life."*
John 8:12

Jesus made extraordinary claims about Himself. For example, He
declared, "I am the light of the world." What a profound statement to issue
forth from the lips of any man. If anyone were to make a statement like that
today, we would suppose that either he was the world's greatest egomaniac
or he was completely deranged.

The astounding thing is that we receive such words as these—"I am
the light of the world...I am the good shepherd...All that ever came before
me were thieves and robbers...I am the resurrection and the life...I am the
way, the truth and the life"—from the lips of Christ as if they were com-
monplace. There is only one of two ways that we can react to this. We must
either draw back in revulsion at such claims or else we must fall down on
our knees and worship.

When the High Priest heard these claims of Christ, he reacted the first
way. He tore his robes and shouted, "Blasphemy!" On the other hand, when
the Magi came and saw the Christ child, they bowed down and worshiped
Him. So too the disciples worshiped Jesus after His resurrection.

Question to ponder: What does it mean to
worship Jesus Christ?

APRIL **20** ═══

Life or Death

> *See, I have set before you today life and good, death and*
> *evil, in that I command you today to love the LORD your*
> *God, to walk in His ways, and to keep His commandments.*
> Deuteronomy 30:15-16

God has set before us the "maker's manual." If you obey the commandments, you will do well. If you don't, you will destroy yourself. The commandments are basically simple, but they are not easy. If we seek to live a godly life, we can only do this by His power and by His grace.

Human success or failure in this life is largely dependent upon the requisite yielding of ourselves in obedience to the commandments of God. It is not some great mystery. It is simply doing what God told us to do. Apparently there are many people in this nation and world who are mostly ignoring those commandments or outright disobeying them. That, of course, is to their own hurt and detriment.

We do not keep the law in order that we might be saved or be acceptable to God; but having been transformed by Christ, having been forgiven and redeemed by Jesus Christ, having been made new creatures by His grace and His mercy, we now desire to live by His commandments and His law. God gives us a new heart, a heart that delights in our God and a heart that desires to live by His statutes.

Question to ponder: We are told to keep God's commandments in word, thought, and deed. Which one is hardest for you?

....

....

....

....

....

"Flame of God"

Then I said, "Here am I. Send me."
Isaiah 6:8

In 1956, five American missionaries were killed in the jungles of Ecuador by fierce Indians. One of them was Jim Elliot, who famously said, "He is no fool who gives what he cannot keep to gain that which he cannot lose."

In his senior year at Wheaton College, Elliot wrote some words in his diary which I recall reading and being awestruck that any college senior could write such words: "[God] makes 'His ministers a flame of fire.' Am I ignitable? God deliver me from the dread asbestos of 'other things.' Saturate me with the oil of the Spirit that I may be a flame. But flame is transient, often short-lived. Canst thou bear this, my soul short life?.... 'Make me Thy fuel, Flame of God.'" Some seven years later, that fuel was consumed.

What is it that holds us back from total surrender or unconditional service? We are often afraid that God will ask us to do something too hard or too difficult.

I'm sure Jim Elliot did not regret his decision. (Certainly, his writings before his death would indicate as such.) Whatever God calls us to do, it will be an adventure, and He promises to go with us every step of the way.

Question to ponder: Can I commit myself to God at a deeper level? Is there anything I am holding back from Him?

....
....
....
....
....
....
....
....

APRIL 22

Many Infallible Proofs

*For we did not follow cunningly devised fables when
we made known to you the power and coming of our
Lord Jesus Christ, but were eyewitnesses of His majesty.*
2 Peter 1:16

It is interesting that in the radical left wing of Protestantism, back about two hundred years ago, they were concocting in their ivory towers all kinds of theories about how the Bible was not the Word of God, how these were but mythological stories, inventions of creative minds, things that never happened in this world at all.

Interestingly, about the very same time, there was another science that was beginning; it was the science of archaeology. In fact, Napoleon contributed to it. When he went to invade Egypt, he took with him scientists who examined all the many wonderful finds in Egypt and gave great impetus to the new science of archaeology. Since then archaeologists have dug up hundreds of thousands of different finds confirming the Bible over and over again and totally demolishing the liberal radical documentary hypothesis of the Old Testament. Today no reputable Old Testament scholar would maintain the kind of things that were taught in many seminaries (including the seminary I attended), because it has been given the *coup de grâce* by archaeology.

Nelson Glueck, the renowned Jewish archaeologist said, "It may be stated categorically that no archaeological discovery has ever controverted a biblical reference." Dr. Paul L. Maier, the noted scholar of ancient history, said, "There is no question but that archaeology is the Bible's best friend."

Question to ponder: How does God defend His own Word?

Self-Image

But seek first the kingdom of God and His righteousness,
and all these things shall be added to you.
Matthew 6:33

There are many people who begin life with a very poor self-image. They are helped along the way by others who criticize them, ignore them, make fun of them, pooh-pooh their ideas, and contribute to their general feeling that they really have nothing to offer, that they are not worthwhile, that nobody wants to hear what they have to say, and certainly that no one could care how they feel. Therefore, they withhold all of these things and the result is a breakdown in communication.

Do you help contribute to a poor self-image in your spouse or in those around you? Many men do so by continually putting their wives down, by being sarcastic and not interested in their ideas. They may find themselves increasingly living in a lonely world and losing out on a great deal. Do you treat your wife that way? There are women, of course, who do the same thing. They enjoy putting their husbands down. They try to lord it over them and belittle them.

I believe that if we seek God's kingdom first and His righteousness, then all things shall be added to us. Included in that list is a healthy self-image. I am uncomfortable with an unhealthy emphasis on self-image. As we love God and our neighbor as ourselves, a healthy self-image tends to emerge, because we are made in His image.

Question to ponder: Can you think of anything you can do to build up anyone around you?

APRIL 24 — *An Adequate Sense of Who We Are*

And the second is like it: "You shall
love your neighbor as yourself."
Matthew 22:39

Our society puts an inordinate amount of emphasis on self-image. Look out for #1 (that is, yourself), cry the pundits. How is a good self-image achieved and does it matter?

A self-image is very much like happiness. Someone once wrote about the "unhappy pursuit of happiness." The unhappiest people are the ones who pursue happiness, because happiness is not something you can find by directly pursuing it. It is something which is a by-product of pursuing something else. It is something we discover when we are not really looking for it.

When we serve God and Christ and help other people, when we fulfill His commandments, when we see our lives being used to build up other people, to transform their lives and to bring in the Kingdom of God, we discover that God has already taken care of our desire for a good self image and we have a very adequate sense of who we are. A self-image is not some balloon inside of us that has to be pumped up; it is simply our reflection of who we are and what we are doing in this world. A right picture of God leads to a correct picture of self.

Question to ponder: What is the relationship between Christ-confidence and self-confidence?

....

....

....

....

....

....

Reconciliation

God was in Christ reconciling the world to Himself,
not imputing their trespasses to them, and has
committed to us the word of reconciliation.
2 Corinthians 5:19

How are we reconciled with each other? By repentance and faith. By faith we rest in the atoning blood of Christ and claim that cleansing stream. We are made one with Him, being one with Christ and one with the Father, and then we can be one with one another.

There must be reconciliation from man to man, woman to woman, individual to individual. That is accomplished by repentance and confession. As you think about your relationship with God, are there things separating you from Him—things you have not repented of, things you have not turned from, things you have not confessed, things you have not claimed His forgiveness for? As you think about your brothers or sisters, are there those from whom you are estranged?

We have been reconciled to God by the death of Jesus. Therefore, we should be reconciled with others—especially to our brothers and sisters in Christ.

Question to ponder: Are there those whom you are holding grudges against? Are there those who have hurt you that you need to forgive or whom you have hurt and need to confess that sin to?

....

....

....

....

....

APRIL 26

Rejecting the Lord

*Today, if you will hear His voice, do not
harden your hearts as in the rebellion.*
Hebrews 3:7-8

I have invited countless people to come to faith in Jesus Christ and
to participate in the great wedding feast of the Lamb, and they have made
light of it. I cannot imagine it, but some do just that.

I talked to a 95-year-old man and invited him to the feast. He said no;
he didn't want to be bored. I tried to deal with that in an intelligent manner,
but I really, upon reflection, think that what I should have said is, "What
would ever make you say a stupid thing like that? Here you are teetering
on the very edge of the precipice of eternity, about to plunge into the lake
of fire, where you won't have time to be bored because you will be howl-
ing and gnashing your teeth forever—and you talk about being bored in
heaven!" When we witness to people we want to make it sound good and
appealing. Remember, we are only the messenger. We cannot scare anyone
into heaven, only invite them.

Question to ponder: How do you feel about people
rejecting the Lord, when you try to witness?

Rejoicing

...Singing and making melody in your heart to the Lord.
Ephesians 5:19

Paul tells us, "Rejoice in the Lord always: and again I say, Rejoice" (Philippians 4:4). When one stops to think about it, that is exactly the opposite of the way we react. For example, if we were teaching a person the secret of success, we would say to them, "This is what you do first...secondly, you do this...thirdly you do thus and so on...." Then success will come and finally, you rejoice. However, Paul says first you rejoice.

The world says that seeing is believing; the Bible says that believing is seeing. So we begin by rejoicing. The reason we can rejoice is because we are rejoicing in the Lord. In Christ we already have success; in Christ we are already the possessors of all things and, therefore, we can and will rejoice. The Lord inhabits the praises of His people. He is near to those who praise Him. Praise and rejoicing is a safe place to dwell because our enemy, the devil, flees before sincere praise.

Question to ponder: In what do you rejoice today?

....

....

....

....

....

....

....

....

....

....

APRIL 28 ═══

Under the Circumstances

We are hard-pressed on every side, yet not crushed; we are perplexed, but not in despair.
2 Corinthians 4:8

I'm sure you've heard the story about the minister who visited a parishioner who wasn't doing well. The minister asked the man how he was doing, and the man replied, "Pretty well—under the circumstances." And the pastor replied, "What are you doing *under* the circumstances?"

The Apostle Paul was an excellent example of a man who never seemed to be under the circumstances. Paul would have us to clearly understand that our rejoicing is not in our circumstances. Paul wrote his admonition to rejoice always from the depths of a Roman prison where he was a prisoner in chains. (We know that when the Roman eagle fixes its claws, it seldom lets go without drawing blood.) Paul had to say that it was quite uncertain as to "how it shall be with me." He was facing a capital trial that could cost him his life. He was obliged to contemplate the fact that he might be offered up—that he might be poured out as a libation. Yet, in spite of the fact that all was uncertain, all was dark, and all was drear, out of the midst of this darkness there chimed the clear notes of his jubilation: "Rejoice in the Lord, always."

Question to ponder: How can we rise above the circumstances of our lives and learn to rejoice?

....

....

....

....

....

....

I Rejoice, You Rejoice

Paul and Timothy, bondservants of Jesus Christ, to
all the saints in Christ Jesus who are in Philippi.
Philippians 1:1

Rejoicing is the theme of Paul's epistle to the Philippians. It could be summed up in four words: I rejoice; you rejoice. This theme of rejoicing is like an underground stream that bubbles its way along and then, ever and anon, it breaks forth into the sunshine, sparkling with joy. It is a continual, reiterated refrain in this harmony of joy that Paul gives to us

It is in the Lord Jesus that we can rejoice. We rejoice in Him...in His goodness...in His grace...in His mercy...in His long-suffering...in His faithfulness. We rejoice in what He has done for us upon the Cross and through the empty tomb.

It is precious to the Lord if we can rejoice when we are going through hard times. If we rejoice only when all is well, that is not such a great accomplishment. We should make thanks and praise a part of our daily life. Even now He is turning the bad things to our good. And He has promised that He will lead us forth to ultimate triumph and bring us forth into that gladsome city where tears shall be no more and singing shall be ever heard. Therefore we can rejoice in Christ Jesus!

Question to ponder: We are to let the joy of God fill our heart—when is it easiest for you to be joyful?

....

....

....

....

....

....

The Only Way

> *Thomas said to Him, "Lord, we do not know where*
> *You are going, and how can we know the way?"*
> John 14:5

All pagan religions have a "way." Whether it is the eightfold path of Buddha, the teachings of the Koran, the Analects of Confucius, or whatever it is, all pagan religions say, "Here is the way. Walk in that way, and you'll make it to..." wherever it is you are supposed to make it to.

If you get to Nirvana or Paradise, and you get there by walking in that way, I have a question: Who got you there? I hope you know. You did. You followed the way. You walked in the path. You kept these teachings. You did it. You...You...YOU saved yourself. You are your savior, because, you see, pagan religions have no savior, except you.

But Jesus says, "I am the way." It is not the teachings of Jesus, it is not the preaching of Jesus, it is not the example of Jesus, it is not the Sermon on the Mount, it is not the Beatitudes, or anything else that He taught or said that is the way. The way is Christ Himself, the divine second Person of the Trinity, the Creator of the galaxies that came into this world. He is the way, He is the Truth, and He is the Life. We have life only ultimately through Him.

Question to ponder: What does it mean in your life that Jesus is the only way?

....

....

....

....

....

....

Only Two Religions in the World

This is a faithful saying and worthy of all acceptance, that Christ Jesus came into the world to save sinners, of whom I am chief.
1 Timothy 1:15

There are only two religions in the world, and it is not the religion of Christ and the religion of Buddha, the religion of Christ and the religion of Muhammad, the religion of anyone and the religion of somebody else. It is either Christ Himself, or it is YOU, because every pagan religion teaches you to save yourself by your own goodness. However, if there is anything that the Bible teaches from one end to the other, it is that you can't do it.

No man can save himself. "All have sinned and come short of the glory of God" (Romans 3:23). "They [we] are together become unprofitable" (v.12). "He that believeth not is condemned already...." (John 3:18).

In the Garden of Gethsemane, Christ was, in effect, saying, "Buddha, come, take a drink. Mohammed, won't you take some of this cup? Confucius, it's yours." But there was no answer. It was not possible that anyone else could drink the cup. Anyone would have been instantly extinguished when the infinite wrath of God fell upon them on the Cross.

Question to ponder: Have you ever tried to save yourself by being "good enough"?

MAY 2 ══

Religious But Lost

Good Teacher, what shall I do that I may inherit eternal life?
Mark 10:17

The story of the rich young ruler (in Matthew 19, Mark 10, and Luke 18) is addressed specifically not to the bum, not to the criminal, not to the person in the jailhouse, but to those who regularly frequent the sanctuary. It is directed toward the religious-but-lost category of which there are millions in our country today.

It is directed toward those who are respectable, reverent, and worshipful. They're not out on the beach on Sunday mornings, but they are frequently at the house of God, offering prayer and praise—at least most do. These religious-but-lost individuals are not in jail, not stretched out with a hangover or some kind of drug addiction. They are respectable, well-dressed, well-traveled, well-accoutered, and rich.

It is a tragedy to be religious but lost. Many in our churches today are. They need to see that they are sinners, and their sins will be punished. Either they let Jesus take the punishment due to their sins, or they will be punished for them. One or the other.

Question to ponder: Do you know anyone who may be "religious but lost." What can you do to try to help them to see Christ and Him crucified?

⊸ ....

....

....

....

....

....

....

A Mother's Impact
〰 MAY **3**

Her children rise up and call her blessed.
Proverbs 31:28

Andrew Murray (1828-1917) of South Africa was a great theologian and writer. He was one of eight or nine children, all of whom grew up to bless their land as the godliest of people because their godly father and mother led Christian lives and gathered the family together for worship each day.

In her old age, Andrew's mother was asked her secret by people who marveled that so many children of such tremendous character, integrity, spirituality, and power and influence could have come from one home. Her answer was that she lived the life she wanted her children to live. And central in that life was the regular worship of God, reading the Word, and prayer together in their home.

We see this same principle in the life of Samuel, one of the great saints of the Bible. This mighty spiritual leader began a whole new epic in the life of Israel, but where did he come from? Like Andrew Murray, he had a godly mother. Hannah prayed for a son and God answered her prayer. Also in the first chapter of I Samuel you will discover three things about Samuel's family. First of all his parents took him regularly to worship with them in the temple. Secondly, his mother and father were praying people. They knew how to pray and to get answers to their prayers. Thirdly, early each morning they gathered together all of the family to worship God in the home. Out of this family life grew Samuel, the prophet, the reformer, the teacher of Israel. His mother Hannah's prayer helped change a nation.

Question to ponder: What can you do to make your home more godly?

〰 ....

....

....

....

MAY **4** ═══ *The Christian and Stewardship*

The earth is the LORD's, and all its fullness,
the world and those who dwell therein.
Psalm 24:1

A key principle of Christian stewardship that is taught throughout the Bible is the principle of the "first fruits." God has said that the first fruits belong to Him. This means that we demonstrate our acknowledgement that the earth is the Lord's and the fullness thereof by returning unto Him what He requires, namely the first fruits of all that He gives to us. Not the middle fruits or the last fruits, and not after "I see if I am going to have something left over" to give. No, we start by, in faith, giving to Him the first fruits.

Here are the five principles of stewardship:

- The earth is the Lord's.
- God wants us before our wealth.
- We are to bring the first fruits of all that we receive.
- They are defined in the test of the tithe.
- If we pass the test, there are great blessings in store for us.

Question to ponder: Have you tried to give to the Lord generously of your time, your talents, and your material blessings?

....

....

....

....

....

....

....

Forbidden Fruit

*So when the woman saw that the tree was good
for food, that it was pleasant to the eyes, and a tree
desirable to make one wise, she took of its fruit and ate.
She also gave to her husband with her, and he ate.*
Genesis 3:6

Many young people today have been enticed to taste the forbidden fruit of sexual immorality. They have been told that it is good, fun, and freeing. As they have followed the siren song of the age right into the marshy swamplands of impurity, they have suffered the consequences, such as seeing their bodies eaten up with sores and sickness, and their souls reduced and shriveled up. "When lust hath conceived, it bringeth forth sin: and sin, when it is finished, bringeth forth death" (James 1:15).

AIDS has devastated much of the homosexual community. Homosexuality reduces the life span of men by almost half. Whereas the average married man in America lives to be seventy-four years of age, the average homosexual dies at forty-three. This is the tragic, natural consequence of their unnatural acts, which God clearly tells us to avoid. So maybe God truly wants the best for us and isn't such an ogre after all. Maybe every good gift and every perfect gift *does* come down from above, and not up from beneath with a hook in it and Satan at the other end of the line.

As Leslie Unruh, founder of the Abstinence Clearinghouse, points out, there is no condom available to prevent a breaking heart. God created sex, and when we play by His rules, things go better for everyone.

Question to ponder: How can we help the people who have suffered so greatly from believing the lies of the sexual revolution?

MAY 6 ══ *Remember. Repent. Return.*

Remember therefore from where you have fallen; repent and do the first works, or else I will come to you quickly and remove your lampstand from its place—unless you repent.
Revelation 2:5

Remember the threefold prescription of our Savior: remember, repent, and return. May God grant that we might remember our first love and from whence we are fallen. What a tragic term "fallen" is. You are a *fallen* woman...a *fallen* man. You have *fallen* from your first love. Repent from your spiritual apathy. Return to your first love for Jesus. Remember . . . Repent . . . Return.

It took the precious blood of Christ to forgive our sins, and nothing less than that will suffice. We cannot be redeemed by contrition or repentance alone, but we cannot be redeemed without them. This is the plain teaching of the Scriptures

If we can catch ourselves and repent from the "small sins"—such as an unkind word or a covetous thought or a missed opportunity to witness or serve, then the return is not so hard. If we do not heed the Holy Spirit and instead we let things slide, we become backslidden, and the return is much harder. If we live in daily repentance, we will continue in His light.

Question to ponder: Have you lost love for Christ and zeal for His work? What can you do to remember, repent, and return?

....

....

....

....

....

....

A Good Name

*A good name is to be chosen rather than great
riches, loving favor rather than silver and gold.*
Proverbs 22:1

In the Bible a name represents a person, just as it does in the third of
the Ten Commandments—"Thou shalt not take the name of the Lord thy
God in vain."

We are all concerned for the reputation of our good name. We have
laws against those that would besmirch our name because they are be-
smirching us. And for those who hold God in contempt and drag Him in
the mud, there is a penalty. God says, "...for the Lord will not hold him guiltless that taketh His name in vain." There is no menace here. It is simply a
statement of a fact.

Ultimately having a good name comes from putting our faith in Jesus.
A good reputation comes from good and sound living. If we are known for
our honesty, hard work, kind words, helpfulness, and generosity, we will
have a good name among people. It takes time and effort. It also takes a
moment to ruin a reputation. We should be as zealous for God's reputation
as we are for our own.

Question to ponder: What type of reputation before
others do you think you have? What can we do to
honor God and His good name?

....

....

....

....

....

....

MAY 8 ══ *Unforgiveness*

And forgive us our debts, as we forgive our debtors.
Matthew 6:12

Jay Adams, a Christian psychologist, tells about a couple, Sue and Wilbur, who came for counseling. She was quite angry and was there because her doctor told her to come. (She had an ulcer).

Reaching down into a shopping bag-sized purse, she pulled out an 8 1/2" x 11" manuscript, about an inch thick, with single-spaced, type-written text on both sides of the page. She slapped it down on the desk and said, "That's why I am here."

Wilbur said, "Oh." He picked it up to see what it was. When he opened it, he saw a careful documentation of every slight, every hurt, every word, every deed he had committed against her for thirteen years—which, by the way, proved in subsequent visits to be an exceedingly accurate report.

She said, "That is what is giving me ulcers."

The counselor said, "I want you to know, young lady, that it has been many a year since I have met anyone—she began to smile and Wilbur slid down even farther in his seat—as hostile and as resentful as you are!" With that Wilbur sort of sat up a little bit straighter. The counselor said, "This is a record not only of the faults your husband has committed against you, but also of the sin you have committed against him and against God and against your own body, for which you are now paying a price."

It is God's job to avenge, and it is because we serve a just God that we can leave it to Him. Forgiveness is never easy, but it is right.

Question to ponder: Is there anybody you are harboring resentment toward? What can you do today to make it right?

Be Nice

*And be kind to one another, tenderhearted, forgiving
one another, even as God in Christ forgave you.*
Ephesians 4:32

Some Christians are not nice; some can't even be civil. Many times people try to communicate with their spouses, or with anyone, but that communication is blocked by that cold and icy wall of resentment which is the memory in the soul of some previous hurt or slight or wound of some sort. That resentment acts like a thermometer that measures within each one of us the level, the degree, of our lack of forgiveness. But Paul tells us in this chapter to be tenderhearted, forgiving one another as God, for Christ's sake, has forgiven us. We are called forgive, even as we have been forgiven.

Think of all that God has given us—pardon, forgiveness, provision and adoption into the family of God, care for all of your needs, and the promise that one day we will be with Him forever in paradise.

When we consider God's gifts to us, it is easier to look kindly on others. When we remember what God has forgiven us for, it is easier to forgive one another. When we consider God's kindness to us, it is easier to be kind to each other.

Question to ponder: How can we develop the heart of Christ toward people around us?

....

....

....

....

....

....

....

MAY **10** ═══

Consider the Butterfly

The body is sown in corruption, it is raised in incorruption.
1 Corinthians 15:42

Recently my wife and I visited Butterfly World, a magnificent spectacle of beauty and color in Fort Lauderdale that houses thousands of butterflies flying freely in an enclosed area. We were each given a little chrysalis in a plastic cup. We observed them. They had already woven their own cerement, created their own winding sheet, built their own coffin. But now they were breaking free. They had utterly transformed themselves. Out comes one wing, and then another. Then they pump up their wings with their own blood and fly off into the sky.

A butterfly is often used as a description of the Resurrection. It certainly is, but it would be a more accurate picture of the resurrection of mankind if we took that chrysalis, ground it to powder, dissolved it in water, mixed it with mud, and splashed it into all the rivers of the world—and then waited for the butterfly to come out. That is the plight of man. Indeed, how shall our bodies ever come together again? Of course, God, who created the world out of nothing, can one day resurrect our bodies, despite the earthly condition of our remains.

Question to ponder: What does it mean to you to know that one day God will resurrect your body?

···

···

···

···

···

···

···

Resurrection From the Dead

*...And what is the exceeding greatness of His
power toward us who believe, according to the
working of His mighty power which He worked in
Christ when He raised Him from the dead and seated
Him at His right hand in the heavenly places.*
Ephesians 1:19-20

Because of Jesus, one day all people will be raised from the dead, either for salvation or damnation. It is not merely a handful of individuals that will be resurrected as was the case in Jesus' earthly ministry when he said *"Talitha cumi"* and a young girl rose from her bed (Mark 5:41), or "Lazarus, come forth" and Lazarus walked out with his graveclothes still on him (John 11:43-44).

No, Jesus said that *all* that are in the graves shall hear His voice and come forth in that day. Everyone. And more than that it will happen instantaneously. In a moment. In the twinkling of an eye it's all going to be done. Surely that seems to be utterly incredible. Yet that is what we are told, and what we are called to believe.

What is the solution to such an apparent impossibility? The apostle Paul said to King Agrippa, "Why should it be thought a thing incredible with you, that God should raise the dead?" (Acts 26:8). There is the other dimension. There is the other factor—God..."that *God* should raise the dead."

Question to ponder: What does it mean to you to know that the same God who raised Jesus from the dead will one day raise you?

....

....

....

....

MAY 12 ≡ *A Third Great Awakening*

O Lord, revive Your work in the midst of the years!
Habakkuk 3:2

There is a great need for a heaven-sent revival by the Holy Spirit of God to sweep across the land. The first thing we can do is pray, and I am glad there are people taking that seriously.

Too often we forget that America became a nation soon after a spiritual revival, the First Great Awakening. Then in the early 1800s, America experienced a Second Great Awakening, which helped bring about a moral revolution—particularly in addressing the evil of slavery. But now we are in need of a Third Great Awakening. Will you join me in praying for that to happen? I believe it is America's only real hope.

People are under the misconception that government will solve all their problems. But I believe that if true change is going to take place it will start with the people through a genuine revival that eventually moves to the halls of government. Not from the government down, but from the people up. God once declared, "If my people, which are called by my name, shall humble themselves, and pray, and seek my face, and turn from their wicked ways: then will I hear from heaven, and will forgive their sin, and will heal their land!" (2 Chronicles 7:14). May it be in our day.

Question to ponder: What are the components of a true revival and how does it happen?

....

....

....

....

....

....

God's Prosperity

This Book of the Law shall not depart from your mouth, but you shall meditate in it day and night, that you may observe to do according to all that is written in it. For then you will make your way prosperous, and then you will have good success.
Joshua 1:8

Are you one to meditate upon God's Word? It is interesting that the book of Joshua is the only place in the Bible where we find the promise to prosper and have good success. God says that if you are careful to meditate upon the Word day and night, you will be prosperous in your goings and you will have good success. That is incredible. What God wants from us is simply faith and obedience to Him. He will take care of our problems.

At the end of the book of Job, God blesses Job, gives him children, his home, and double his flocks, his wealth and what he had before. We should remember that the Old Testament temporalizes the blessings of God. In the New Testament they are more spiritualized and we're called upon to take the long look to understand that the things of this life will not be balanced until eternity. God has reserved for us in Heaven rewards beyond anything Job ever even dreamed of, and we can never lose sight of that promise.

Today, the success God grants to us is not always in the form of material blessings. Often it is spiritual. But He always provides what we need. Spiritual rewards are not less; they are more.

Question to ponder: What does it mean to meditate on God's Word?

....

....

....

....

....

MAY 14 — *A Right Way, A Wrong Way*

*There is a way that seems right to a
man, but its end is the way of death.*
Proverbs 14:12

I remember one time, not too many years before she died (she was probably about 75 at the time), my mother came to visit us. One day, she had a headache and she asked for two aspirin. After I gave her the aspirin, she put one in her mouth as far back as she could on her tongue, and then tried to swallow it. Guess what? She gagged and choked and sputtered. Finally, red in the face, she was able to get most of it down. The rest of it was smeared across the back of her throat, I suppose, in the attempt.

I said, "Mother, that's not the way to take an aspirin. Let me show you." I took some vitamins, threw them in my mouth, and drank them right down. She was amazed. "Mother, it's all in the technique," I said. "You don't put the aspirin on the back of your tongue, you put it in the concavity of your tongue and it just floats down. She tried it and it worked. It isn't difficult to swallow an aspirin when you do it the right way. It's ghastly when you do it the wrong way.

So it is with virtually anything in life. It isn't that difficult when we do it the right way, but it's terribly difficult when we do it the wrong way. God's Word shows us the right way for virtually everything we deal with in life. Let us trust God today. Let us do things God's way, and see the truth of His Word.

Question to ponder: Can you think of anything in your life right now that you may be possibly attempting to handle in a ***wrong*** way?

〰️ ....

....

....

....

....

The Ascension of Christ ═══ MAY 15

Now when He had spoken these things, while they watched,
He was taken up, and a cloud received Him out of their sight.
Acts 1:9

When Christ Jesus was finished with all His work on earth, He ascended in triumph to heaven. The day of his ascension ought to be celebrated as the coronation day for the King of kings.

Christ, who was once despised and rejected of men, a man of sorrows and acquainted with grief, now occupies a most exalted position where there is joy forevermore. Jesus Christ, once derided by sinners, is now celebrated by saints. The scoffing and the hissing of the reprobate have given way to the panegyrics of angels. The flailing of whips and the pounding of hammers have been replaced by the flourish of trumpets, the beating of drums and the flying of colors. The Son of God has come home to sit at the right hand of His Father—until all His enemies are made a footstool for His feet and Christ becomes all in all.

It is this Christ in all His glory, and with all His authority and might, who will one day come back to earth. But not as He came the first time. Not in humility, but with all His splendor and glory.

Question to ponder: How do you picture the exalted and glorified Christ?

....

....

....

....

....

....

....

MAY **16** ═══ *Sin and Happiness?*

*...Choosing rather to suffer affliction with the people
of God than to enjoy the passing pleasures of sin.*
Hebrews 11:25

I believe the greatest deceit Satan has ever perpetrated upon the human race, the most successful lie he has ever used and which impinges upon our consciences from a thousand different directions, is simply this: We shall find happiness and fulfillment through sin and by disregarding the commandments and precepts of God. And it is by throwing off the chains that bind, letting ourselves go and following our own passions, ignoring Christ and His Word that we will find satisfaction and joy in this life. Satan's most successful lie would have us believe that joy shall be ours through sin. I am sure that most of us have believed this lie a thousand times or more in our lives.

Yet, the great truth of the Word of God is that at the right hand of God there is joy forevermore. There is happiness in holiness. It is through submission to the will of Christ that man will find his true joy and fulfillment. These are two totally and completely antithetical propositions. One is truth, the other a lie.

Question to ponder: Can you think of a time in your life when you believed sinning would make you happy?

〰...

....

....

....

....

....

....

The Monster of the Old Nature ══ MAY 17

*And do not present your members as instruments
of unrighteousness to sin, but present yourselves to
God as being alive from the dead, and your members
as instruments of righteousness to God.*
Romans 6:13

There is a little couplet which I like so much, but it contains a good word—forgotten by many today—the word "mien" (pronounced "mean"). It means "countenance" or appearance. Listen to the couplet:

"Vice is a monster of such horrible mien, that to be hated it needs but to be seen. But seen too oft, grown familiar with its face, first we endure, then we embrace."

Familiarity with the face of the monster of vice is the very essence of just about every talk show on television I have seen or know anything about (except the news or Christian-oriented ones). But Christians do not seek such familiarity. Instead, we should turn away from our old vices, our old habits, our old sinful nature.

The diminishing of our old nature is called mortification. The growing of our new nature is called vivification. Put the two together (mortification and vivification) and you get sanctification—one of the great glorious doctrines of the Christian faith.

Sanctification is a process that goes on and on throughout this life. It is never even perfected in this life. It is not until we cross that river that there, in a final act of glorification, the final vestiges of sin are removed and we are declared to be perfect.

Question to ponder: Is there any vice that you could possibly have grown too familiar with?

⑂ ....

....

....

MAY 18 *Energy for Good or Evil*

> *We know that we are of God, and the whole*
> *world lies under the sway of the wicked one.*
> 1 John 5:19

The ungodly world is energized, unknowingly in most cases, by Satan. Too often, the world under that energizing force accomplishes more than many Christians do. This has given rise to the belief among many, especially among the younger people of our country, that Satan is actually able to do more for them than God. This is a great shame. Christians have not believed enough and have not called upon God for great things nor have they demonstrated the might and power of God in this world. God is glorified by great things accomplished by Christians.

We know that Satan is the great mimic. He mimics God and he would try to destroy people by substitution. On Christmas, we have the great ersatz savior, Santa Claus, the substitute for Christ. Satan substitutes everything that is Divine. On Easter, we have the Easter Bunny and the Easter Egg, all to divert the thoughts of men away from that which is most significant.

We also know that Satan has been defeated by Christ in His death and resurrection. Christ came to destroy the works of the devil.

Question to ponder: How do we know that good will triumph over evil?

....

....

....

....

....

....

A Much Needed Advocate

My little children, these things I write to you, so
that you may not sin. And if anyone sins, we have an
Advocate with the Father, Jesus Christ the righteous.
1 John 2:1

Satan is the accuser of the brethren. Even as he appeared before God accusing Job, he accuses us of all manner of sins. All our iniquities and all our transgressions are picked up by this malignant spirit and hurled against us in utter condemnation before God's Throne.

Who shall plead our case? Where is the advocate for our defense? Not only does Satan accuse us, but all about us are unbelievers who claim we do not live up to the ideals we profess. They say that there are hypocrites in the Church, and that each believer is also a sinner. Our own sinfulness is used to vilify us. Furthermore, at times our own conscience condemns as well.

Who shall plead our case? Thank God, there is One who is at the right hand of God, acting as our advocate. His blood ever intercedes on our behalf. Jesus Christ is our sure defense against all these enemies: the world, the flesh, and the devil.

Question to ponder: What comfort does it give you to know that Jesus is ever pleading your case before the Lord?

....

....

....

....

....

....

....

MAY 20 — *Kept Through All These Years*

*God is faithful, by whom you were called into
the fellowship of His Son, Jesus Christ our Lord.*
1 Corinthians 1:9

When I look back at my life, what amazes me is that, throughout all these long and sometimes difficult years, Christ has been with me, He has never forsaken me; He has kept me in the way everlasting. I am amazed, considering how weak I am, that I have not been totally overwhelmed by temptation and sin. I have seen others who have fallen by the wayside. I thank God that He has kept me through these years. Why? "I have prayed for thee, that thy faith fail not" (Luke 22:32). Jesus is our great intercessor with the Father.

By His grace, we are saved. By His grace, we are preserved. In this world, in this life, the temptations to stray will continue. We must be careful not to fall for the devil's attempts to lure us away. Until Satan is restrained, he will continue to try. But know this: God's ability to keep us is greater than any temptation. His hand is stronger than the tug from our enemy.

God's faithfulness is greater than our frailty. His arm is strong enough; His counsel is wise enough to lead us all the way home.

Question to ponder: How have you experienced God's faithfulness?

....

....

....

....

....

....

Fanatics and the Second Coming ≡ MAY 21

*But of that day and hour no one knows, not
even the angels of heaven, but My Father only.*
Matthew 24:36

It is unfortunately true that there have been some in the lunatic
fringe who have dwelt continuously upon the doctrine of the Second Coming and brought it into disrepute. There have been others who have ignored
it completely, and still more who have distorted and perverted it. And yet
it remains an inescapable and ineluctable fact that Jesus Christ will come
again. Over 300 passages in the New Testament alone testify that Christ
will come again, this time as a conquering King.

John boldly declares in Revelation: "Behold, he cometh with clouds
and every eye shall see him...and all kindreds of the earth shall wail because
of him" (Revelation 1:7). The Bible even concludes with this same promise,
"Surely I come quickly. Amen" (Revelation 22:20). And Christians every
week across the globe affirm their belief in this great fact of His return,
found in the Apostles' Creed: "From thence He shall come to judge the
quick and the dead."

When will Jesus return? This is the question that has puzzled the
minds of innumerable people throughout the centuries. Our Lord said that
no man knows the day or the hour of His coming. This is reserved for the
Father alone. And yet He does tell us when it will be. He says that He will
come in an hour that you think not.

Question to ponder: Is there anything in your life you would
do differently if you knew Jesus were coming tomorrow?

⑂ ....

....

....

....

MAY 22

The Great Day of Judgment

And I saw the dead, small and great, standing before God, and books were opened.
Revelation 20:12

At the time of the Second Coming, many will wake up on that day ignoring Christ, as they have ignored Him for years, and then suddenly, without warning, unexpectedly, there shall come a sound that will chill the blood of every unbeliever, but will cause God's own to leap with joy.

It will be the sound of a trumpet as the Scripture says. It will be a sound that will be heard around the world. Then suddenly there shall appear in the heavens the sign of the Son of man, for the Lord, Himself, shall descend from heaven with great power and glory. His glory will eclipse the sun, and every eye will be lifted up to behold His great glory as He comes.

Then all around the world, graves will be opened and the dead in Christ shall rise first with their bodies reconstituted and glorified. And then we, which are alive, shall be caught up together with Him and we shall be changed in the twinkling of an eye. We shall be changed, and all that is corruptible will put on incorruption and all that is mortal will put on immortality. From homes, and kitchens, and cars, and planes, they will be taken up to be with the Lord in the air, who shall come with His angels and cherubim and seraphim and with ten thousand times ten thousand of His saints. In magnificent splendor and glory, He will come.

Question to ponder: What difference does it make to you that history is marching toward its great climax, the return of Christ and the final judgment?

....

....

....

....

The Wrath of the Lamb

*Do not harden your hearts as in the rebellion,
in the day of trial in the wilderness.*
Hebrews 3:8

I am sure that in the great day of the Second Coming, there will be millions who will cry, "Oh, God, have mercy upon me; oh, Lord, help me." But, my friends, it will be too late. It will be everlastingly too late for the door of grace will irretrievably have been shut. There will be no time for repentance then. There will be no tomorrow. There will only be the endless ages of eternity without God and without hope.

People will see that the Son of man will come to this earth, not as a lamb to be slain, but the Lamb in His wrath and anger. They will then cry out unto the hills and unto the mountains and rocks, "Fall on us, and hide us from the face of him that sitteth on the throne, and from the wrath of the Lamb" (Revelation 6:16).

If you are a Christian, you can say with joy, "Even so, come, Lord Jesus. Come quickly," and the very thought of His return brings rapturous joy. But for those who are not followers of Christ, they will be filled with terror and awe.

Either we let the Lamb receive the wrath of God for our sins by trusting in Jesus and His finished work on the Cross, or we will face the wrath of the Lamb of God when He returns.

Question to ponder: Does it sober you to think that Jesus Christ, who allowed Himself to be man-handled by sinful men, will one day execute the wrath of God against unrepentant sinners?

....

....

....

....

MAY 24 ══

"*To Forgive is Divine*"

"Lord, how often shall my brother sin against me, and I for-give him? Up to seven times?" Jesus said to him, "I do not say to you, up to seven times, but up to seventy times seven."
Matthew 18:21-22

Not only do we have a great reward in Heaven when we forgive, but we present a great witness right here. Nothing witnesses so powerfully to the glory and truth of the Gospel as when a Christian forgives his enemy.

Some years ago there was a war between Muslim and Christian Turks. One of the Christian officers was captured and became a prisoner of a Turkish official. This Muslim officer treated the Christian with the utmost cruelty and hatred and tortured him.

Then the circumstances of the war changed. The Christian prisoner was released; the torturer was captured and placed before the Christian. The Tukish officer's face and eyes showed the fear and dread that filled his heart. He knew this man was going to retaliate against him with great vengeance. However, the Christian man said to him, "You do not need to be afraid. I am a Christian and I will not return evil for evil. I forgive you for what you did to me."

The Muslim was so astonished, he said, "I will not die a Muslim, but I will die a Christian, for there is no religion but that of Christ which teaches forgiveness of injuries."

What a marvelous testimony it is to do good to them who have done evil to us. Remember my friends, "Forgive us our debts as we forgive our debtors."

Question to ponder: Have you ever prayed, "Father, forgive them, for they know not what they do?"

⸙ ....

....

....

....

The Indestructible Word of God ═══ MAY 25

I will delight myself in Your statutes;
I will not forget Your word.
Psalm 119:16

We are living in a time when biblical ignorance is widespread. Except for a small proportion of those who faithfully and daily study the Word of God, Americans are a biblically illiterate people. But the Bible is the greatest of treasures. It is the indestructible Word of God, the unconquerable Word of God. Dr. A. Z. Conrad said this about the indestructible Word of God:

> Century follows century—there it stands. Empires rise and fall—there it stands. Dynasty succeeds dynasty—there it stands. Kings are crowned and uncrowned—there it stands. Emperors decree its exterminations—there it stands. Despised and torn to pieces—there it stands. Storms of hate swirl about it—there it stands. Atheists rail against it—there it stands. Agnostics smile cynically—there it stands. Profane, prayerless punsters caricature it—there it stands. Unbelief abandons it—there it stands. Higher critics deny its inspiration—there it stands. Thunderbolts of wrath smite it—there it stands. An anvil that has broken a million hammers—there it stands.

Not only is the Word of God indestructible, but its vital importance extends to every phase of our lives.

Question to ponder: In your opinion, what is the greatest truth of the Bible?

....

....

....

....

....

....

MAY 26 ≡   *The Sin of Ingratitude*

And one of them, when he saw that he was healed,
returned, and with a loud voice glorified God, and
fell down on his face at His feet, giving Him thanks.
And he was a Samaritan. So Jesus answered and said,
"Were there not ten cleansed? But where are the nine?"
Luke 17:15-17

This passage shows something of the nature of ingratitude. It is an astonishment to God that His beneficences do not, indeed, call forth expressions of gratitude. Ingratitude is a very serious sin.

This is certainly brought out in the first chapter of Romans, where Paul describes the sinfulness of the heathen world and catalogs a great list of sins. Read the last half of the first chapter of Romans and you will see how the heathen world had sunk deeper and deeper into the vilest forms of depravity. Finally, when you trace it all back, what do you find? "When they knew God, they glorified Him not as God, neither were they thankful.... Wherefore God gave them up to vile affections" (Romans 1:21, 26).

Ingratitude and thanklessness are wellsprings out of which flowed eventually all of these other sins. The person who commits all these sins mentioned in Romans 1 is a person who is not grateful. You cannot be praising God and thanking God for what He has done for you while engaging in the type of activities described this chapter.

Question to ponder: Why is ingratitude a gateway sin into what Scripture calls "vile affections"?

....

....

....

....

....

If the Lord be God

If the Lord is God, follow Him; but if Baal, then follow him.
1 Kings 18:21

Examine all history, sacred and profane, and you will find few, if any, contests comparable to the one described in 1 Kings 18 when Elijah confronted the prophets of Baal. It was a matter of life and death for the people involved, for the nation itself, and through them for the whole world, as Satan made this grand attempt to destroy the faith of Israel.

Elijah asked the Israelites a classic question: "How long halt ye between two opinions? if the LORD be God, follow him: but if Baal, then follow him" (1 Kings 18:21). With that, the contest was on.

Baal was the god of the sun, the "giver of life," the god of fire. So the religion of Baal worship was threatening to crush out the religion of Jehovah, the worship of the true God. Elijah, one of the few prophets of Jehovah left in the world, was the only one who was willing to stand up and confront the overwhelming odds against him—the power of the throne, the power of the false temple of Baal, and all the people who were against him. But God was with Elijah and God gave him the victory.

Question to ponder: How can we stand for Christ in an increasingly hostile world?

....

....

....

....

....

....

....

....

Pain is Never Wasted

Your rod and Your staff, they comfort me.
Psalm 23:4

Human beings are often in need, in trouble, in pain. People need comfort. We try to find it in various places, from a mother's hug to a bottle of wine.

We can certainly get comfort from each other. But Christ is the only source of real comfort for us. What is the purpose of His comfort in our lives? Of course, it is to assuage our heart's needs, to ease our aching spirits, to uplift us, to reanimate us, to encourage us, to help us on the way to continue fighting the battle. Also, it is, as Paul says, "that we may be able to comfort them which are in any trouble."

There's nothing more painful than suffering that seems to be without purpose. Let me tell you, however, there is no such thing. Paul says that we are comforted in all of our tribulation so that we may be able to comfort others in their trouble with the same comfort wherewith we have been comforted of God.

God's comfort works because God can handle our pain and trouble. When it is past, we can look back and see His hand and then reach out and comfort others.

Question to ponder: Can you think of some difficult time in your life which later enabled you to help someone going through the same thing?

Encourage Each Other

...Strengthening the souls of the disciples, exhorting them to continue in the faith, and saying, "We must through many tribulations enter the kingdom of God."
Acts 14:22

Probably few of you would know who the New Testament character Joseph of Cyprus was. But you probably would recognize him if I used the other name given to him: Barnabas, meaning the "Son of Consolation," or the "Son of Encouragement." That was his name and he was famous for comforting other people. Does anyone like that come to your mind?

I know a Christian who is always encouraging others. I can't think of this individual without thinking of the fact that this man is an overflowing reservoir of comfort. He is always concerned about other people and about their difficulties and trials. You would never find out about his trials because he's so concerned about others. He's a blessing and benediction to all who know him. He is truly a Barnabas, a son of consolation.

Go out and be a blessing as you encourage someone this day.

Question to ponder: Can you think of a person to imitate who is an encourager of others?

MAY 30

Lest We Forget

Now the Lord is the Spirit; and where the Spirit of the Lord is, there is liberty.
2 Corinthians 3:17

Memorial Day is a time to remember those brave men and women who paid the ultimate price for our freedom. Tragically, hundreds of millions of people do not live in liberty. Ironically, freedom is something that is easily taken for granted. It is like the air we breathe. It is not until it is gone that we even think about it.

John Adams, our second president, made a declaration to future years, saying this: "Posterity: You will never know how much it has cost my generation to procure your freedom. I hope you will make good use of it."

One great truth that Americans have forgotten, I believe, is that the source of liberty comes from only one place: it comes from God; it has come from Christ, who alone can make people free. Wherever the pure Gospel of Jesus Christ with its emphasis upon grace and the Cross has been preached, it has been followed by civil and political liberty.

Would that the flame of freedom and liberty that burned so brightly in the hearts of our founders be fanned into a flame again in America. This Memorial Day is a good time to begin.

Question to ponder: Are you thankful for your freedom? Is there any survivor of a fallen soldier that you can thank today?

....

....

....

....

....

All Things Through Christ

I can do all things through Christ who strengthens me.
Philippians 4:13

We were created by God to do great things, to soar high and to make an impact upon our world for Him. In fact, most of the great men and women who have accomplished impressive things in this world have been men and women who have dreamed dreams of what God, by His grace, could do in their lives.

I suppose everybody has dreamed dreams. The problem is that we all as children had great visions, but alas, as we grew up, most of those dreams faded away. They are destroyed by that pesky voice that whispers, "You can't do it. You never have, you never could, and you never will."

So like acid rain that falls upon our dreams, they slowly disappear. Our great visions fade and our ambitions corrode because we believe the negative words of the devil: "You can't, you can't, you can't." And so, we invent all kinds of reasons why we can't.

The apostle Paul had no such limitations. He said, "I can do all things through Christ which strengtheneth me" (Philippians 4:13). Paul is not talking about PMA—a "Positive Mental Attitude." He did not say, "I can do all things through PMA" —but through Jesus.

May God help us to realize we can do all things through Christ. He is the creator of dreams and the source of our strength.

Question to ponder: Is there something, great or small, that God has put on your heart to accomplish for Him?

....

....

....

....

....

JUNE **1** *Even the Moon Praises Him*

The heavens declare the glory of God....
And night unto night reveals knowledge.
Psalm 19:1-2

We all look at the moon, admire the moon, sing about the moon—the moon in June. It brings out tunes and all of that, but what does the moon really mean to us? Let me say this: If there were no moon, there would be no you. For example, the moon is God's cleaning-maid for the earth. It cleans up the oceans with its tides. Without those tides and without the moon, all of our shores and all of our bays would be filled with billions of tons of garbage, stench and debris. The highest priced landscape would be as far from the seashore as you could get, especially on the leeward side.

Furthermore, the moon's gravitational pull mixes the atmosphere. Just as it works on the sea, it works on the atmosphere and mixes oxygen with the water in the waves breaking on the shore. When you watch waves breaking on the shore, you are watching the ocean's lifeline in progress. Oxygenated water is required by plankton, which is the foundation of the whole marine food chain, without which all marine creatures would die. The moon, which just "accidentally" happens to be there, just "accidentally" happens to be the right size in the right place and the right distance away from the earth to exert the proper gravitational force on tides and the atmosphere.

Day by day, night by night, God's creation itself brings Him glory for those who will but listen.

Question to ponder: What aspects of creation fill you with awe about God?

....

....

....

....

....

The Triumph of Good Over Evil

Do not be overcome by evil, but overcome evil with good.
Romans 12:21

A man who was having great trouble with a neighbor who was doing him dirt came to me one time. I told him of the principle of returning good for evil and he said, "I just couldn't to that." He was right. The natural man can't. It is spiritual; it is the greatest evidence of a truly regenerate heart to respond positively or kindly to enemies, to love our enemies, to bless them that curse us, to do good to them that hate us and despitefully use us. This is, however, what Christ tells us to do.

It is a defensive shield, so that no matter what anybody does to us, we can turn that into a blessing. We can transform that person by going the second mile, by turning the other cheek, by returning good for evil.

When we do good to those who hurt us, we are a part of the greatest triumph in the world. When Christ triumphed on the Cross over all evil powers and the devil himself, He proved that good is stronger than evil. Every time we do a kindness instead of "getting even," we are triumphing over evil.

Question to ponder: Can you think of something good you can do today or in the near future for someone— maybe even for someone who has hurt you?

....

....

....

....

....

....

....

....

JUNE 3

Entropy

> *The heavens will vanish like smoke,*
> *the earth will wear out like a garment.*
> Isaiah 51:6 (NIV)

In this world, the Second Law of Thermodynamics constantly works and everything is running down, wearing out, growing old, and perishing. There is no escape from the law of entropy. In this contest, you can never win; you cannot even break even.

With the fall and the curse came the current order of things. We go from order to chaos, from clean to dirty, from new to old, from fresh to rotten, from living to dead. Everything breaks down, even heaven and earth itself will wear out.

Thankfully, this is not all there is. For we have a Savior who declares, "Behold, I make all things new" (Revelation 21:5). This means the reversal of entropy. Paul says that "the creation itself also will be delivered from the bondage of corruption into the glorious liberty of the children of God" (Romans 8:21).

In heaven, we'll experience freedom from entropy. In heaven, all things will be continuously new. A new heaven and a new earth—without entropy.

Question to ponder: When you think of all that breaks down, from the earth to our bodies, what does freedom from entropy mean?

....

....

....

....

....

....

....

Hope Beyond the Grave

For I am persuaded that neither death nor life...shall be able to separate us from the love of God which is in Christ Jesus our Lord.
Romans 8:38-39

If Christ had not come, there would be no sure hope of eternal life. For Christ has brought life and immortality to light. Only He can give the blessed assurance of everlasting life. I have never met a person who knows what is going to happen to him beyond this life who was not a believer in Jesus Christ who said, *"I am he that liveth, and was dead; and, behold, I am alive forevermore"* (Revelation 1:18).

If Christ had not come, then the dark and dank tomb would be the end of each and all. There would be no hope beyond the grave. If Christ had not come, you could look down into that six-foot hole and see your future; beyond that there would be but speculations and vague hopes. Jesus brought us an absolute certainty: *"I am the resurrection and the life... Because I live, ye shall live also."* Only in Christ is there the assurance and certainty of everlasting life. What a magnificent promise that is.

Amazing to say, because of His grace in Jesus Christ, God is willing to wash me whiter than snow, to forgive me, to cleanse me, and to accept me as His child, now and forevermore. When the stars have burnt into cinders, and this universe has collapsed, I will still be with God and will have only just begun to live.

Question to ponder: In light of the promises of Christ and His resurrection, what does death mean?

JUNE 5

The Elder Brother

But he was angry and would not go in. Therefore
his father came out and pleaded with him.
Luke 15:28

Jesus knows the heart. The parable of the Prodigal Son shows us that very frequently, prodigals are not welcome even today. We are quite willing to have the respectable folks come into the church, those who are well-clothed and come from good families and upbringings, but bring the drunk in off skid row, bring in the person who has destroyed his body with vice, drugs, and sinful living, and some people will raise their eyebrows. Sinners are told to come into the warm harbor of God's love, and they run smack-dab into the iceberg of the elder brother.

"What are you doing here in our nice church?" Some people don't really believe in conversion. You talk to them about the thief on the cross and they become very upset, even as some of the early Christians did not believe Saul had been converted.

For 24 years I lived without the slightest shadow ever crossing my mind that I was separated from God and on my way to perdition. Not until I came to that realization did the door of God's mercy open to me. Let us always be open and welcoming to those who seek after God. He always welcomes a repentant sinner.

Question to ponder: If someone came to church from from a life of sin, would you welcome them as a God-seeker?

You're It

And He said to them, "Go into all the world
and preach the gospel to every creature."
Mark 16:15

I've always liked the story—it's not factual, but it is based on truth—
the story of when Jesus Christ returned to Heaven after His resurrection
and His ascension. When He arrived in heaven, as the story goes, all of the
angels gathered around to hear about His great exploits on the earth below.
He told them about His birth in a manger, about the life He lived, about His
work as a carpenter, His mission as a prophet going out and preaching and
teaching, the gathering together of His disciples, His betrayal, His scourg-
ing, His mockery, His condemnation, the Cross, the spikes, the sword, the
tomb, and finally the glorious resurrection and His return into Heaven.

He said, "I have told my disciples that they are to go into all the world
and tell everyone that through what I have done, they may have pardon and
forgiveness and reconciliation and may receive the free gift of eternal life."

Then there was quiet among the angels. Finally, one of them said,
"Lord, but what if they don't do that? What other plan do you have?"

Jesus Christ replied, "I have no other plan."

Dear friends, *you* are it.

Question to ponder: How does it make you feel to
know that you are privileged to be His channel of
eternal blessings to others?

JUNE 7 === *"Voiceless Christianity"?*

...You shall be witnesses to Me.
Acts 1:8

Some professing Christians are members of the club called "Voiceless Christianity." They say, "I can't witness with my mouth. I just witness by my life."

Dear friend, if you witness by your life, you only witness to *yourself*. Christ told us that we are to point beyond ourselves, unto Him and to His Cross, and that requires the use of our mouths.

Many claim that words don't accomplish anything; it is the life that we live that gives a powerful witness. So, is it the case that most of you who are part of the "Voiceless Christianity" group have had dozens of people just this past year coming up to you and saying, "Oh, what a wonderful person you are. I am so amazed. Please tell me how I can be like you and how I can have whatever makes you that way?"

No, our Lord has entrusted us with the responsibility and the joy of leading others to Himself. Before He left this earth, Jesus said to His disciples:

> All authority has been given to Me in heaven and on earth. Go therefore and make disciples of all the nations, baptizing them in the name of the Father and of the Son and of the Holy Spirit, teaching them to observe all things that I have commanded you; and lo, I am with you always, even to the end of the age (Matthew 28:18-20).

Voiceless Christianity is a myth by which the lazy or fearful justify their silence.

Question to ponder: Do you practice "voiceless Christianity?" Why or why not?

....

....

....

....

"I Don't Want to Get Involved"

Deliver those who are drawn toward death,
and hold back those stumbling to the slaughter.
Proverbs 24:11

In March 1964 a young New Yorker named Kitty Genovese came home from work, put her key into the lock on the front door of the apartment building she lived in. Suddenly a man grabbed her from behind and when she screamed he cut her with a knife. She screamed louder and said, "Help, I'm dying. Help me. Somebody help me. This man is killing me."

Windows went up all over the huge building. People looked down at her as she screamed for help. The police finally arrived thirty minutes later. It had taken thirty minutes of screaming for Kitty Genovese to die. No one in the building called the police.

Thirty-eight residents of that building said they saw the murder. When asked why they didn't intervene or call the police, each answered, "We didn't want to get involved." Don't you feel like going up and punching those people in the nose? I do. "This woman is being carved into pieces, and you didn't want to get involved?"

As Christians we are called to get involved in the lives of others. We are called to a life of service and witness for Him.

Question to ponder: How can you "get involved" today or this week to help people in need?

The Fly in the Ointment

*Continue earnestly in prayer, being
vigilant in it with thanksgiving.*
Colossians 4:2

Sir Noel Paton was an outstanding artist. His paintings always have one unusual feature: There are beautiful flowers and gorgeous birds, knights and ladies, gossamer-winged fairies, and children of seraphic beauty. However, always, somewhere down in the corner of the painting, or at the feet of these beautiful characters, is a form that is uncouth, repulsive, and repugnant, a loathsome creature such as a toad or a lizard or a slimy snail to render, by contrast with their repulsiveness, greater beauty to the rest.

This is how it is with the New Testament. We see Christ in all of His glory crucified between two thieves. There are twelve apostles, and one of them is a devil.

Rather than thank God for all His blessings, it is much easier to have a "fly complex." I do not know if you have ever detected this in your own life, but I have. The old "fly in the ointment."

Many of us, it seems, spend a great deal of our time counting the flies in the ointment of life. We need to realize that there is never going to be a jar of ointment in this world that does not have some flies in it. The question really comes down to whether we see the flies or the ointment. You can almost divide people into two kinds: There are the "fly people" and there are the "ointment people." Which are you?

Question to ponder: What is the "ointment" you are thankful for today?

....

....

....

....

....

No Fear of God in Their Eyes ═ JUNE 10

Therefore, since we are receiving a kingdom
which cannot be shaken, let us have grace, by
which we may serve God acceptably with reverence
and godly fear. For our God is a consuming fire.
Hebrews 12:28-29

Some years ago I was on the Merv Griffin Show talking about prayer in schools. Merv asked, "What good is a couple of minutes of prayer going to do, anyway? What difference does it make?"

It makes a great deal of difference whether one believes in God and when one prays, or a class of students prays, one thing they are saying is that there is a higher authority than the state.

Does that really make any difference? There have been many, many indirect consequences of the Supreme Court's 1962-1963 decisions to ban school prayer. And the fallout has literally amounted to expelling God *in toto* from our entire school system and beyond that, from the public life of America. God has been thrown out, and so the metal detectors have been installed.

Have you ever wondered why our society is going downhill so fast? I think a major part of it is that so many today lack a fear of God. They act as if they will not be held accountable. In this, they are totally wrong. Part of the reason some people get upset with Christians speaking out on moral issues from a biblical perspective is that they want to be able to sin with impunity. Jesus put it this way, "the light has come into the world, and men loved darkness rather than light, because their deeds were evil" (John 3:19).

What we need in our land is more "God fearing."

Question to ponder: What does it mean to you when the Scriptures say that our God is a consuming fire?

⟋ ....

....

....

....

JUNE 11 = *Is Christianity Unscientific?*

It is the glory of God to conceal a matter, but
the glory of kings is to search out a matter.
Proverbs 25:2

Sometimes we hear the accusation that Christianity is unscientific. What people who make such claims don't realize is that science got its birth during the Christian era. All of the early modern scientists were Christians who believed that they were, in the words of astronomer Johannes Kepler, "thinking God's thoughts after Him." They believed that a rational God had made a rational universe, and it was the role of science to discover the rules He had impressed on the material world.

Who invented science? It was Francis Bacon who is credited with having been the inventor of the scientific method, that combination of induction and deduction, of hypothesis and proof (empirical proof). Bacon was a devout Christian. He believed in God. He believed in Christ, he believed in the Bible, and he believed in Creation. He said that God had given us two books—He has given us the book of nature to understand the world, and the book of Scripture—and we are to read both of them.

Who was the greatest scientist who ever lived? A poll taken of scientists just a few years ago concluded that the greatest scientist was Sir Isaac Newton. Newton believed in God, he believed in Christ, he believed in the Bible, and he believed in creation. The beliefs were the foundation for Newton's work as a scientist.

Question to ponder: What does the phrase "laws of nature and of nature's God" mean?

....

....

....

....

The Transforming Power of Scripture === JUNE 12

Man shall not live by bread alone, but by every word of God.
Luke 4:4

The Bible is the greatest book in the world.

In the midst of the many marvelous texts that make up the Scriptures, there are some verses that are often overlooked and seldom quoted compared to other well-known verses. These verses lie nestled away like timid little flowers. However, these timid little flowers give off a marvelous fragrance—a fragrance that, if inhaled deeply, can utterly transform your life. Sometimes I like to pick one such little flower from the pages of Holy Writ, lift it up, analyze it, and sense its fragrance and its transforming power.

Psychologist William James once stated: "The Bible contains more true sublimity, more exquisite beauty, more morality, more important history, and finer strains of poetry and eloquence than can be collected from all other books, in whatever age or language they may have been written." Sir William Gladstone, considered by many the greatest prime minister England ever had, said, "I have known 95 great men of the world in my time. And of these, 87 were followers of the Bible."

Question to ponder: Can you list ten reasons why you read and study the Bible?

JUNE **13** ═══

In Remembrance of Me

*With fervent desire I have desired to
eat this Passover with you before I suffer.*
Luke 22:15

The Lord's Table is a memorial, but obviously it is also a supper, as it is a sacrament. It is a meal unlike any that has ever been celebrated before. How wonderful it is that we can eat with Him. Even as John laid his head upon the bosom of Christ, so we can eat with the Lord Jesus Christ.

The Great Pyramid was built to honor a man to his everlasting re-membrance—can you remember his name? It was the mighty Khufu. The Taj Majal is perhaps the most beautiful building built. It took 20,000 people 22 years to build it. It is a magnificent place. It was built by Shah Jahan to memorialize and cause to be brought to everlasting remembrance his beautiful young wife, whose name is not remembered by most of us.

Our Lord Jesus Christ, however, He left for us a very simple, tiny by comparison, memorial—the Last Supper. But when the stars shall have burnt out of Heaven, when the end of all of the ages shall have come, when the Great Pyramid shall have crumbled into dust, this memorial will still be known, and everyone who sees it will know precisely who it is that is to be remembered in the simple bread and wine of the Lord's Table.

Question to ponder: How do we benefit spiritually from the Lord's Supper?

Absolute Truth in a Relative World — JUNE 14

And you shall know the truth,
and the truth shall make you free.
John 8:32

Sadly, a majority of Americans today believe that truth and morality are relative. Even many professing Christians have fallen prey to this myth.

Virtually all of our high school students have learned that there are no absolutes.

You probably heard about the teacher who said to his class, "You can know nothing for certain."

One student responded, "Teacher, are you sure?"

He said, "I'm certain."

Sometimes students don't realize that when a teacher or professor says there are no absolutes, he is also saying there is no God. Because, you see, God is the ultimate absolute.

If there are no absolutes, how is it that the Holocaust was wrong?

If there are no absolutes, how could 9/11 be wrong?

It becomes very difficult to live in a completely relativistic world. Suppose you are waiting in your car at a train crossing, and a train is coming down the tracks at 60 miles an hour. You know that if you drive your car out in front of that train, you are not going to be "relatively" dead—you are going to be "absolutely" dead. We can't live as relativists in this world.

Truth is revealed to us in God's Word. Christ says, "Ye shall know the truth, and the truth shall make you free" (John 8:32).

Question to ponder: Why is truth so important to God?

JUNE 15

Belief vs. Unbelief

*...Whoever believes in Him should
not perish but have eternal life.*
John 3:15

We have been exposed repeatedly to the humanistic thesis that belief in God is irrational and unbelief is rational. Is that true? I would like to expose it for what it really is: an unmitigated fraud, an unalloyed lie that rises right up from the father of all lies.

To believe that God has made us, that there is a purpose for our lives and that we go to be with Him when we die—that is the Christian world-view.

This belief leads to meaning in life, joy, and satisfaction, purpose, and peace. Unbelief leads to hopelessness, lack of meaning and purpose, and fear of death. Unbelief is not sophisticated, it's devastating, and the result of unbelief is grief and pain. The result of belief in the God of the Bible is contentment, peace, and joy. Belief in God is life-giving and life-sustaining.

Question to ponder: Contrast belief and unbelief in people you know. Can you see the difference?

Sin Has Consequences

"Where did you go, Gehazi?" And he said, "Your servant did not go anywhere." Then he said to him, "Did not my heart go with you when the man turned back from his chariot to meet you? Is it time to receive money and to receive clothing, olive groves and vineyards, sheep and oxen, male and female servants?"
2 Kings 5:25-26

Many people think they can get away with all sorts of crimes today. Perhaps they do for a while. But in the big picture, God sees, and He will one day bring it to light—whether in this life or the next.

In 2 Kings 5, Gehazi ended up with Naaman's leprosy because of his greed. When David sinned, he was forgiven—yet "the sword" never left his house. Even though God forgives us for our sins when we come to Him with repentance, God does not always remove the consequences of our sins. Sin is always serious and always destructive.

Certain sins can follow families and be repeated for several generations. Yes, God can break the cords of sin. Chains can be loosed at Calvary, but it is much better to keep ourselves from sin in the first place.

Question to ponder: Have you seen situations where one sin has brought trouble to many?

....

....

....

....

....

....

....

JUNE **17**

A Day of Reckoning

So then each of us shall give account of himself to God.
Romans 14:12

The Bible makes it plain that we shall, each one, have to give an account of ourselves. It will not be your wife, your husband, your parents, your neighbors, church members, or preachers, it will be you yourself that you will be giving an account of in that great day. No other statements will be allowed. I guess the Corinthians are still around today. How many people walk out of church and make comments such as: "Well, what did you think of that sermon?" "How did you like the preacher?" Are we not back to Corinth again? My friends, do you come to judge God's servants or do you come to place yourself under the judgment of God's Word? What a difference there is in those two attitudes.

In a worship service, to paraphrase Soren Kierkegaard, it is God who is the audience, the congregation, the performer, and the preacher. God is the one to judge. We who are covered by the blood of Christ will be forgiven, but we are still accountable and will face the day of reckoning.

Question to ponder: What is frightening and what is comforting about the accountability of believers?

....

....

....

....

....

....

....

....

A Surprising Witness from Antiquity === JUNE 18

When I consider Your heavens, the work of Your fingers,
the moon and the stars, which You have ordained...."
Psalm 8:3

The Bible condemns astrology. It says that we are not to consort with astrologers; we are not to consult them; we are not to have anything to do with it. And, yet, behind all of that, there is a great revelation of God and His glory and of His salvation in what has come to be known as the Zodiac. This is often described as a circle of animals. But that is not really what the word "Zodiac" means. Rather it comes from a primitive root, *zoad*, which comes from the Hebrew *sodi*, and in Sanskrit means: "a way; a step; a path." It is the path, or the way, and it is the way of salvation which is revealed in the heavens.

I hope that as you go out and look at the starry skies above, you will be impressed anew and afresh. You will become amazed at the God who hath written on high these things for all the world to see. For surely His voice has gone out unto the ends of the earth and the invisible things of Him are plainly seen from the creation of the world. God has placed in the constellations of the Zodiac, which He brought forth with His own hand, pictures of the great salvation which He has wrought in Jesus Christ.

Before it was corrupted and twisted, the Zodiac presented a clear picture of God's story. It shows the virgin who gives birth to a son and is attacked by the evil one. And there is much more, as we will show in the following devotional reading.

Question to ponder: The horoscope is a tool used by Satan to deceive. How did it become so twisted?

....

....

....

....

....

JUNE 19

The Gospel in the Stars

*The heavens declare the glory of God; and the firmament
shows His handiwork. Day unto day utters speech, and night
unto night reveals knowledge.*
Psalm 19:1-2

The Zodiac has twelve major signs. The first is Virgo, depicting a woman who has in her right hand a branch and in her left hand sheaves of corn. In Hebrew she is called Bethulah, which means "virgin," even as *virgo*, from Latin, means virgin.

Everywhere her name is the same. She is called "the virgin." This is of course, the picture of Mary, the virgin mother of Christ. So we have Virgo, the virgin woman, holding the branch and seeds in her hand. We find next to her, Coma, "the desired one" (the desire of all nations, who shall come) who is now an infant being nourished in her lap. Thirdly, we see him grown to manhood—a very unusual man, however, one with two natures: One who is the great hunter, teacher, physician; one who gives his life voluntarily and conveys his immortality to others; one who is the great High Priest, slaying the victim over the Southern Cross.

Finally, we see him, also full grown, coming mightily and in power, and rapidly as Bootes—the coming One, the ruler, the governor, the harvester of the earth, coming with a sickle in his hand in judgment to harvest the world. Thus, there is the Gospel presented in the stars, in the Zodiac—none of which has anything to do with reading your horoscope.

Question to ponder: How do the stars "reveal knowledge"?

....

....

....

....

A Father Who Loves the Mother === JUNE 20

...Rejoice with the wife of your youth.
Proverbs 5:18

The best thing a father can do for his children is to love their mother. If you are going to be a godly dad, you need to forsake all others with heart and mind and soul and love your wife. We are to love our wives as Christ loved the church and gave Himself for us.

It is in loving each other that parents create a stable and good home. Besides loving his wife in order to be a good father, a man must commit to be there for his children.

It is really very easy to become a father, but it is very difficult to be a godly father in the home. You must, first of all, be a godly man. Second, you must–very obviously, but today, importantly—be in the home, because if there is one place where tens of millions of American fathers aren't today, it is in the home. Eighty percent of all of the families in the inner city are fatherless. Eighty percent.

Without fathers in the home, children will lack the emotional center a father provides, crime will go up as will all the troubles that lack of guidance and fathering bring upon a family.

Question to ponder: What happens to a society where men are not present in the home?

....

....

....

....

....

....

JUNE 21 — *Rejoice in All Circumstances*

Rejoice always.
1 Thessalonians 5:16

Trouble comes to us all, saved or unsaved. But people react differently.

We know that the same sun that bakes bricks melts butter. Adversity causes some people to become embittered and hardened, to become hateful toward God and man. Others it sweetens and softens and enriches.

The world finds it very, very strange that even in the midst of the most painful circumstances, there can be rejoicing. In fact, Paul tells us that we can be sorrowful and rejoice at the same time: "As sorrowful, yet always rejoicing" (see 2 Corinthians 6-10).

Regardless of the pain of the circumstances, there can be deep-seated joy. In the midst of an illness, at the very nadir of my experience, a time when I was in such pain that I absolutely did not know what to do and tears were coursing down my cheeks, I could honestly say to my wife, "I yet believe that God is good and will lift me up out of this."

What kind of problems have you had this past week? Did you face them like Paul, or like the world faces them? How do we deal with our problems? Faith comes from our realization that God is with us, whatever the problems we may face. When we face them, do we become better or do we become bitter?

Question to ponder: Are you going through a difficult time? Can you find something to thank God for in the midst of your adversity?

....

....

....

....

....

Propitiation ══ JUNE 22

In this is love, not that we loved God, but that He loved
us and sent His Son to be the propitiation for our sins.
1 John 4:10

God's forgiveness is astounding. I hope that you realize that all of your sin is wiped away by a God who cannot forget anything because He is omniscient and knows all things. One of the great mysteries of the Scriptures, a paradox indeed, is that He has said, He will cast all our sins "into the depths of the sea" (Micah 7:19) and He will remember them no more.

In Christ we have the assurance that all of our sin has been wiped away and we are reconciled unto God, invited back into His favor, into the fellowship of His communion, adopted into His family, given His name, invited to His table, made His heir everlastingly. Our inheritance in Christ cannot possibly be measured. That is what Christ has done for us on the cross.

What I have just described is called propitiation. This means that the wrath of God toward us is set aside and falls not on us, but on our substitute, Christ. Secondly, it means our sin is wiped away forever, as when one would wash a blackboard. Thirdly, we who had our backs to God are reconciled and drawn into the fellowship of His love. This is God's forgiveness; this is God's love.

Question to ponder: What does it mean that God is appeased?

....

....

....

....

....

....

=====   *An Absolute God*

> *Who is this King of glory? The LORD*
> *of hosts, He is the King of glory.*
> Psalm 24:10

W hat exactly are absolutes? If you were to check the word "abso-lute" in Webster's Dictionary, you would discover that "absolute" comes from the two Latin words *ab* ("from") and *solvere* ("to set free") from which we get the word *dissolve*. So *absolute* means "to be set free."

But set free from what? It means to be set free from imperfection. To be pure. It means to free from any admixture. It is perfect. It means to be free from any limit, restriction, or qualification as in an *absolute* monarch. And it means to be positive, certain, authoritative.

That is what absolutes are, whether we are talking about persons or truth. To be absolute is to be free from any kind of error, admixture, imper-fection, or limit.

If there are no absolutes, there is no God, because God is the ultimate absolute. His *omnipotence* is without limit, restraint, or qualification. His *omniscience* is unlimited. His *omnipresence* is without restraint or restric-tion. God is the altogether absolute One. He is the absolute Monarch, the absolute God.

Question to ponder: What are the consequences in a world without absolutes?

Anger Management

He who is slow to anger is better than the mighty,
and he who rules his spirit than he who takes a city.
Proverbs 16:32

When it comes to anger, someone has said that people tend to be of two different types. There are those who blow up and there are those who clam up. Some people do both. Paul deals with that in Ephesians 4:26. He says, "Be ye angry, and sin not" (Ephesians 4:26a).

There is such a thing as righteous anger but the sin related to anger is when this bursts forth in all sorts of vicious speech. When we rail against another person, give place to malice, explode, and tell other people off. We have then given way to sin; we have given place to the devil.

So Paul tells us in verse 26 that we are not to let our anger explode. Furthermore, he says, "Let not the sun go down upon your wrath" (v. 26). That is, do not close up like a clam and keep that hot boiling anger within you. There are some people who can keep it in for years, blocking any sort of communication.

But by His grace, many people are able to control their anger, to "be angry and sin not."

Question to ponder: How has the Holy Spirit worked in your life to control your temper?

....

....

....

....

....

....

....

JUNE 25 ═══ *An Anthropic World*

So God created man in His own image; in the image of
God He created him; male and female He created them.
Genesis 1:27

The 500th anniversary of Copernicus' birth was celebrated in 1973. Copernicus showed that the earth was not at the center of the universe, a scientific finding used to displace the earth and man from their presumed place of central importance in the cosmos. In celebrating the Copernican revolution, his followers were celebrating the demise of man and, more importantly, the demise of God.

At the celebration, Brandon Carter, a highly reputed astronomer from Oxford, discussed his discovery of certain strange and almost inexplicable things in the world of particle physics and astronomy. They all seemed to that suggest that this world, and the whole universe, have been made for the purpose of hosting intelligent life on this planet—namely man.

He noted, for example, that if the mass of the proton were just a tiny fraction larger or smaller, the entire solar system would collapse. Many similar physical constants which appear optimized for human existence point to the fact that this universe seems to have been designed for mankind.

His "anthropic principle" says that this universe has a "purpose." That is a dirty word to evolutionists who have substituted chance for design and purpose.

But suddenly, at the 500th anniversary of the Copernican revolution, when the final spike was being driven into the significance of man, the anthropic principle was born. Despite man's attempts to deny God, He has left His fingerprints all over the universe.

Question to ponder: Why did God create the world?

The Straight and Narrow

*Enter by the narrow gate; for wide is the gate and broad
is the way that leads to destruction, and there are many
who go in by it. Because narrow is the gate and difficult is
the way which leads to life, and there are few who find it.*
Matthew 7:13-14

We live in a time when the majority report is virtually always un-godly, unChristian, immoral and defeatist. We hear it all the time. It blares at us from our radios, our television, our newspapers, and magazines. The majority report is ever before us, which is: Forget about what God has said. Forget about Him altogether.

This is the "popular" way. Sometimes we have agreed with the major-ity and said yes, God's way is too hard. But His way is the straight and nar-row road that leads unto life. It is the wide gate, the broad way that leads to happiness. It is the broad way which the Bible says leads to destruction.

Every one of us has to decide: Are we going to go with the popular view, the majority view, or are we going to follow the minority report, which is a report of faith?

Are you able to face the real difficult things of life, to stand for Christ when it is unpopular to do so? God has a special blessing for those who stand firm for Christ and the truth, even in the face of great unpopularity.

Question to ponder: How can you stand for Christ, when it is unpopular to do so?

....

....

....

....

....

JUNE 27

Defender of the Faith

*...Always be ready to give a defense to everyone who asks you
a reason for the hope that is in you, with meekness and fear.*
1 Peter 3:15

Some years ago I heard Dr. Somebody or Other taking calls from Christians on a radio show. They were calling in and challenging him on various things, and he was chewing them up and spitting them out. Not one Christian could answer any question he asked them.

They would explain why they believe with statements like, "Well, because I've got it down in my heart."

This atheist answered, "Well, I don't have it down in my heart, and I don't believe it either"—and he hung up.

The Scripture says that we should always be ready to give an answer as to why we believe anything we claim that we believe. The Bible is not based upon blind faith, but on God's acting in history, past and present.

Just to give one example: When Jesus was born, carried out His ministry, was crucified and raised back to life, He fulfilled hundreds of prophecies that were written hundreds of years before He came. Only God knows the future. Only God could have written that story.

All around us we have unbelievers today challenging us on what we believe. We hear challenges on television, radio, books, magazines, motion pictures, and the Internet as to why we believe any of this "stuff" we say that we believe. Let us always be ready with reasons for our faith.

Question to ponder: How can you prepare to give a good answer to people who challenge your faith?

....
....
....
....
....

Available for God

As your days, so shall your strength be.
Deuteronomy 33:25

What is the greatest ability we can have when it comes to serving God? Is it the ability to preach great sermons and lead thousands to Christ? Is it the ability to cross the ocean and serve in some great missionary enterprise? Is it the ability to stay home and rear children in the Christian faith? All of these things are important and have their place.

But I believe that the greatest ability that the Christian needs is *availability*. Are you available to God? Are you available to Him today and each day to use you?

When we make ourselves available to God, He equips us for every good work He wants us to do. He gives us the strength to accomplish that which He has set before us.

"I can do all things through Christ which strengtheneth me" (Philippians 4:13). Someone recommended taking that verse and repeating and emphasizing separately each succeeding word. "*I* can do all things through Christ," not merely the apostles, or the martyrs or super saints, but "*I* can do all things through Christ."

That is a promise to you. Do you believe it? "I *can do* all things ... I can do *all* things." I can do all things through *Christ* which strengtheneth me.

Question to ponder: If you knew you couldn't fail—because God was in it—what great thing would you attempt for His glory and others' good?

....

....

....

....

....

....

God and the Arts

> *One thing I have desired of the LORD...to behold
> the beauty of the LORD, and to inquire in His temple.*
> Psalm 27:4

Christianity has been a great patron of the arts—from paintings to music to the great cathedrals.

Now there are those who have supposed that the second commandment against graven images forbids the use of visual arts altogether. But God also gave all of the instructions for the building of the tabernacle. And in that tabernacle were all manner of visual arts. On the veil that separated the holy place from the holy of holies there were flowers and pomegranates and palm trees and many other things. Note what it says about the high priest's clothing: "And you shall make holy garments for Aaron your brother, for glory and for beauty" (Exodus 28:2).

God is a God of beauty. He changed the chaos into the cosmos—a thing of beauty. The very word means order and beauty. Cosmology is the study of beauty. God is the great artist who gives us the magnificent sunsets He paints for us every evening. He gives us the glory of the budding flowers, the beautiful trees and plants that we all enjoy. God is not opposed to art. He is the great artist. What God forbade was idolatry, the worship of an idol, or even of the true God through an idol.

Question to ponder: What place does art play in your life in general and in your spiritual life particularly?

....

....

....

....

....

The Second Mile

And whoever compels you to go one mile, go with him two.
Matthew 5:41

Centuries before Christ, Cyrus the Great was a mighty monarch of the Persian Empire, which stretched from one end to the other of the known inhabited world. He invented the first national postal system, probably because the decrees of the king of the Medes and the Persians were inviolable and could not be changed, so it was important that the people heard about it when the king made a decree. In the process of putting that huge postal service in place, Cyrus the Great issued a decree that the couriers could require any person to carry any burden on his person, his mule, his cart, a horse, in a ship or whatever, for one mile. After that, he could not impress or compel him any further.

The Romans adopted this postal system, along with the custom of compelling a person to carry a burden for a mile. It was a very onerous thing for the Jews, who already detested the fact that they had to pay taxes to the despotic and tyrannical Roman conquerors.

When Jesus said we should go a second mile, it was unthinkable to His Jewish hearers. It was unconscionable. Then they would have to walk two miles back, That's four miles. Does Jesus know what He is asking? Ah, yes, He knows. Jesus not only taught it by precept, he taught it by example. It is one of the most difficult things anyone will ever learn to do. It is the art of true Christian forgiveness carried through to the end.

Question to ponder: How can you apply the second mile principle in your life today—showing kindness to someone who may not deserve it?

The Threat of Humanism

Thus says the LORD: "Cursed is the man who trusts in man and makes flesh his strength, whose heart departs from the LORD."
Jeremiah 17:5

For every effect there must be a sufficient cause. What is the reason, the etiology, of this disease which is eating away at the very core of America? There is, without question, an absolutely new philosophy, a philosophy of secularism, of humanism—or, as it is called, "secular humanism." This philosophy has taken over the educational elite of this country and if they have their way, it will be imposed upon virtually every teacher, school and textbook in America.

There are those who like to decry this and say that secular humanism is a myth. I read an article recently that said secular humanism is something invented by television evangelists. The American people are often so credulous that they will believe such an idea in spite of the fact that there is in existence the American Humanist Association—of which John Dewey was the first president. There is also *The Humanist Magazine*, which must obviously have dropped out of the sky because, according to them, there is no humanist organization printing it.

Humanism is not to be confused with humanitarianism, which is doing good for humanity. Humanism is trust in man, in opposition to God. But God's Word declares: "There is no wisdom or understanding or counsel against the LORD" (Proverbs 21:30).

Question to ponder: Are there any ways in which you trust in yourself rather than in God?

At the Right Hand of the Father JULY 2

Therefore He is also able to save to the uttermost those who come to God through Him, since He always lives to make intercession for them.
Hebrews 7:25

The Apostles' Creed declares that Jesus "sitteth on the right hand of God the Father Almighty." What does that mean? It indicates a completion of His work of atonement and the beginning of His work of intercession. Hebrews 10:11–12 tells us that every priest stands daily ministering and offering sacrifices, which can never take away sins. But Jesus, after He had offered one sacrifice for sins forever, sat down at the right hand of God.

Christ has finished His work as our High Priest. His blood made full atonement for all our sins. Now He sits in the seat of authority at the right hand of God. Not only has He taken away our sins and made us right with God, He invites us to come boldly before His throne. Christ Himself hears our prayers and intercedes with the Father on our behalf. Jesus is our advocate with the Father and therefore we can pray with confidence.

Question to ponder: Picture yourself clean and spotless, standing before God Almighty Who awaits your prayer. How will you pray and what will you ask for?

....

....

....

....

....

....

....

JULY 3

"Duty is Ours"

If the foundations are destroyed, what can the righteous do?
Psalm 11:3

All nations that have ever existed have either been founded upon some theistic or anti-theistic principle. This is true whether we think of the Hinduism of India, the Confucianism of China, the Mohammedanism of Saudi Arabia, or the Atheism of the former Soviet Union.

If we know our history, we know that America was a nation founded upon Christ and His Word. Those foundations, indeed, are crumbling in our time. There are those in our country today who are busily tearing apart that foundation, those who would gnash their teeth at the idea that this is a Christian nation. They will not be satisfied until they have removed every vestige of our Christian heritage not only from the minds of the people but also from the monuments of this country.

We see the hatred people have for God and His Christ, and we tremble at the enormous assault on all things godly. What can the righteous do? Often in history God has raised up one person who has turned things around. One person is not too small. He has called us to be faithful to Him. John Quincy Adams once said, "Duty is ours. Results are God's."

Question to ponder: Is God calling you to help make a difference "for such a time as this"?

Christian Heritage of America

Blessed is the nation whose God is the LORD.
Psalm 38:12

John Quincy Adams, sixth President of the United States, said: "The highest glory of the American Revolution was _____." What? It secured our independence from England? It got rid of the Stamp Tax? The Tea Tax? It dissolved our bonds with Parliament and the king?

No.

What was the highest glory of the American Revolution? Listen well to what President John Quincy Adams said: "The highest glory of the American Revolution was this: it connected in one indissoluble bond, the principles of civil government with the principles of Christianity." "One indissoluble bond"—government and Christianity. Well, today there are those who have come with their solvents of unbelief, skepticism, atheism, Marxism, humanism, and secularism, and they are doing everything in their power to totally dissolve that indissoluble bond.

You and I were born in a Christian nation. That may not be said for our children or grandchildren unless we who have received this marvelous patrimony do something other than let it sift through our fingers like sand because we are engaged simply in the pursuit of own "personal peace and prosperity," as Dr. Francis Schaeffer used to say.

The price of freedom is eternal vigilance, and we should never take our freedom and our great heritage for granted.

Question to ponder: How can we pass Christian heritage on to the next generation?

....

....

....

....

....

JULY 5 ≡ *America: A Christian Nation*

*...Although they knew God, they did not glorify Him
as God, nor were thankful, but became futile in their
thoughts, and their foolish hearts were darkened.*
Romans 1:21

"America: A Christian Nation" is a concept that has been so systematically blotted from the collective memory of this country as to sound in the ears of most Americans like an alien philosophy, an intrusion of religion into the tranquility of a secular nation.

This is a nation that was born of the Bible. In 1982 *Newsweek Magazine* observed that some historians are now coming to realize that it was the Bible, even more than the Constitution, that founded this nation.

Today as we look at our country, we see a nation which has ceased to glorify God. When a people forget God, their hearts become darkened. But God still has many of His own in our land—many who are calling on His name and living humbly before Him, just as the Pilgrims, the Puritans and other godly settlers, along with many of our founding fathers did.

We should endeavor to remember that the secret of America's greatness is the creed that our rights come from God. God-given rights are non-negotiables. This is a great heritage that we can pass on to our posterity.

Question to ponder: What does it mean to be a "Christian nation"?

A Longing for the Word of God

As the deer pants for the water brooks,
so pants my soul for You, O God.
Psalm 42:1

Several years ago, around the time that the Soviet Union was imploding, American Christian booksellers were invited for the first time to show their wares at the Moscow Book Fair. One of those booksellers brought 50,000 Bibles to give away to people there. After several hours, the police stopped the give-away for the simple reason that there was such a mob of people clamoring for Bibles that every aisle of the Book Fair was jammed and traffic was gridlocked. So they were required to stop giving the Bibles away for two hours, then they were allowed to resume for another hour, then another break, then resume for another hour. The police weren't trying to prevent them from distributing Bibles—they were simply trying to keep the Moscow Book Fair open.

Further down the same aisle of the Book Fair, at the American Atheist Society booth, Madalyn Murray O'Hair was displaying their wares. Someone who was there told me that virtually no one even stopped to see what she had to offer, because they knew all too well. They had had atheism for seventy years and they wanted nothing more to do with it.

What a privilege it is to have the Bible. Let us never take it for granted.

Question to ponder: Do you feel a longing for the Word of God?

....

....

....

....

....

....

JULY 7 ═══ *See No Evil, Hear No Evil, Speak No Evil*

And do not be drunk with wine, in which is dissipation; but be filled with the Spirit.
Ephesians 5:18

When we receive Christ, we are baptized by the Holy Spirit into one body, but, alas, we are leaky vessels. Every hole is caused by sin, and so we need to be filled with the Spirit. By the way, the verb "be filled" is what is called a "continuous, repetitive tense." It means not just a one time action, but something that occurs over and over again. So, too, we need to continuously ask God to fill us with His Spirit.

How vital that prayer is. You can do nothing for Christ—you can't teach Sunday school, bear witness, preach, or anything without the Spirit of God enabling you to do so. We need to obey Him, which means a determination to turn from whatever it is God shows us by His Word and Spirit is wrong.

We need to place a guard on our eyes—what we look at; on our ears—what we listen to; on our lips—what we say; on our hearts—what we think; and on our feet—where we go. When we do, God's Spirit will fill our hearts and minds, and He will guide our steps.

Question to ponder: How can we continually be filled with the Holy Spirit?

Oneness in Christ

For by one Spirit we were all baptized into one body—
whether Jews or Greeks, whether slaves or free.
1 Corinthians 12:13

We need to have caring and sharing and burden bearing, even rebuking and correcting in the church. We need to have affection demonstrated in love—in the love of the family of God. But it all begins in our reconciliation to God through Jesus Christ.

His broken body, His shed blood, are the means by which that oneness occurs—that ultimate perfect oneness when we are in Christ and together in Heaven. It is a oneness where there will never be the slightest ripple of division or dissension, when all sin will have been taken away forever. In heaven, we will enjoy forever with Him such a joy and a love in that fellowship and family and communion that we cannot even imagine it now!

Many of us have experienced the pain of separation. The world is full of different churches and denominations. From the Great Schism in 1054 onward, we have kept dividing. We are separated from fellow believers by everything from church splits to geographical distance. Nevertheless, the pain of separation and distance will one day be removed, and how we long for that to happen.

Lord, make us one.

Question to ponder: What pain of separation have you experienced? Does the hope of heaven help you overcome that pain?

....

....

....

....

....

JULY 9

The Great Babylon

The king spoke, saying, "Is not this great Babylon,
that I have built for a royal dwelling by my mighty
power and for the honor of my majesty?"
Daniel 4:30

An example of biblical prophecy fulfilled is the magnificent city of Babylon, perhaps the greatest city in ancient times. The walled city consisted of 196 square miles of the most beautiful architecture, hanging gardens, palaces, temples and towers. Babylon drew her stores from no foreign country. She invented an alphabet, worked out the problems of arithmetic, invented implements for measuring time, and advanced beyond all previous peoples in science. Yet there are more than one hundred specific prophecies concerning Babylon's fate. God said of Babylon, even when it was the greatest city in the world: "Babylon, the glory of the kingdoms, the beauty of the Chaldees' excellency, shall be as when God overthrew Sodom and Gomorrah" (Isaiah 13:19).

The great walls of Babylon, Herodotus the historian tells us, had towers that extended above the 200-foot walls to a height of 300 feet. The city was laid out in a square with walls that were 187 feet thick at the base and 14 miles to a side. The city of Babylon was impregnable. But God said of those towers: "The broad walls of Babylon shall be utterly broken…it shall be desolate for ever" (Jeremiah 51:58, 62). There is nothing vague or ambiguous about this prophecy and even though it took centuries for it to be completely fulfilled, today not a remnant of that wall remains.

Question to ponder: How does Biblical prophecy strengthen your faith?

....

....

....

....

God's Sovereignty in History ⟹ JULY 10

*The king's heart is in the hand of the LORD, like the
rivers of water; He turns it wherever He wishes.*
Proverbs 21:1

Babylon became a symbol in antiquity of the world's evil power. The
inhabitants were described as enslaved to witchcraft, magic, idolatry, and
sacrilege (Daniel 5:1-3). From the Tower of Babel to the fall of Babylon in
Revelation, Babylon is described as the mother of harlots and of the abomi-
nations of the earth.

In the fourth century A.D., Julian the Apostate came to the throne
of Rome. His one great overwhelming desire was to destroy Christianity
and reestablish the pagan religions of Rome. While engaged in a war with
the Persians near the remains of Babylon, Julian completely destroyed the
remnants of the wall of Babylon, lest it afford any protection in the future
for the Persian army. And thus the prophecy from Jeremiah was brought to
fulfillment by one of the greatest antagonists of Scripture of all time.

But God had much more to say about this city: "Because of the wrath
of the Lord it shall not be inhabited, but it shall be wholly desolate.... It
shall be no more inhabited forever" (Jeremiah 50:13, 39). Babylon was
situated in the most fertile part of the Euphrates valley, and yet 2,500 years
have come and gone, and Babylon to this day remains an uninhabited
waste. Nothing but "heaps" remain of the city, as the prophet Jeremiah
prophesied (Jeremiah 51:37).

Question to ponder: How does this prophecy validate the
Word of God?

Who Cares for the Sick?

...I was sick and you visited Me...
Matthew 25:36

A famous atheist was quoted as saying: "An atheist wants a heaven on earth, a hospital instead of a church. He wants disease conquered, poverty vanquished and war eliminated." Now, that expresses a very noble sentiment.

But what say the facts? This person says atheists want heaven on earth. To bring it about they want a hospital instead of a church. Isn't that an amazing thing? As far as I know, there is not a single hospital anywhere on the face of this globe that has ever been built voluntarily by atheists.

That is not to say that some government, committed to atheism, may not confiscate by taxation some of the wealth of the people and build a hospital. But atheists, voluntarily banding together and contributing their own money freely to build a hospital? There's not one that I know of on the face of the earth.

Christians, however, have built tens of thousands of hospitals all over the world, even in the most remote parts of the farthest jungles on the earth; hospitals that minister to the sick and to the lepers and to the blind and to the deaf and to the crippled and the maimed of every sort.

We can thank the Lord for the love of Christ which has motivated Christians to care for the sick and advance modern medicine so that His love and mercy may be demonstrated all around the world.

Question to ponder: Would you be alive today if it weren't for modern medicine?

....

....

....

....

A Leap of Blind Faith

The fool has said in his heart, "There is no God."
They are corrupt, and have done abominable
iniquity; there is none who does good.
Psalm 53:1

One of the fruits of evolution has been the proliferation of atheists. Do you realize that before Darwin, an atheist was as scarce as a hen's tooth? Oh, there were a few around, but very, very few. Do you know why? Because if you said you were an atheist, all I had to say to you was, "Look around, buddy. Where did all of this come from?" And the atheist said, "Ah... bu... da... I don't know."

Then came Charles Darwin, who, as one evolutionist said, "made atheism respectable." I would not want to be Charles Darwin on Judgment Day. Think of all the people whom he has led astray. It is true that some were led astray quite willingly, but he is responsible for a lot of unbelief, ungodliness, and misery.

To say that tiny changes in all organisms (micro-evolution, if you will) prove gigantic changes from one species to another species (macro-evolution) is a gigantic leap of blind faith. The missing links were missing in his day; they're still missing in our day.

We believe in God, the Creator of heaven and earth. We should do all we can to counteract the false teaching that has been so readily accepted at every level of our society.

Question to ponder: How did you come in your journey of faith to believe in God the Creator?

....

....

....

....

JULY 13 —

Is That You, David?

Wash me thoroughly from my iniquity,
and cleanse me from my sin.
Psalm 51:2

There is an inevitable sadness connected with sin. Theologian Clarence McCartney reminds us of David, a man after God's own heart and the beautiful Psalm-singer of Israel. But who is this that we see lying prostrate on the ground in the dust, weeping out his penitential tears and crying to God for mercy: "Cast me not away from thy presence; and take not thy holy spirit from me" (Psalm 51:11) "...all my bones are out of joint; ... my strength is dried up like a potsherd" (Ps. 22:14,15).

Is that you, David? You, the man after God's own heart? Can it be? Is that you—the one who watched over your father's flocks as a young shepherd and so courageously killed the lion and the bear? Is that you, David, who with your sling destroyed that blasphemer, Goliath? Is that you, David, who with your lyre drove out the evil spirit from King Saul?

Alas, it is you, O, David. What sorrowful sight is this that the one who was the man after God's own heart should thus be brought low, covered with sadness and impurity. Let us mourn over him: this adulterer, this murderer; this one who has cast himself in shame; this one who has been told that because of his sin the sword shall never depart from his household; this one who weeps because he knows that his own sin has plunged the knife into the body of his infant child.

In the end, David discovered mercy and forgiveness from the Lord, while the consequences of his sins remained.

Question to ponder: Can you think of a sin in your life that God forgave you for, but you still had to live with the consequences?

The Walking Dead

Have the gates of death been revealed to you?
Or have you seen the doors of the shadow of death?
Job 38:17

A distinguished professor of psychology was telling his class of a rather striking case of somnambulism (sleepwalking). A man got out of his bed, went down the stairs, opened his front door, walked across the lawn and out into the street. He walked right out of town and on through the fields and meadows. He never woke up until his bare feet stepped into the cold water of a stream that crossed his path. Then, suddenly, he awakened and looked around terrified at the strange surroundings. He wasn't in his bedroom. He was standing in the midst of a stream.

I thought, then, that there are many people like that. The "walking dead," asleep while supposedly awake, who walk through life oblivious of where they really are in the eternal scheme of things. They never wake up until suddenly they find their feet in the cold stream of death. Then they awaken—started by strange surroundings—to find themselves in the midst of death and judgment and condemnation.

Death is a wake-up call. When we are confronted by our own mortality or the death of a loved one, it puts life into perspective.

Question to ponder: How does the thought of death wake us up?

....
....
....
....
....
....

JULY 15 ═══   *Saved By Grace*

God, who has saved us and called us with a holy calling, not
according to our works, but according to His own purpose and
grace which was given to us in Christ Jesus before time began.
2 Timothy 1:8-9

The meaning of grace is totally unmerited favor to those who deserve disfavor. To the undeserving, to the ill-deserving, to the Hell-deserv-
ing, God offers eternal life, but not because of anything that we have done.

If biblical passages could be likened unto mountains, Ephesians 2:8-9,
"For by grace are ye saved through faith; and that not of yourselves: it is the
gift of God: Not of works, lest any man should boast," would be the Himala-
yas. One text stands out above them all, rising high into the sky, snow-clad,
surrounded with clouds of mystery. It is, I think, the very pinnacle of biblical revelation, and it shares with us that great truth, that one central truth,
that God wants us to know: "By grace are ye saved."

Question to ponder: How is the grace of God manifest
in your life?

....

....

....

....

....

....

....

....

....

Accepting God's Grace ≡ JULY 16

*For all have sinned and fall short of the glory
of God, being justified freely by His grace through
the redemption that is in Christ Jesus.*
Romans 3:23-24

Grace means looking away from yourself unto the cross. It means being accepted because of what God is, not because of what we are. It means being accepted, not based on what we have done, but in spite of everything we have done. It is the free gift of eternal life.

If you have never received that grace, I urge you to receive it now. You don't have to plead your virtues; you don' have to plead your great accomplishments. You see, there's only one thing you can add to your salvation—your sin for which Christ died. By God's grace, He changes our hearts. By His grace, He brings us to repentance and faith.

God's grace is really all we need. It is all sufficient.

Grace is the most important concept in the world. It is the most important concept in the Bible. Some of you are saying, "Did not the Apostle Paul say that the greatest concept was love?" No, he didn't. What he actually said was: "And now abideth faith, hope, charity [love], these three; but the greatest of *these* is charity" (1 Corinthians 13:13). What a glorious concept that is. If grace had entered into the list, love would have had to step into the shadows, for grace is greater than love.

Question to ponder: Explain in your own words: What is grace?

〰 ....

....

....

....

....

JULY 17 *The Addictiveness of Sin*

For the good that I will to do, I do not do;
but the evil I will not to do, that I practice.
Romans 7:19

One of the tragic things about sin is that it is addictive. It doesn't matter what kind of sin a person gets into—not just alcohol or drugs—all sin is addictive. The more we do a particular sin, the stronger becomes our addiction and the more its chains hold us and the greater our desire for that sin. Some of you know exactly what I am talking about; you have been there or you are in bondage right now. The good news is that every shackle is broken at Calvary.

There on the Cross, Christ having been affixed—hand and foot—for us, broke the chains that bind the captive to sin. And He can set you free. You can go to that fountain which has been opened at Calvary's Mount, and you can be washed and cleansed. You can be clothed in the perfect righteousness of His white robes of purity and become whiter than snow. You can be in-filled with the power of the Holy Spirit and delivered from the bondage and addiction of sin. Only at the Cross is there hope for a sinful world.

I invite you in His name to come to the Cross to find forgiveness, to find a new life, to find the purity and freedom you desire. Come and find the truth and the love of Christ, and the life abundant and everlasting.

Question to ponder: Have you surrendered your life fully to God? How does it make you feel to know you are cleansed and forgiven?

....

....

....

....

The Great Unmentionable

The last enemy that will be destroyed is death.
1 Corinthians 15:26

Death is our enemy, but praise be to the Lord, He has conquered death.

Death is something that causes the human mind to recoil. We do not like to think about it. The great English poet and dramatist Ben Johnson said that man spends all of his life in one effort after another trying to avoid the thought of his own mortality.

The great English preacher Charles Spurgeon, however, would call us to look upon it. He said that the time comes, erelong, when these shining orbs by which I look out upon you and through which you look into my very soul, will become a "carnival for worms," This body of mine will be inhabited by loathsome things, the brother of corruption, the sister of decay. These cheeks now flushed with life will soon be sunken in death. Beneath the skin there will be going on such activity that, could we look upon it, we would recoil in horror. This same death of the body is the condition of our soul as we come into this world.

But ultimately the Christian need not have the same fear of death that the non-Christian has. Because Jesus conquered the grave, we have new hope in the face of death.

Question to ponder: Is death still our enemy?

JULY **19** ═══ *The Final Step in Salvation*

...Whom He justified, these He also glorified.
Romans 8:30

The final part of our salvation is glorification. This will take place when we are finally home in heaven and made perfect through Jesus Christ.

I have always known that in glorification we would be perfect. I knew that we would have perfect bodies; we would never be sick; we would never be weary; we would never tire nor need sleep. All of that, of course, is true but I never thought about the face being perfect. I thought that if we were perfect we would all look the same. Of course, that is not really so. Each one of us is a certain type that God has made. We are unique like snowflakes, but each one of us also is marred: a little twist to the nose, or bulge to the ears, or a crook to the teeth, or whatever it might be. But just think what would happen if all those imperfections were corrected. Perfection. Paradise. A perfect body in a perfect environment forever—all compliments of Jesus Christ.

And that is just the physical part of our glorification. Our darkened mind will be sharp and perfectly able to function at top capacity. Our will shall finally be free from all evil influences and unable to rebel again. Our emotions will be healed of all hurt and pain. Most of all, our souls will be sinless and sin-free forever.

Question to ponder: Think of your own glorification. What do you look forward to most?

⑃⎪⎪⎪...

....

....

....

....

....

To See the Savior's Face

They shall neither hunger anymore nor thirst anymore;
the sun shall not strike them, nor any heat; for the Lamb
who is in the midst of the throne will shepherd them and
lead them to living fountains of waters. And God will
wipe away every tear from their eyes.
Revelation 7:16-17

For believers, death is only a transition, a glorious step into His world and our eternal home. But millions who do not know Christ are afraid of death. Woody Allen once made light of it by remarking, "I'm not afraid of death. I just don't want to be there when it happens."

We see death symbolized as the caped skeleton with his bony finger beckoning us to go where we don't want to go. This is captured dramatically in Charles Dickens' *A Christmas Carol* when Scrooge is visited by the Ghost of Christmas Future, who shows him his own grave.

To many, death is indeed the King of Terrors. But the Christian need not be afraid of death. Afraid of death? Afraid to see the Savior's face? Ah my friends, there is no tragedy, no pain, no suffering, no depression or disconsolation that Christ cannot heal. One of my favorite hymns states it this way:

Come, ye disconsolate, where'er ye languish,
Come to the mercy seat, fervently kneel.
Here bring your wounded hearts, here tell your anguish.
Earth has no sorrow that heaven cannot heal.

This is what we have to look forward to—the healing of all our hurts, emotionally, physically, and spiritually. Total healing and perfection: that is what Jesus Christ wants for us and that is what He has in store for us.

Question to ponder: What major hurt in your life
do you long for Jesus to heal?

A Great Light

*The people who walked in darkness have seen
a great light; those who dwelt in the land of the
shadow of death, upon them a light has shined.*
Isaiah 9:2

Jesus came into this dark world of sin, yet even more wonderful to tell, He is willing to come into the dark world of our hearts—our hearts of sin—bringing a light which will never go out. Christ brings the light of life to those into whose hearts he comes. Behold, they that "sat in darkness saw a great light" (Matthew 4:16).

We as Christians are called "children of light." In one sense, the sun, warmth, light, and day are all symbols of God, and pictures of all that is good. We have all been called out of the darkness into light.

Because the light of the world has come, we have hope. In *The Inferno* of Dante's *Divine Comedy*, the famous inscription over the Gates of Hell reads, "Abandon all hope, ye who enter here."

Without hope, we have nothing. Hopelessness, darkness, and despair are tools of the devil to keep people away from God, away from Jesus Christ and His marvelous light. Jesus is the light of the world, and without Him we walk in darkness. Jesus has come and He has brought light and life to our dark world.

Question to ponder: What is the connection between physical and spiritual light?

....

....

....

....

....

On the Side of Truth

*And my speech and my preaching were not with
persuasive words of human wisdom, but in demonstration
of the Spirit and of power, that your faith should not be in
the wisdom of men but in the power of God.*
1 Corinthians 2:4-5

There are many arguments for the Christian faith, for the Bible, for the existence of God, and for the resurrection of Christ. And I am very thankful that after spending a great many years of study, I am not afraid to talk to anybody or debate anybody on these matters, because I know that the truth is God's and that God is truth. The truth is on our side, which makes it far easier to win a debate.

In every debate I have ever seen between a Christian and an unbeliever, the Christian has won because truth is on our side. When Jesus (the *Logos*—or Logic) was incarnated in human form, it was Love.

The truth of Christ stands: not because the messengers are eloquent and wise. The Truth is eternal and strong, in spite of the messenger. We do not win debates because we are better debaters. We win because we have the Truth.

At times it might seem that we fail by human standards, but God incarnate, Truth with a capital T, is Jesus Christ. He is the Logos that came into the world and even though we are weak and stammering, the message is true, eternal, and mighty.

Question to ponder: Can you think of a time when your words felt totally inadequate, but God used them anyway?

....

....

....

....

JULY 23 ====   *In the Ark or Not*

> *By faith Noah, being divinely warned of things not yet seen,*
> *moved with godly fear, prepared an ark for the saving of his*
> *household, by which he condemned the world and became*
> *heir of the righteousness which is according to faith.*
> Hebrews 11:7

In Noah's day vast multitudes were invited to come into the ark. As many as would, Noah invited to come and join him, but they would not. When the great fountains of the deep were broken up, and the windows of heaven were opened, and the floodwaters came upon the earth, I am sure they beat upon the sides of that ark and cried out to be admitted, but God had shut Noah and his family in, and there was no opening the door.

There is coming a day when the period of grace shall be irrevocably, irretrievably, ended. Now the sun shines and the day of grace is still upon us, and all that will come into the ark are invited to come. But the decision must be made by us.

While you are deciding whether or not to surrender your life to Jesus Christ, you have two options: reject Him or accept Him. Nevertheless, in truth, you have already taken the option of having rejected Him, for until you accept Him you have done precisely that. "He that is not with me," said Christ, "is against me" (Matthew 12:30).

There is no middle ground. There is no fence upon which to sit. We are either the friends of Christ or we are His enemies and adversaries; we either gather in or we scatter abroad. There is no third choice.

Question to ponder: For Christ or against Him: what were some of the factors that helped you respond to His call?

....

....

....

....

The Alchemy of God

The Lord will fulfill his purpose for me.
Psalm 138:8 (NIV)

Alchemy, the precursor of chemistry, stands in relation to chemistry somewhat the same way that astrology stands to astronomy. The great quest of the alchemists was to transmute the base metals into the noble—to change lead into gold. As you may surmise, they failed in their quest. However, God is the great cosmic alchemist who never fails. Romans 8:28 is the alchemy of God. He changes the lead of our lives into gold.

What is the great comfort in our lives? Ultimately, it is His divine deliverance that is our great comfort—all things that come to us He is able to turn to our good. No matter what it may be, Christ can deliver us. What a marvelous promise this is—even from the greatest tragedy, the tragedy of death—Christ can deliver His people.

If Christ can turn to good even death itself, how much more can He take the problem we are facing today and bring resolution? It seems like life presents one problem after another, whether it is our health, our finances, our relationships, our work, our family, or our loved ones. As soon as we solve one problem, another presents itself. Jesus never promised a problem-free life; but He did promise that things will work together for good for those who love God and are called according to His purpose. If we are His, He will make all things right in the end. He has given us beauty for ashes.

Question to ponder: What problem are you facing today for which you need divine deliverance?

....

....

....

....

JULY **25**

Delighting in the Lord

*Delight yourself also in the Lord, and He
shall give you the desires of your heart.*
Psalm 37:4

We live in a culture where people are profoundly dissatisfied; we have an unsaturated lust for more and more. However, we are encouraged by the Lord to present our needs to Him, and He has promised to provide for us. To be satisfied by little or much, to learn contentment—this is a Christian virtue. The key is to delight ourselves in the Lord.

Thanks be to God! There is an antidote to covetousness, and that antidote is found in Jesus who brings peace and joy and rest to our hearts. To rest in Jesus is to find the answer to all of our desires.

The most astonishing thing that happened to me in conversion was that God reached down and changed my "wanter." Suddenly, all of the things I had always wanted and never had enough of, I did not want anymore. I saw them for the lies and deceits they really were. Suddenly, my affections were set on Someone above, and the things of this world grew strangely dim in the light of His glory and grace. At last I found contentment.

Christ gives us new desires, new affections. He sets our affections on things above, not on things here below. That is why Pilgrim, when he comes to Vanity Fair in Bunyan's *Pilgrim's Progress,* passed through without being enticed by all of the baubles therein.

Question to ponder: How can you delight yourself in the Lord today?

The Poverty of Discontentment

Now godliness with contentment is great gain.
1 Timothy 6:6

Unless the discontented person learns the secret of contentment, he is never going to be happy, because he is never going to get enough. Whenever he gets one thing, the devil is going to let him know there is something else—a newer car, a bigger house, a boat—that is going to make him happy. But he never will be happy.

I remember reading about a man who was very, very rich. I think he had about $900 million dollars, an extraordinary amount of money at that time. A TV interviewer asked him, "Are you satisfied, contented, with what you have?"

"Well, not yet."

"How much would it take for you to be content?"

"Just a little more."

Do you see the truth in that? If you are discontented, then even if you had $10 billion, you would still need "just a little more" to be satisfied.

Ben Franklin said, "Who is rich? He that rejoices in his Portion…. Content[ment] makes poor men rich; Discontent[ment] makes rich Men poor."

Not only is there a great sorrow involved in discontentment, but we also need to realize the sin of discontentment. Discontentment leads to grumbling, complaining, and unhappiness.

To be content in such a discontented culture is to shine for God, because little is much when God is in it.

Question to ponder: Have you noticed how thankfulness and trust drive away discontentment?

....

....

....

....

JULY 27 — *"Not in Our Stars, But in Ourselves"*

For from within, out of the heart of men, proceed evil thoughts, adulteries, fornications, murders, thefts, covetousness, wickedness, deceit, lewdness, an evil eye, blasphemy, pride, foolishness. All these evil things come from within and defile a man.
Mark 7:21-23

The greatest minds have known that man was sinful. Albert Einstein said: "The real problem is in the hearts and minds of men. It is not a problem of physics but of ethics. It is easier to denature plutonium than to denature the evil spirit of man."

Shakespeare, who was a masterful student of human nature, had Cassius tell Brutus the truth: "The fault, Dear Brutus, is not in our stars, but in ourselves that we are underlings" *(Julius Caesar)*. And how very true that is.

The problem is within us that we are underlings, that we are sinners, and not in our environment. I think of the man a hundred years ago who was driving into Maine with his wagon and his horses. He was laboriously beating his horses, and they were straining mightily to climb this long hill. Finally, as he passed a farmer who was standing on the edge of the road watching him in some amazement as he furiously drove his horses, he cried out to the farmer. "Sir, how long does this hill last?"

The farmer said, "Hill, nothing. Your hind wheels are off."

Are you having problems, my friend? You had better check your hind wheels. They may be off. The problem may be within. The only hill may be in your heart.

Question to ponder: What do you find most troublesome about the evil within?

〰 ....

....

....

"Your Sword, Sir"

Therefore I urge you, brothers, in view of God's
mercy, to offer your bodies as a living sacrifice.
Romans 12:1 (NIV)

When the Revolutionary War was over, the British general came to surrender to Washington. The general began to praise Washington for his leading of his troops (a much smaller army than the British), the tactics that he employed, and the incredible things that had been done, which amazed even him. In the midst of the praise, Washington interrupted him and said, "Your sword, sir."

It is not for us to begin to praise God until first we have surrendered ourselves and our sword to Christ. This is the army of the conquered—those that have been conquered by Christ.

When our hearts have been won and our wills have been taken over by Christ, when the sword of our rebellion is knocked from our hands and we are brought to the ground, only then will we abandon all lesser goals and all lesser aims, and give ourselves over to the highest and the best. Those who are most thoroughly surrendered to Him are the greatest trophies of grace and will have the greatest victories.

Our will was created good, but in Adam's fall, the will of man became rebellious and self-serving. Only when our will is submitted to God are we free again to offer ourselves as our spiritual worship.

Question to ponder: Is there any area of your life that is not surrendered to the Lordship of Christ?

....

....

....

....

....

JULY **29** ══ *Controlling Our Tongues*

*Even so the tongue is a little member and boasts great
things. See how great a forest a little fire kindles.*
James 3:5

Tact can go a long way in solving a lot of problems, as one man who worked in a grocery store discovered when an elderly lady came up and wanted to buy half a head of cabbage. "But Madam," he said, "we only sell the whole head."

"I just want half a head of cabbage," she replied. "I live by myself and I only need half a head of cabbage."

He tried a number of times to dissuade her. Finally, with some exasperation, he said, "Well, I'll go and ask the manager."

So he walked to the back of the store and found the manager. "Can you believe that some old idiot wants to buy half a head of cabbage?" he exclaimed. Then he noticed out of the corner of his eyes that the woman had followed him and was standing right behind him. Recovering his tact quickly, he said, "And this dear lady has agreed to buy the other half. Would that be all right?"

May God grant that we learn to control our tongues. May He help us to use them to build people up, not to tear them down. May He give us the grace to glorify Him and to use our tongues tell others of Jesus.

Question to ponder: How can you use your tongue
for someone's good today?

....

....

....

....

....

Using God's Name to Honor Him　　≡ JULY 30

You shall not take the name of the Lord your
God in vain, for the Lord will not hold him
guiltless who takes His name in vain.
Exodus 20:7

The law of gravity says that if you step off the roof of a 30-story building, you will be dead. That is not a threat. It is a fact—a very simple fact. And if you take the name of God in vain, it is a fact that God will not hold you guiltless. What does that mean? It means you shall not go unpunished.

As a young man in my late teens and early twenties I, on occasion, used profanity and used the name of God in vain. Then I learned of the immense love of Jesus Christ. I learned that when He was on that Cross, He was agonizing for me; that what He endured there, He was enduring for my sake and in my place. As my substitute, in my stead the wrath of God fell on His head for my sins. And with many tears I fell to my knees and invited Him into my heart to be the Lord and Savior of my life. That was many years ago. To the best of my remembrance, and I think in this case it is accurate, since that time I have not once in all these years taken the name of Jesus Christ in vain. That's because I love Him, and I want to honor His name.

Question to ponder: How can we honor God's name?

JULY **31** ═══ *Fishers of Men*

Follow Me and I will make you fishers of men.
Matthew 4:19

One of the greatest needs of the human soul is the need for adventure. We long to be a part of something big, a grand epic, something beyond us. This is what Jesus offered Peter.

Jesus said to Peter, "Fear not, from henceforth thou shalt catch men" (Luke 5:10). "No more slimy, scaly, smelly fish for you, Peter. You shall catch men—such men as you never even dreamt to speak to in your life you shall catch, for I will give your life a meaning and a significance and a purpose that you can't even dream about. Your life with Me will be an adventure, not a humdrum, because you have taken Me at My word."

The Lord offers us a part in this great adventure. He has a purpose for our lives. What He has for us is way beyond simply going to work and coming home. He wants us to be kingdom-builders. God will reveal Himself to all who seek Him diligently.

Question to ponder: How can you open your heart to God's big adventure? How do we find our purpose?

Using Wealth for God's Kingdom ═ AUGUST 1

Whoever can be trusted with very little
can also be trusted with much....
Luke 16:10 (NIV)

Jesus didn't say to everyone what He said to the rich young ruler: to sell all he had, give to the poor, and come follow Jesus (Luke 18). I think that what we really have in the story of the rich young ruler is the story of the taproot sin.

Some trees that have taproots have other roots that extend out a little bit on the surface. But they have one root that goes deep down into the earth. You can cut all of the surface roots, and you can't remove that tree to save your life unless you cut the taproot. In His encounter with the rich young ruler, Christ put the axe to the taproot of sin. The rich young ruler trusted in his possessions.

What we have been given is for our benefit and for the good of God's people and His Kingdom. Numerous times I have seen how much good one committed Christian can do for God using his wealth. Whether we have little or much, the important thing is: Can God trust us to manage what He has given us?

Question to ponder: How can you use your possessions for God and His Kingdom?

....

....

....

....

....

....

....

Taproot Sins

For out of the heart proceed evil thoughts, murders, adulteries, fornications, thefts, false witness, blasphemies.
Matthew 15:19

Some sins are at the taproot of the heart. When is comes to these sins, the devil will say to you, "Oh, you may get rid of this sin, or give up that sin, or quit doing this, or quit doing that,… but when it comes to this particular sin, you'll never get rid of it!" This is your taproot sin. Has it been cut? If not, Jesus is the master gardener.

I don't know what your taproot sin is: maybe it is greed or lust, perhaps it is gluttony, perhaps it is alcohol, perhaps it is addiction—you're addicted to something, and that taproot sin holds you right down in the earth. You can't grow in your spiritual life because you are bound by that taproot.

Maybe the sin is criticism or gossip. Oh, what a cutting taproot that is. Perhaps it's anger. You're angry at someone who has done you in.

I don't know if you are struggling with a taproot sin, but I do know that unless it is cut, you cannot rise up and follow Christ.

Jesus has conquered all sin, and there is no sin that you cannot overcome in His name and by the power of His blood. Let Jesus deal with your sin, and His victory will shine in your previously defeated heart.

Question to ponder: How can we learn to detect the root sin in our heart?

....

....

....

....

....

....

Born, Dead, Buried, Raised ⟹ AUGUST 3

For I delivered to you first of all that which I also received: that Christ died for our sins according to the Scriptures, and that He was buried, and that He rose again the third day according to the Scriptures.
1 Corinthians 15:3-4

The Apostles' Creed is the oldest condensation of all of the beliefs of Christianity. What does it have to say about the teachings of Jesus or the preaching of Jesus or the example of Jesus? Absolutely zilch. Nothing. It says, "[He was] conceived by the Holy Ghost, born of the Virgin Mary [that's His birthday]...." Immediately contiguous with that, "[He] suffered under Pontius Pilate, was crucified, dead, and buried...."

And so it goes from His birthday to His death day with absolutely nothing in between, because Christianity is based upon Christ and Him crucified. He came not to teach, but to die. In the mind of God, He was crucified before the world began.

This does not mean that Jesus' teaching or preaching was unimportant. What it does mean is that it is His person—who He was, is, and will be—that outshines what He said and thought. As the Apostle's Creed states, we believe in our crucified and resurrected Savior who is coming again with life and liberty to all who believe.

Question to ponder: What place, if any, do the historic creeds of the Christian church have in your life and worship?

How Happy the Angels Will Be

All the angels stood around the throne....
Revelation 7:11

The picture of the angels of God worshiping and rejoicing before God and the Lamb is a beautiful image. Imagine these angels rejoicing over a human—a man or a woman.

"Oh, Mommy, how happy the angels will be!" These words burst spontaneously from the lips of a little five-year-old girl on hearing about the death of a very godly man. The man was Boston-born, Harvard-educated professor of Latin, the Right Rev erend Phillips Brooks, Bishop of Massachusetts for the Episcopal Church, composer of the classic hymn "O Little Town of Bethlehem."

May we so live for Christ that when we die that someone could make a similar exclamation, "Oh, Mommy, how happy the angels will be!"

May God help us live in such a way that we not only please the angels, but we please the Lord. For example, if we want to please the Lord, we should be encouragers. Paul's letter to the Galatians says, "Bear ye one another's burdens" (Galatians 6:2). Most of us would immediately set out to help somebody who was doubling over because of a heavy burden. Oftentimes, however, we do not see the burdens people are struggling with that are not visible to the physical eye.

If our eyes were open, we would realize that opportunities abound to please the Lord in our daily lives. May we truly live in such a way as to please Him.

Question to ponder: It's one thing to talk about making angels happy. Is there anything we can do to make the Lord happy?

⸎ ....

....

....

....

A Vale of Tears

Put my tears into Your bottle....
Psalm 56:8

As far as we know, God does not cry. As far as we know, neither do angels. I also believe that in the sense that we know the term, animals don't cry either—though I confess that some of them do something that looks like it. Tears seem to be, in the economy of God's providence, something reserved for the human race. Perhaps that is because of sin. Before the fall, there were no tears.

We need to have our hearts melted and our souls strengthened, and somewhere in there are going to be tears when we really see ourselves as we are. A soft heart brings tears to our eyes. We weep for our own sins. We weep for others. We weep because we live in a fallen, sinful world, where sorrow and pain are all around us. Tears belong to this world, and when this life is over, God Himself will wipe our tears away, and there will never be any more reason for crying, weeping, or wailing.

In the mean time, God numbers our tears and keeps them in His bottle.

Question to ponder: What is most frequently the cause of your tears?

AUGUST 6 ======

No More Tears

And God will wipe away every tear from their eyes;
there shall be no more death, nor sorrow, nor crying.
Revelation 21:4

In this life, because of sin, there is much sorrow. Between our far from God, sin-laden souls, and the joy that is at the right hand of God, there is, I believe, almost of necessity, a vale of tears to be crossed. Just as icicles hanging on the frosted branches drip forth water when the sun shines on them, even so the sin-filled soul, when it is brought close to the Son of Righteousness, will invariably drip with tears.

All the sins of man eventually turn into tears. For some, the tears come in this world. For those with harder hearts, they come in the next world. However, they will come, for God has so ordained that sin must bring tears of contrition and repentance. Don't misunderstand: I would have you to clearly know that it takes more than our salty tears to wash away the stains of all our sins. It is only when we place our trust in Christ, and Him alone, that we can find forgiveness and the confident hope of eternal life with Him in Heaven.

The Bible tell us that in Heaven there shall be no more tears, for God shall wipe them away with His own finger.

Question to ponder: What kind of tears are good and beneficial?

....

....

....

....

....

....

Flee Temptation

Therefore let him who thinks he
stands take heed lest he fall....
1 Corinthians 10:12

We need to stay as far away from sin as we possibly can. Flee temptation. For none of us are immune to the tempter's snare.

Joseph faced the temptations of Potiphar's wife, who wanted him to have sex with her. But he resisted, even at the cost of going to jail. Daniel in Babylon resisted the temptations of a godless society. Countless millions of others have, likewise, taken a stand for Jesus Christ. The responsibility ultimately is ours.

The Bible is very clear about temptation. There is a theological phrase that describes what we are supposed to do about temptation. I want you to remember it. I want you never, ever to forget it. It is not all that difficult. I think it should be understandable to everyone. That is, whenever you are confronted with temptation, remember this phrase: Run like crazy. "Flee temptation," the Scripture says. "Flee also youthful lusts" (2 Timothy 2:22).

Many people have supposed they could flirt with temptation. How many among the army of addicts to alcohol, tobacco, and drugs have thought they could flirt with temptation: "Oh, it will never get the best of me." They have fallen ignominiously on their faces before it. How many have flirted with sexual temptations and have found themselves falling headlong into an abyss of sin that has ruined their lives.

Question to ponder: Have you ever thought that you would never fall into one sin or another?

AUGUST 8 — *This Life Versus Eternity*

> *As for man, his days are like grass; as a flower of the
> field, so he flourishes. For the wind passes over it, and
> it is gone, and its place remembers it no more.*
> Psalm 103:15-16

Once, when leaving a building, I opened a door thinking it was an exit, only to discover that I had stepped into a tiny broom closet! Of course, I stepped out instantly and closed the door. I probably was in there only one or two seconds at the most. Now, wouldn't it be extraordinarily odd, if I were to spend the rest of my life talking about that little closet?

Since it is without doubt, if we have placed our trust in Christ, that we will spend more than 99.99% of our lives in Heaven, why do we spend all of our time talking about this "little closet," which will be but a fleeting moment in the prospect of eternity?

According to the Bible, this world is simply the foyer to eternity—a testing ground where the talents and the abilities that God has given to man are to be used and exercised. What is important in this life is what we do for God's glory with the talents that God has given to us. But what we do about Jesus Christ in this life determines our eternal destiny.

When we view our earthly existence as a prelude to eternity, we see this world in an entirely different light, and this affects our view of this life as well.

Question to ponder: How much of your time do you spend thinking about eternity?

....

....

....

....

....

Giving

Give, and it will be given to you: good measure,
pressed down, shaken together, and running over will
be put into your bosom. For with the same measure
that you use, it will be measured back to you.
Luke 6:38

Tithing is God's method of sanctifying and maturing Christians, and making us more like Christ. Since selfishness and covetousness are two of the root problems of humankind, we need to learn how to cut out that taproot and be set free.

Malachi 3 is the only place in the Bible where God says, "Prove me." Can you believe that? What an incredible condescension. God says to put Him on trial—"Prove me now herewith...if I will not open you the windows of heaven, and pour you out a blessing, that there shall not be room enough to receive it" (Malachi 3:10).

Those who will trust in the Lord will find that He indeed will "open you the windows of heaven, and pour out a blessing, that there shall not be room enough to receive it." God's challenge to give is a test of faith that proves whether our god is gold or the true God, because where your heart is, there your treasure will be also.

Question to ponder: Have you experienced that it is more blessed to give than to receive?

....

....

....

....

....

....

AUGUST 10 ═══

Redeeming the Time

*I must work the works of Him who sent Me while it
is day; the night is coming when no one can work.*
John 9:4

My friend, have there been kind and loving things you have planned
to say to your child? Have you been planning to spend time with your son
before he becomes a man? Has there been some praise you wanted to give
to your wife or husband? Has there been some kindness you have been
thinking about doing but have always put it off. You were just too busy.

We have no tomorrow. There is no yesterday. We have only *today*.
"This is the day which the Lord hath made..." (Psalm 118:24). We always and
only live in today.

There is a thought that has impacted my life, and I would like to share
it with you. I would like for you to seriously consider what this day would
be like if at midnight tonight you knew you would die. How would you
change this day? What would you do today that you have not really been
planning to do at all? Or tomorrow? Or the next day? Or the next?

If each day were the last day we were to live on this earth, can you
imagine how much more kindness, how much more love, how much more
encouragement, how much more praise there would be in our homes?

Question to ponder: Is there anything you have put off
that you need to do today?

⑾ ....

....

....

....

....

Do not Boast about Tomorrow ══ AUGUST 11

*Today, if you hear his voice, do not harden your hearts as you
did in the rebellion, during the time of testing in the wilderness.*
Hebrews 3:7-8

I remember some years ago a young man from a Christian home came
to see me in my office. He was living a wild life and I spoke with him for a
good while. I explained to him the Gospel and urged him to turn his life over
to Christ. He said to me, "Dr. Kennedy, I want you to know that I believe
everything you said. I know it is all true. I know it because my parents taught
it to me as a child, and I want you to know something else. I have every
intention of receiving Christ as my Savior. I have no intention of leaving this
world without doing that—but not now; I've got some real living to do first."

He got up to leave, and as he opened the door, I stopped him. I said, "Let
me leave one text with you as you go. The Bible says, "A man who remains
stiff-necked after many rebukes will suddenly be destroyed—without remedy"
(Proverbs 29:1 NIV). He paused, looked back at me, turned again, and left.

A few days later I received word that he was riding his motorcycle
on the freeway when a truck with the tailgate down stopped unexpectedly
in front of him and he was instantly decapitated. I couldn't help but think
of my parting words to him: "He, that being often reproved hardeneth his
neck, shall suddenly be destroyed, and that without remedy."

"Do not boast about tomorrow, for you do not know what a day may
bring forth" (Proverbs 27:1 NIV). Now is the accepted time. Today is the day
of salvation.

Question to ponder: Do you know of any people you
should talk with about the state of their souls?

....

....

....

....

AUGUST 12 ═══

Tolerance

> *Nevertheless, I have this against you: You tolerate*
> *that woman Jezebel, who calls herself a prophet.*
> Revelation 2:20 (NIV)

We live in a very tolerant society. One example of this is that you will never see anybody on a talk show, no matter what they have done—whether they've committed murder, adultery, or rape—you'll never hear a whisper that they are sinners. It is because we are a "tolerant" people. All other virtues have disappeared except that of tolerance. Nobody would dare say, "Tch, tch, you shouldn't have done that. That is a sin, and you are a sinner." That is never heard in this society.

God is not tolerant, however. Every single sin of whatever kind that is perpetrated on this earth will be punished by God. Every single sin that you have committed and I have committed will be punished by God, either on us in hell, or on Christ at Calvary. God is infinite justice. He cannot tolerate sin. He lives in a totally 100 percent spotless, pure and holy heaven. Sin is not tolerated there.

We Christians do believe in and practice a tolerance; but remember this: tolerance is the last virtue of a completely immoral society.

Question to ponder: What is the difference between tolerating a person and tolerating sin?

....

....

....

....

....

....

A Glimpse of His Glory

*Did I not say to you that if you would
believe you would see the glory of God?*
John 11:40

Matthew, Mark, and Luke all record the "transfiguration" of Christ.
Jesus took the disciples north of the Sea of Galilee to Mount Hermon, and
there they went up to the top of that Mount of Transfiguration. He left the
other disciples and took the inner circle, John, James, and Peter, a little bit
farther. There they saw Christ with Moses and Elijah, who appeared from
the dead and talked with Him. At that time, Christ allowed something of
His divinity to shine through the veil of flesh and His garments were glis-
tening white. They were so brilliantly white that the disciples could hardly
bear to look upon them.

But when that was over, Peter felt a speech coming on, and so he said,
"Master, it is good for us to be here: and let us make three tabernacles; one
for thee, and one for Moses, and one for Elias [Elijah]" (Mark 9:5). Then
there came a thundering sound out of the clouds. It was the voice of the
Father, saying, "This is my beloved Son: hear him" (v.7), which is gracious,
heavenly language for "Peter, shut up and listen. Maybe you might learn
something."

Peter might not have been very eloquent, but his heart was right—it
is the longing of every Christian that we might stay, that we might dwell
where God is.

Question to ponder: How do we dwell where God is in this life?

....

....

....

....

AUGUST 14 ═══   *Fiery Trials*

Consider it pure joy, my brothers,
whenever you face trials of many kinds...
James 1:2 (NIV)

Peter, as well as James, tells us that we should not be amazed when the fiery trials come upon us. It should be expected that our faith would be tried by fire that it might come out as pure gold. Therefore, God puts us through these trials of fire, that we may be sanctified and refined.

Christ looks into our hearts. Is your heart troubled this day? Is it filled with anxieties, with insoluble problems? Christ, indeed, empathizes with you. Not only does He feel your trouble, He alone is sufficient and adequate to deal with it. He has promised that He will turn all things together for our good.

There is no one who does not face troubles in this world. "A man is born unto trouble as the sparks fly upward," as the saying goes, and this is true. We don't get through this "valley of tears" without learning why it is so named. But Christ is there with us. He has promised, "I will never leave thee, nor forsake thee" (Hebrews 13:5). He is right here with us. He will see us through all our trials.

Question to ponder: Have you ever looked back at a trial and understood why you could "consider it pure joy"?

....

....

....

....

....

....

....

A Trinity of Comfort

> *...The Father of mercies and God of all comfort, who*
> *comforts us in all our tribulation, that we may be able*
> *to comfort those who are in any trouble, with the comfort*
> *with which we ourselves are comforted by God.*
> 2 Corinthians 1:3-4

Many people are desperately in need of comfort. They may be experiencing financial pressure, homelessness, physical suffering, sorrow over a handicapped child, bereavement, disgrace due to sin, a life of loneliness, the aftermath of an abortion, fear and uncertainty, marital breakup, weariness of the flesh, a besetting temptation, a family suicide, the death of a spouse, a shattering divorce, or grief over a prodigal child. The list goes on and on and on. Surely, it is true that people need comfort.

The Holy Spirit is called the Comforter, and the Father is the God of all comfort.

Jesus comforts us by His presence. Thus, we have a whole trinity of Comfort.

In the very early years of our church, a wonderful young Christian mother had a two-year-old son climb the fence in their back yard when she was on the phone. He fell into the canal and drowned. I sat in her home for hours the next day trying to comfort her.

Person after person came in, but she later told me, "There were only two people who were really able to comfort me, and they were both mothers who had lost a child." They knew how it felt and they were there in her time of need. Just by our presence we can comfort people in the time of their grief.

Question to ponder: Can you think of someone who might need comfort and how you could possibly help?

Let God Be True

He is the Rock, His work is perfect; for all His ways are justice, a God of truth and without injustice; righteous and upright is He.
Deuteronomy 32:4

It doesn't matter if everyone in the world joins hands and votes unanimously that God's truth is false—it still remains true. It remains true whether I believe in it or I don't believe it. Whether you accept it or you reject it does not alter the fact that God's truth does exist and never changes.

Over against the relativism of our time, I think we need desperately to reassert what Jesus Christ said. "Ye shall know the truth, and the truth shall make you free" (John 8:32).

Jesus is declaring here that *there is truth.* He didn't say, "You will know *a* truth." He didn't say, "You will know *your* truth." We hear this today by those who say, "Well, that's true for you, but it's not true for me." Jesus said, "Ye shall know *the* truth."

God's truth is true for everyone. Jesus Christ said, "I am the way, the truth and the life: no man cometh unto the Father, but by me" (John 14:6). He is not *a* truth, *part* of the truth, or *somebody's* truth but not somebody else's truth—He is *the* Truth. How ironic it is that Pontius Pilate could say with a sneer, "What is truth?"—when standing before him was Jesus Christ, Incarnate Truth.

Question to ponder: Why is it so hard for people in our culture to fathom absolute truth?

When Nothing Makes Sense ══ AUGUST 17

*...But their thinking became futile and
their foolish hearts were darkened.*
Romans 1:21 (NIV)

One of the consequences of modern unbelief and the failure of rationalism is that modern man has been plunged into an irrational worldview that now dominates the culture all about us. This can be seen very clearly in the development of painting. If you go from Rembrandt, for example, to modern times and to Cezanne, the cubists and all other forms of modern art you will find that paintings become more and more incomprehensible.

How many people have stood in modern art galleries looking at a painting one way and another, sideways, and sometimes almost standing on their heads, ultimately concluding that it must have been hung upside down.

What are these artists doing? They are very sensitive to current philosophies, so what they are doing is portraying through their art the world as they see it. These modern artists show us in their pictures a worldview which has left God out. Their paintings reflect a world without meaning, full of sound and fury, signifying nothing.

The next time someone tells you that unbelief gives you a rational, intelligible view of the world, think of the last modern painting you looked at and puzzled over.

Question to ponder: If our rational God made a rational universe, why can people no longer see it?

⊣⊢ ....

....

....

....

....

AUGUST 18 — *The Central Figure of History*

And he made known to us the mystery of his will according to his good pleasure, which he purposed in Christ, to be put into effect when the times will have reached their fulfillment—to bring all things in heaven and on earth together under one head, even Christ.
Ephesians 1:9-10

The entire history of mankind before the advent of Jesus can be seen as nothing other than a preparation for His coming into the world. All history since His coming has simply been the unfolding of the progress of His Spirit in the hearts of men and the establishment of His Kingdom in the world.

Jesus Christ is the center of all history. All others are coming and going, while Christ remains. His Kingdom is grown, and He is the ultimate ruler, not only of our world but of the universe. The whole goal of history is to bring together all in Him, all things in heaven and on earth. This will be fulfilled at His second coming.

We pray the Lord's Prayer. We pray "Thy kingdom come...." But do we truly desire it? Do we work for it? Christ is the King, not only of the world to come, but of this world as well. Do we pray that His kingdom will come in this world, in this land, in this century, in our time?

The word "kingdom" comes from the two words "king's dominion," and where the King holds dominion over the hearts of men, there His kingdom has come. It is come by the gracious influence of His Holy Spirit, by the Gospel of His love.

Question to ponder: Do you see evidence of all things in heaven and on earth coming together under Christ here in our world? Where is it clearest?

Unbelieving Scholars

With the pure You will show Yourself pure; and
with the devious You will show Yourself shrewd.
2 Samuel 22:27

Dr. Maurice Roberts, minister of the Church of Scotland once said about unbelieving scholars:

> Till their eyes are opened by faith [the critics] will go on with the age-old mischief of cutting the Jesus of the Gospels down to a size they can cope with. They grace their [so-called] science with the title of "scholarship"; in reality it is nothing but hatred of Christ's authority and Godhead [emphasis mine]....
> The Higher Critics and the liberal theologians...have placed Christ on their Procrustean bed and lopped off his Godhead, glory and grace.

A "Procrustean bed" is part of Greek mythology. In Procrustes' inn he had a room with a metal bed. When anybody came to sleep in that bed, he wanted to make everything nice and neat and fit the way he thought it ought to, so he cut off their legs if they were too long. Or if they were too short, he would stretch them until they fit his bed. This is a marvelous metaphor that describes the way a lot of people think and act. And so it is with skeptics and atheists down through the centuries.

When the skeptics are dead and gone, however, Jesus will be going on from glory unto glory. How wonderful, how infinite He is! As Roberts also said, "Jesus is not in the smallest degree diminished by their low opinions of him. He remains the Lord of glory still."

Question to ponder: If you have any questions, seek the answers. St. Augustine said, I believed, and then I understood (not visa versa). Are you disturbed by the skeptics?

Question to ponder: If you have any questions, seek the answers. St. Augustine said, I believed, and then I understood (not visa versa). Are you disturbed by the skeptics?

AUGUST 20 — *The Dumbing Down of Our Schools*

The words of the wise are like goads, and the words of
scholars are like well-driven nails, given by one Shepherd.
Ecclesiastes 12:11

One scholar pointed out that in our public school system in America, we have been dropping one month per year academically ever since around the time they threw prayer out of the schools. It is interesting to look at tests that were given to students fifty or eighty years ago and see that many of today's college graduates couldn't pass a high school *entrance* examination given in 1900. Many college graduates today could not read *McGuffey's Reader* [6th grade level], because they wouldn't understand many of the words.

For example, when John Adams entered Kings College one of the *entrance* requirements was to translate the first ten chapters of the Gospel of John from Greek into Latin.

We live in a time when there are powerful forces engaged in an effort to see that that Christian education is nullified and, instead, children receive a godless education. This has, of course, been a cause of great concern to many. We might ask ourselves, "How did it come about that so many of our children today are brainwashed in godless secularism in so-called 'Christian America'?"

Question to ponder: How can we impart wisdom to the next generation?

The Bible and Education

For the Lord is the God of knowledge.
1 Samuel 2:3

If we are to secure the well-being of our children and the generation to come, we must teach them the Scriptures. The very reason education for the masses was created in the first place was so that people could read the Bible for themselves.

I think we need to take more seriously what the Bible says when it tells us that we, as parents, are to train up a child in the way he should go. We need to consider Christian education, beginning in the home, as we train our children in the Word of God, as we train them to pray, as we train them to walk the Christian life. Besides the home, we need to teach them in Sunday school and church and in Christian school, if possible.

We are told that Jesus grew in wisdom and stature and from that simple statement there has come a desire to teach children. Education was taken away from the few and given to the many. And it wasn't the slave that was to teach but it was given over to mothers. And children grew in the knowledge of God and in the knowledge of the things of this world. There is no doubt that wherever the Bible has gone, education has gone with it. And wherever the Bible has not gone education has lagged behind.

Question to ponder: How has the Bible made you wise?

....

....

....

....

....

....

AUGUST 22 — *The Battle for the Children's Education*

The kings of the earth set themselves, and the rulers take counsel together, against the LORD and against His Anointed [Christ].
Psalm 2:2

Do you realize that teachers in the public schools were being encouraged to become proselytizers for a new religion? Do you realize that secular humanism has been virtually established as the state national religion of America? In a classic statement in *The Humanist Magazine,* one of the humanist educators said this:

> I am convinced that the battle for humankind's future must be waged and won in the public school classroom by teachers who correctly perceive their role as the proselytizer of a new faith; a religion of humanity...for they will be ministers of another sort, utilizing a classroom instead of a pulpit to convey humanist values in whatever subject they teach, regardless of the educational level—preschool, day care or large state university. The classroom must and will become an arena of conflict between the old and the new—the rotting corpse of Christianity, together with all its adjacent evils and misery, and the new faith of humanism.

I am afraid many parents don't know what is happening. The secular humanists continually say that there is no such thing as humanism. Adolf Hitler said, "Let me control the textbooks and I will control Germany."

Since secular humanism has had virtually full reign in our public schools, true learning has plunged. But that makes sense, since the Scriptures declare that the fear of the Lord is the beginning of wisdom.

Question to ponder: Why have so many of our schools become God-free zones?

In His Dwelling Place

Because you have made the LORD, who is my refuge,
even the Most High, your dwelling place....
Psalm 91:9

God invites us to know His protection, as seen in Psalm 91. I would want you to understand that this psalm is not saying that everybody has the protection of the Almighty. It is not even saying that all Christians have this protection, since apparently only a few, relatively speaking, really enjoy it,

As Spurgeon said, "Here are the elect of the elect." Here are the three of the twelve. Here are those special ones who enjoy this protection from God and are delivered from the snare of the fowler and the noisome pestilence.

Who are these who dwell in the secret place of the Almighty? It doesn't say those who visit it occasionally, but rather the promise is given to those who dwell there. His promise of protection is very similar to the promise of peace found in Isaiah 26:3, where we read: "Thou wilt keep him in perfect peace, whose mind is stayed on Thee: because he trusteth in Thee."

He doesn't say He will keep everybody in perfect peace. Rather, He will keep in *perfect peace* those "whose minds are stayed upon Thee," who are leaning heavily upon Him. The Hebrew word for "stayed" means those who cling to Him, those who rest upon Him.

Question to ponder: How do we dwell with God?
How do we live in His presence?

....
....
....
....
....
....

AUGUST 24 — A Message for All Worriers

Be anxious for nothing, but in everything by
prayer and supplication, with thanksgiving,
let your requests be made known to God.
Philippians 4:6-7

Are you a worrier? Perhaps you are beginning to realize that you have been victimized. Our enemy wants us to give in to fear and to let go of our trust in God. We must cling to Him.

Who was this that made such a statement? He did not know about the kind of problems that I face in my life. Well, maybe and maybe not. His name was Paul. He wrote these words from a dungeon in a Roman prison where he was incarcerated for Christ. Ahead of him he had a trial to look forward to—a trial before that most excellent and fair-minded judge, Nero, that lover of truth and light. Indeed, Nero must have been a lover of light because he enjoyed covering Christians with tar, tying them to poles and lighting his garden with them.

This "humanitarian" Nero was the one that Paul was preparing to stand before. He knew that the outlook was certainly very dim; ahead of him was absolute calamity and disaster. And yet, from that dungeon he cried out, "Be anxious for nothing," and "Rejoice in the Lord evermore."

Question to ponder: What are you worried about right now? How can you place these worries into the Lord's care?

....

....

....

....

....

God is Love

*And we have known and believed the love
that God has for us. God is love, and he who
abides in love abides in God, and God in him.*
1 John 4:16

Truly, the most profound words ever spoken are—not with complex syntax or intricate convoluted grammar—but a simple sentence: "God is love." Only three words: *"God is love."* And those words, like a magician's wand, forever changed the way the world thought. But they were backed up by deeds; the love of God was manifested in the life and love of Jesus Christ.

We are so used to hearing about God's love for us that we view it as our right and privilege to be loved by God. But the world into which Christ came was not at all familiar with that concept. The pagan gods were temperamental, capricious, and unpredictable. They were to be appeased, not loved. The idea of a God that loved was strange.

Then Jesus came, and now we know: God is love.

Question to ponder: How do you experience God's love in your life?

....

....

....

....

....

....

....

....

....

AUGUST 26 — *Plunging Headlong Away from God*

*Every one of them has turned aside; they have together
become corrupt; there is none who does good, no, not one.*
Psalm 53:3

God is the source of knowledge and wisdom. But we seem to be in a major hurry to forget that these days. Since the early 1960s, America has been plunging headlong away from God, religion, and the Bible—at least, officially—into materialism, atheism, evolutionism, and a godless secular philosophy of life. We are reaping the terrible consequences of that philosophy.

My friends, the seeds of secularism, grounded in evolution, have been and are producing a most pernicious and deadly harvest in America today. Years ago I read an interesting illustration by Dr. Ernest Gordon, dean emeritus of the Princeton University Chapel. He said that in the late 1950s, he spoke at a public school:

> Twenty years later, I was invited to the same school for the same purpose. I again presented myself to the same office, but it was no longer the habitat of an educator [of the assistant headmaster]. It was the command post of a police inspector. Corridors and classrooms were monitored by police officers who reported regularly to the inspector. The reasons for the change were obvious: violence, assault, rape, drug-induced madness…. The demoralized school is the tragic consequence of a society's rejection of the biblical worldview that provided the intellectual dynamic of Western education.

The Word of God is the source of true wisdom and even knowledge. David said, "I have more understanding than all my teachers, For Your testimonies are my meditation" (Psalm 119:99).

Question to ponder: If there is no belief in God, how will humanity be held accountable to be good?

....

....

....

"Seeing is Believing"

And Jesus said, "For judgment I have come into this world, that those who do not see may see..."
John 9:39

There is an old mariners' chart drawn in 1525 by an unknown cartographer that now resides in the British Museum. It depicts the coast of some forbidding and unknown continent. The cartographer wrote in various places on the chart, "Here be giants" and again, "Here be fiery scorpions," and, "Here be dragons." Somehow, during his lifetime, it fell into the hands of the then-renowned scien¬tist, Sir John Franklin, a Christian, who put a line through each of those fearsome statements and wrote across it all: "Here is God." What fearsome, unknown continent was that? It was the east coast of the United States. When God is near, dragons, scorpions, and giants flee.

The world says, "Seeing is believing," but the Bible teaches believing is seeing, and when God enables us to trust in Jesus Christ, we begin to see things we have never seen before. The fear of the unknown gives way to a trust in Him who is there.

The spiritual world with dangers and foes we can not even imagine are all overcome by Christ when He made a spectacle of them on the Cross. So put on the full armor of God, and thus we can stand.

Question to ponder: What are the "dragons" and "giants" you may fear?

....

....

....

....

....

AUGUST 28 ====== *Others' Day*

He died for all, that those who live should live no longer for themselves, but for Him who died for them and rose again.
2 Corinthians 5:15

General William Booth, the founder of the Salvation Army, wrote a telegram when he was on his death bed and had it sent worldwide to every officer in the Salvation Army. It consisted of just one word: "Others."

After I mentioned the telegram in a sermon, a young lady came up to me several weeks later and said, "You know, when you preached about Booth's telegram, I decided right then and there that I was going to make that day "Others' Day."

"Good idea," I thought. She said, "And so I tried to focus throughout all of that day on the needs and wants of other people. "I was so blessed by the end of the day that I decided to make it 'Others' Week.'" Then she said, "By the end of the week, I was so filled with joy that I couldn't believe it. It was the happiest week of my life."

I am convinced that one reason so many people are lonely is because they are so self-centered. If they would only turn their eyes outward and consider that the world desperately needs comfort, they would find that they wouldn't be lonely at all. They wouldn't be rejected at all if they really showed the love of Christ to others. The key to Christian service is being focused on "Others."

Question to ponder: What could you do today to make it "Others' Day"?

....

....

....

....

....

Christ-confidence

Some trust in chariots, and some in horses; but we will remember the name of the LORD our God.
Psalm 20:7

Self-confidence is not the virtue that modern man has made it into. In fact, there have been no doubt hundreds, if not thousands, of books written on self-confidence and how to obtain it. Do you have self-confidence? The Bible has little to say about it other than the fact that it is a curse, not a virtue.

The word "confidence" is a combination of two Latin words: con (with), and fides (faith), so "Self-confidence" means "with faith in yourself," and that is misplaced faith. Our faith should be in Christ. What we need is not self-confidence, but Christ-confidence. If you have self-confidence, you are always going to run into somebody bigger than you are, stronger than you are. You are going to run into a problem that is bigger than you can handle; your self is going to give way and the result of that is often despair and despondency.

But if you succeed, that's even worse. What do you get then? You get pride. The Bible tells us "Pride goeth before destruction, and an haughty spirit before a fall (Proverbs 16:18), and can be deadly for the spiritual life. Sadly, in America today, we have hundreds of books teaching people how to have self-confidence, and thousands of parents are teaching their children to "Be proud."

Question to ponder: Which comes easier to you— self-confidence or Christ-confidence?

....

....

....

....

....

The Perseverance of the Saints

And I give them eternal life, and they shall never perish;
neither shall anyone snatch them out of My hand.
John 10:28

We believe that God will enable us to persevere to the end. He began a good work in our lives and will continue that work until the end. Jesus Christ is perfectly able to care for His own. Under His wings, the saints can rest secure.

We have all heard stories of people who have been kept safe in the midst of horrible danger. We might never see the car that almost hit us or the angel that kept us from violence, or the temptation God steered us away from. We do know that God is protecting us and that His hand will lead us home.

He protects us from spiritual as well as physical danger. We should never presume upon God's grace, but we can count on His faithfulness. In Philippians 1, Paul tells us that He who began a good work in us will complete that work until the day of Christ Jesus. What a great promise!

Question to ponder: Does it comfort you to know that no one can snatch you out of the hand of Christ?

A Self-Examination

*Examine yourselves as to whether
you are in the faith. Test yourselves.*
2 Corinthians 13:5

When I told a lady in the church that my sermon was going to be on self-examination, she said, "Oh, that's going to hurt!" Well, lassies and laddies, I assure you that I come not to hurt you, but to help you, and if you cannot stand the interrogation of a mere mortal like me, how will you do in that great day when you are compelled to stand before the Great Assize of God? If you cannot stand the probing finger of your own conscience, how will you stand the shafts of the divine inquisition?

We need to examine ourselves and prove ourselves. We need to examine our hearts and minds. Do we live lives worthy of our calling? Have we allowed sin into our lives? Have we been unkind to anyone? Are we serving the Lord? Is there fruit in our lives?

May we pray along with David in Psalm 139: Search me, O God, and know my heart. Try me and know my anxious thoughts. And see if there is any wicked way in me, and lead me in the everlasting way (a paraphrase).

Question to ponder: Is there a difference between God's Spirit examining our lives and self-examination?

SEPTEMBER 1 ⸺ *Labor Day Considerations*

And whatever you do, do it heartily,
as to the Lord and not to men.
Colossians 3:23

Your work matters before God. We should do it for His glory.

Look at the difference the Savior has made in reference to labor. Jesus Christ picked up the saw and the hammer and the plane; and in so doing He wrought a miracle in civilization. Most people are totally unaware of what that did. But it changed the whole concept of work. Do you realize that in ancient Greece or Rome honest work was despised as servile and was consigned to slaves?

But Christ came and He gave a new dignity to labor. Before the word of God had come and taken over countries there were only slaves. Half the Roman Empire at the time of Christ was slaves and serfs. But those slaves and serfs in the lands where the Gospel of Christ has come have been translated into the working classes. And in America where the Word of God has come more fully, they were translated into the middle class—out of poverty and into economic well-being.

All honest labor is holy unto the Lord.

Question to ponder: How do you feel about your work? Do you see it as a service to God?

....

....

....

....

....

....

Is Work a Curse?

Whatever your hand finds to do, do it with your might.
Ecclesiastes 9:10

The earth is under a curse, and we experience that curse in one way or another each day. God declared to Adam in judgment: "Cursed is the ground because of you; through painful toil you will eat of it all the days of your life. It will produce thorns and thistles for you, and you will eat the plants of the field. By the sweat of your brow you will eat your food" (Gen 3:17-19).

Ecclesiastes describes a bleak picture of man's daily existence as he toils every day under the sun in order to enjoy for a moment fleeting pleasures.

A bumper sticker declares the daily grind of many people; "I owe, I owe, so off to work I go!"

Many people suppose that work is a curse to be avoided, if at all possible, and an activity to be involved in only when necessary. This is not the case. God ordained work before the fall. It is not part of the curse. Adam was commanded to tend the garden before he fell into sin. Even after sin, though it is greatly aggravated by the results of the fall and the curse, it is still true that work occupies a very important position in man's life. Without work, it is impossible for any human being to fulfill the probation that God has given him in this life.

Question to ponder: Is work a curse to you? Is work a joy to you?

If a Man Will Not Work...

But his lord answered and said to him,
"You wicked and lazy servant...."
Matthew 25:26

Paul minces no words about loafers: *"For even when we were with you, this we commanded you: that if any would not work, neither should he eat" (2 Thessalonians 3:10).* You would have to listen a long time before you heard those words today. The Apostle knew that man inclines toward evil and so he inclines toward idleness and laziness. A man will avoid all opportunities to work if he can, but the Apostle makes it clear that if a man will not work, he is not to eat.

This does not refer to a person who is not able to work. The Scripture has a great deal to say about caring for the lame, the blind, the sick, the infirm, the aged, and the young. But if anyone *will not* work, then neither let him eat.

Because of the prevailing politics of guilt, most people will feel a twinge of guilt when they hear those words, as if they were words without compassion. May I say to you that this is the most compassionate statement on the subject of economics that has ever been made. Were it not to a large degree followed, there would be wholesale famine and starvation plaguing the world. So let it be underscored and proclaimed in bold and capital letters: if any will not work, neither let him eat.

Question to ponder: Do you find laziness a temptation to you in any way?

···

···

···

···

···

No Sin, No Sadness

For the wages of sin is death....
Romans 6:23

"When lust hath conceived, it bringeth forth sin: and sin, when it is finished, bringeth forth death" (James 1:15). So it was in the world of the spirits before man was created, and so it was also at the beginning of the human race. This is the source of all manner of sadness. Grief has but one primary root, and tears have but one primary source; and that root, that source, is sin.

No sob ever mingled with Eden's breezes. No tear ever dripped from the eyelids of Mother Eve 'til sin first reared its ugly head. No heartache was ever known until the serpent made a conquest of the human will. Then sobs and sighs and tears and weeping and wailing and mourning and all of the woeful progeny of sin were born into the world. After sin, sadness reigned on the face of the earth.

Where there is no sin, there is no sadness or sorrow or grief, but this world teems with sin, and so sadness rolls down like a river. Sin has robbed man of honor and dignity. Sin has cleft such a chasm between mankind and God and has cloaked mankind with such impurity and sadness that it is no wonder this world is called—and is actually found to be—a vale of tears, sorrow, and sadness.

Question to ponder: In heaven sadness and sorrow will flee away, but what about this life? Is there less sadness in godly living?

....

....

....

....

SEPTEMBER 5 === *"More Alive Than I Have Ever Been"*

I have come that they may have life, and
that they may have it more abundantly.
John 10:10

Note *from Dr. Jerry Newcombe: What a difference Christ makes in this life and in the next. These words spoken by Dr. D. James Kennedy several years before his home-going to heaven speak volumes about the confidence Christ gives as we face the prospect of death.*

Now, I know that someday I am going to come to what some people will say is the end of this life. They will probably put me in a box and roll me right down here in front of the church, and some people will gather around, and a few people will cry. But I have told them not to do that because I don't want them to cry. I want them to begin the service with the Doxology and end with the Hallelujah chorus, because I am not going to be there, and I am not going to be dead. I will be more alive than I have ever been in my life, and I will be looking down upon you poor people who are still in the land of dying and have not yet joined me in the land of the living. And I will be alive forevermore, in greater health and vitality and joy than ever, ever, I or anyone has known before. That is what Christ offers us.

Question to ponder: Can you affirm with Paul that to live is Christ and to die is gain?

....

....

....

....

....

....

....

....

Living Zombies

Then the serpent said to the woman, "You will not surely die.
For God knows that in the day you eat of it your eyes will be
opened, and you will be like God, knowing good and evil."
Genesis 3:4-5

Those who walk in the land of the half-dead—the half alive—are living zombies who live according to the course of the world animated by the spirit of this world, which is Satan. They are engaged in fulfilling the desires of the flesh and the lusts of the mind. What is their motto? "If it feels good, do it."

God has given to us the amazing and marvelous gift of imagination, and by that gift, we may entertain unholy fancies and lay the reins upon the neck of the steeds of passion, always stopping short of the act.

Underlying this is a subtle tool of the devil. He places fear in human hearts along this line: If you get too close to God, you are going to be unhappy; if you live life His way, you are going to be miserable. Satan's first lie is: God will make you miserable; the other side of this lie is: sin is good.

The truth of the matter is, it is only sin that is harmful; it is only sin that will hurt us, ultimately, because God loves us with an infinite love. His banner over is us is love and He desires nothing but good for us.

Question to ponder: How do we come to believe that good is bad and bad is good?

....

....

....

....

....

....

....

In Your Face

*Then the LORD saw that the wickedness of man
was great in the earth, and that every intent of the
thoughts of his heart was only evil continually.*
Genesis 6:5

There was sin around when I was growing up, but you had to go looking for it. Now, we have home delivery, just like pizza. Sin is brought right into your house through a conduit you pay for called cable television and the Internet. They dump it right in your lap in your easy chair. They spray it all over you.

There are very few decent movies. Sin is everywhere—on billboards, in magazines and books, and in conversations. We live in an unclean and unholy and ungodly and immoral world like we've never known in America before. There are evil people who kill in the name of their god and think they are serving him by doing such.

Most of the readers of this book worship Sunday morning, as is good. But what have we been doing during this week? Any dishonesty? Any deceit? Any lies? Any lusts? Any immorality? Any malice? Any envy? Yet we come to worship the all-holy God?

Before we come into His presence, we must repent and be cleansed. In such a culture where sin is so often predominant, we are not always able to see our sin. We must ask the Holy Spirit to show us our sin, so we can be cleansed.

Question to ponder: What is the result when we ask God to reveal our sin to us?

....

....

....

....

Horizontal Comparisons

*Therefore you shall be perfect, just as
your Father in heaven is perfect.*
Matthew 5:48

Now it is clear that horizontally we can look around ourselves and we can see there are some people who, morally and ethically, stand head and shoulders above others. Therefore, we can see that they are superior. Some people are more righteous than others; they shine in comparison. However, vertically, it is different. There is one prayer you never want issued from your lips, one prayer you never want to utter, and that is: "Lord, give me what I deserve."

God does not grade on the curve. He doesn't say we are good compared to our neighbors. He judges by perfection. If you're not perfect, then you can't go to heaven. But then who could possibly get there, since no one's perfect? No, not one.

Martin Luther said the most damnable and pernicious idea that has ever plagued the minds of men is the idea that we sinful, fallen, depraved creatures could ever make ourselves good enough to stand in the presence of an all-holy, sin-hating God. But God has provided a way to get rid of our sin by punishing it on His own Son. The Old Testament tells that God has devised means by which His banished ones, who were expelled from the Garden because of their sin, should not ultimately and totally and finally be separated from Him. These means are called "the Gospel," "the Good Tidings," "the Good News" of the love of Christ and His death and resurrection.

Question to ponder: How do we live with the goal of perfection in an imperfect and sinful world?

....

....

....

....

SEPTEMBER 9 ⟩⟩ *The Dread Disease*

You are of purer eyes than to behold evil,
and cannot look on wickedness.
Habakkuk 1:13

How terrible is sin. We haven't got a clue, however, for we live in it. We wallow in it. It's up to our necks. Only those who live in a perfect world like Heaven would have the foggiest notion of how horrific sin really is. But when we look at this One who came all the way from Paradise to heal us of this dread disease, we begin to get a new view of just how terrible a thing sin really is. May we see in Christ a mirror of our own souls and stand amazed that such a one as He, the altogether perfect One, could love such ones as us.

We need to come to grips with what Christ endured—that this terrible thing called sin might be taken away because sin inevitably draws upon itself the wrath of God. May we never forget that even if we become complacent in the face of sin, even if we accept it broadly as a people, God is a God who is infinitely holy and has an infinite hatred for sin. He is of purer eyes than even to look upon iniquity and has promised that He will visit our transgressions with the rod, and that His wrath will inevitably fall upon our sins. So we stand in His presence, amazed that He could want us fallen creatures and that He found a way to make us cleansed, radiant, and free of sin.

Question to ponder: What power is in the blood of Christ that it would be strong enough to cleanse us?

The Gospel According to Isaiah === SEPTEMBER 10

Surely He has borne our griefs and carried our
sorrows; yet we esteemed Him stricken, smitten by God,
and afflicted. But He was wounded for our transgressions,
He was bruised for our iniquities; the chastisement for our
peace was upon Him, and by His stripes we are healed.
Isaiah 53:4-5

Imagine, if you will, writing the details, the minute details, of the life of someone who would live in the 28th century A.D. What do you know about anyone? You know absolutely nothing whatsoever. But now, hear the Word of God, who knows the end from the beginning: "Who hath believed our report? And to whom is the arm of the LORD revealed? For he shall grow up before him as a tender plant, and as a root out of a dry ground" (Isaiah 53:1–2).

There is no way Isaiah 53 could be said to have been written after Christ was born. I have seen the actual Isaiah manuscript taken from the Dead Sea Scrolls—sealed and hidden before Christ was born.

Furthermore, in the Septuagint translation (begun in the 300 B.C.), the Old Testament was translated into Greek and spread around the world. It would have been impossible to insert anything at a later date. This was, indeed, written seven centuries before Christ was born.

It is truly remarkable. It obviously proves that the Scriptures are inspired by God. There is no other way a writing such as this could exist.

Question to ponder: How does the inspiration of Scripture make the reading and studying of it different from any other book?

Jesus in Isaiah

Then Philip said, "If you believe with all your heart, you may." And he answered and said, "I believe that Jesus Christ is the Son of God."
Acts 8:37

In Acts 8, Philip was out in the desert and saw the Ethiopian eunuch in a chariot. The Holy Spirit said to him, "Go near and join thyself to this chariot" (Acts 8:29). The eunuch was reading from Isaiah 53: "He was led as a sheep to the slaughter; and like a lamb dumb before his shearer, so opened he not his mouth" (Acts 8:32). Philip asked him, "Understandeth thou what thou readest?" (v. 30).

Then the eunuch asked Philip a question: "...of whom speaketh the prophet this? of himself, or of some other man?" (v. 34). Then we read: "Then Philip opened his mouth, and began at the same scripture, and preached unto him Jesus" (v. 35).

Beginning at that Scripture, Philip preached unto him Jesus. So we see that the authoritative New Testament Scripture makes very clear that this passage is talking about Jesus Christ. Just the very content of it makes it absolutely plain—crystal clear, that that is what it is about.

This Ethiopian treasurer might have been the first person that we know of who was converted to Christ by the words of Isaiah 53, but millions have followed in his footsteps.

Question to ponder: How has Isaiah 53 impacted you?

....

....

....

....

....

The Great Deceiver

When he speaks a lie, he speaks from his own resources, for he is a liar and the father of it.
John 8:44

Satan is a great deceiver. He first blinds his victims before he binds and leads them unto destruction. The great and mighty Samson discovered that. Before he could be bound and set to grinding in the prison house, he first was blinded. Gehazi saw only the shiny Syrian raiment; he didn't see the leprous scars that would cover his face. Achan saw only the goodly Babylonian garments; he didn't hear the execrations of the people and the lamentations of his wife and children or the crackling of the fires of the funeral pyre that would consume him and all of his. Judas saw only the glitter of silver; he did not see the darkness of remorse or the blackness of the pit into which he plunged.

The deception can be very small at first. At Stone Mountain in Decatur, Georgia, there is a warning railing that keeps sightseers from getting anywhere near the edge of that great rock. So gradually does it slope downward that if one were to get within 75 or 100 feet of the edge, he would already find himself slipping toward the precipice and would be unable to recover himself. With no way to stop, he would continue to slide downward until he plunged over the edge to his death hundreds of feet below. Sin, like this same slippery slope, pulls us down into things that we never expected we would do.

Question to ponder: How can we be alert to the deceptiveness of temptation?

SEPTEMBER 13 ═══ *Overcoming Selfishness*

*...Those who live should live no longer for
themselves, but for Him who died for them....*
2 Corinthians 5:15

Selfishness is the universal form of human depravity; it lies at the base of all of our sins. Every sin that can be named is only a modification of it. What is avarice, but selfishness decorating and indulging itself—a man sacrificing to himself as his own god? What is sloth, but that same god asleep, and refusing to attend to the calls of duty? And what is idolatry, but that god enshrined—man worshipping the reflection of his own image?

Sensuality—indeed, all the sins of the flesh—is only selfishness setting itself above law and gratifying itself at the expense of all restraint. And all the sins of the spirit, are only the same principle impatient of contradiction, and refusing to acknowledge superiority, or to bend to any will but its own. What is egotism, but selfishness speaking? Or crime, but selfishness without its mask, in earnest and in action? Or offensive war, but selfishness confederated, armed and bent on aggrandizing itself by violence and blood?

Indeed selfishness is the universal form of all sin. Jesus Christ said, "Beware of covetousness." It is covetousness and unbelief combined that keep people from obeying many of God's commands to their own hurt. But God rewards obedience to His Word.

We are called to live for Christ and not ourselves. It is by focusing on Jesus that we can overcome selfishness.

Question to ponder: Are you as selfish now as you were before Christ came into your life?

....

....

....

....

....

Christian Stewardship

> *"Bring all the tithes into the storehouse, that there may*
> *be food in My house, and try Me now in this," says the*
> *LORD of hosts, "If I will not open for you the windows*
> *of heaven and pour out for you such blessing that*
> *there will not be room enough to receive it."*
> Malachi 3:10

What an incredible promise we see here in Malachi. If you have never "tried" the Lord in this, you have missed probably the greatest temporal blessing you can know in this life...a deliverance from all anxiety and worry and concern about your own finances. All of those things are encapsulated in that marvelous promise and the provision for all of your needs. "My God shall supply all of your needs," cried the Apostle Paul, "out of His riches in glory."

God owns all things—the earth is the Lord's and the fullness thereof. He gives them to us as a stewardship to be used for His glory and our testing as to our faith. The tithe is not just God's way of raising money for His work; it is also His way of raising Christians in His image. God commands that a tenth or the tithe, be returned unto Him. The word "tithe," whether in Hebrew, Greek, old Anglo-Saxon, or modern English, means the same thing. It means a tenth—a tenth of our income is the tithe. And God says that it belongs to Him, and we are not to touch it, but to give generously.

As we become more generous in all ways, including with our tithes and offerings, we become more like Jesus.

Question to ponder: Are you pleased with the level of your giving to the Lord?

SEPTEMBER 15 ══ *Words Without Knowledge*

*Who is this who darkens counsel
by words without knowledge?*
Job 38:2

People believe what they want to believe whether they have studied the particular issue or not. When it comes to origins (creation-evolution), more and more scientists and respectable scholars see the flaws of evolution and draw different conclusions.

Dr. Karl R. Popper, who, according to one evolutionary scientist, is incomparably the greatest philosopher of science the world has ever known said that evolution is not a theory; it doesn't even rise that high. It certainly is not a fact. It is not a theory; it is not even a hypothesis; it is nothing more than a "metaphysical research program." So said one of the most widely regarded philosophers of science the world has ever known.

In a sense, some evolutionists are saying, "Don't confuse me with the facts." Facts like the missing links that are completely missing, or the improbability against life just arising by chance, or how mutations are virtually always harmful, but according to the evolutionary scheme they proved beneficial, and so on.

Question to ponder: How can we stand up for the truth in a world of lies?

"Looking for Loopholes" === SEPTEMBER 16

And do you think this, O man, you who judge
those practicing such things, and doing the same,
that you will escape the judgment of God?
Romans 2:3

W. C. Fields, the old-time comedian who in his professional persona seemed to be in a continual state of inebriation, came to the final illness of his life. He was in the hospital and neither he nor his friends or doctors gave him much hope. One of his friends, who had known him for many years and had seen his disdain for religion and everything godly and moral, walked into the hospital room. He stopped as if he had run into a pane of glass, because there before his eyes was W. C. Fields in his hospital bed reading the Bible. His friend said in utter amazement, "W. C., what in the world are you doing?" And he replied, "I'm looking for a loophole...looking for a loophole."

It seems that there are lots of people who are looking for loopholes—who are trying to find some way to escape the just consequences of their sins.

There is no way around God's judgment, but there is one who went under it and has promised a way of escape.

Question to ponder: What would your response be if you could have talked to W. C. Fields?

....

....

....

....

....

....

....

SEPTEMBER 17

Dust in the Wind

Vanity of vanities, all is vanity.
Ecclesiastes 1:2

It was left to that mournful Dane, Søren Kierkegaard, the father of existentialism, to say that all is vain and the quest has ended in utter despair; rationalism is dead and human reason has failed in its great effort to grasp and comprehend the universe in which we live.

It was at the time of the bloody First World War that Kierkegaard's ideas began to take root, slowly at first, until today existentialism is without question the regnant, the dominant philosophy of our time in the world. Existentialism teaches that because of the finiteness of man and his understanding, he will never be able to grasp ultimate reality—that there is nothingness out there. The world is unintelligible, the cosmos cannot be comprehended, and ultimately all things are without meaning and significance. This has been the great contribution of existentialism to our time.

It is a philosophy of despair.

A young woman told me that when she was in college she embraced the existential philosophy. Certain pressures then came upon her and she endeavored to take her life. She ended up in a mental institution having shock treatments. All this because existentialism had robbed her of any meaning to life and ripped from her grasp any hold she had upon transcendental significance or purpose in this world. She knew the blackness and emptiness that the worldview of existentialism offers.

Question to ponder: Can you be a Christian existentialist? Is there such a thing as meaninglessness with God?

The Pied Pipers

*They would have none of my counsel
and despised my every rebuke.*
Proverbs 1:30

We go to all kinds of sources to find out how we ought to do things in this country. Decades ago, we went to Dr. Benjamin Spock to find out how to rear children and produced the most rebellious generation of young people this country has ever seen. We have gone to Marx and other socialist writers to find out how to run our economy, and to one radical teacher after another to learn how to do the various things we do in this nation. The results have, for the most part, been disastrous. Just because someone has a degree or writes a popular book does not mean that we should necessarily follow him or take her wisdom to heart. We have seen the liberal theological scholarship dismantle our biblical foundation in the minds of many. People listen because they are the "ones who know." You can find a scholar and expert who says virtually anything. Therefore, be careful who you listen to and whose advice you take.

> *Question to ponder:* Who are the people you take advice from and whose scholarship do you trust?

SEPTEMBER 19 — The Myth of "Quality Time"

Remember how short my time is....
Psalm 89:47

When we look back, it always seems that time was so very short. The years the children were home—gone. The years of school and study—over. We must remember to redeem the time we have.

It is interesting that what children most remember about their parents when they grow up is not so much what they said, but what they did with them—the time they spent with them. One recent study has shown that the average father spends 37 minutes a day with his child. That would be tragic, except the truth is he spends 37 seconds a day talking to his child. That truly is a tragedy.

What is worse, this is given the name of "quality time." But it has also been discovered that children are totally incapable of recognizing "quality time." From their perspective, what concerns them is how *much* time you spend with them.

Time is a gift and time spent with a child, a parent, a spouse is never wasted. Our families are our first priority under the Lord. These are the people God us put in our lives for us to minister to. Time spent with family is time well spent.

Question to ponder: How can you show love by spending time today with a family member?

....
....
....
....
....
....

With All Your Mind

Teach me Your statutes. Make me understand the way of Your precepts; so shall I meditate on Your wonderful works.
Psalm 119:26-27

The idea is repeatedly and almost constantly put forth by the secular media in all of its forms that belief in God and in the Christian faith is somehow irrational, obscurantist, and un-intellectual. By contrast, it is held that unbelief in God and the Christian faith is the rational, enlightened and intelligent view of life. Though the thesis is hardly ever set forth as clearly and precisely as that, it very subtly seeps into the mindset of modern man from multiple sources.

But is it really so? I am sure that many people have been convinced that it is, including people within the Church. They have concluded that to believe in God and Christianity is to commit intellectual suicide. One must, somehow, have had a frontal lobotomy or parked their brain in the narthex when going in to worship God to hear the preaching of His Word.

This, of course, has a very adverse effect upon human beings because, instinctively, we know that if God has created us, He has obviously given us intellects as well as hearts and souls. It seems inconsistent that we should short-circuit our intellect and leap into a blind faith of some sort.

True worship of God always involves our mind. We are to love God with all our minds. We are to learn, to understand, to meditate, and to wonder at His greatness.

Question to ponder: How can we love God with all our minds?

....

....

....

....

....

SEPTEMBER 21 ═══

Fault Finding

So the governors and satraps sought to find some charge against Daniel concerning the kingdom; but they could find no charge or fault, because he was faithful; nor was there any error or fault found in him.
Daniel 6:4

Several Babylonian officials were on a fault-finding mission, to bring Daniel down. They found nothing. People love to find faults in others, especially in people who are in the Church. We Christians should be blameless ourselves, nor should we find fault in others. Sad to say, very few people are in Daniel's league. We are told not to judge others and not to point out their faults. That should be left to the Lord.

Every commandment in the Bible also contains a commandment to do the opposite good. Not only is it true that we are not to find fault (do not judge, or you will be judged), we are to find good. We are to be "good-finders."

Andrew Carnegie said that when gold is mined, tons of dirt are moved to get one ounce of gold, but they are not looking at the dirt, they are looking for the gold. The faultfinder is looking for the dirt, and he never finds the gold. We have to become a good-thinker and a good-seeker so that we are looking for the good.

Just think of how many good things you could find about relatives, fellow workers, fellow students, friends, neighbors and others that you could bring to their attention and thereby bless their lives.

Question to ponder: Can you find some good in another today and share that good with them?

....

....

....

....

Fear of God

*And do not fear those who kill the body but cannot
kill the soul. But rather fear Him who is able to
destroy both soul and body in hell.*
Matthew 10:28

The Scriptures admonish us to fear God and keep His commandments. Jesus tells us to fear God who has the power to cast people into hell.
"The fear of the Lord" does not mean a slavish dread of Him. Rather, it is a
reverential awe of God that should be part of every true believer's faith in
the living God. We believe in the Great, in the Mighty, in the Terrible, in the
august, in the all-powerful God of this universe.

In a very real sense, God inspires all true believers with a certain
reverential awe—an awe not unlike the awe a child feels for his father on
this earth. That is not to say, however, that we live in dread of our Heavenly
Father without care for Him. Rather, because of our reverence for Him, His
righteousness, and His holiness, we fear to do evil. So, it is well that each
one of us who believes in the living God should fear to do evil.

Dostoyevsky said famously, "If there is no God, then all things are
permissible." That is why the fear of God is good, and to be a God-fearing
person is healthy.

Question to ponder: What is the relationship between the
love and the fear of God?

....

....

....

....

....

....

Thy Will Be Done

O My Father, if this cup cannot pass away
from Me unless I drink it, Your will be done.
Matthew 26:42

In his agonized prayer in the Garden of Gethsemane, we see the total submission of Christ to the Father. We see a struggle between life and death, a cosmic struggle with millions of souls in the balance. The victory was in submission.

This short little prayer, "Your will be done" has been called "the prayer that never fails." God always honors and answers this prayer. Throughout our life, we need to pray it many times as we again and again give control of our lives to God.

We need to pray, "Lord, use me today for Your great purposes and for Your glory." When we do this, we will be amazed at the opportunities we have to do good. We will meet people in need. We will meet people who are lost—people with whom we can share the Good News. There are always all kinds of opportunities to serve His plan.

This prayer demonstrates the difference between a Christian prayer and a pagan prayer (or incantation). When a pagan prays, he tries to harness the spiritual powers of the universe to do his bidding and proclaims, "As I will so it must be." In other words, "My will be done." Contrast that with the Christian prayer: "Thy will be done."

Question to ponder: Is there any area of your life where you need to pray this prayer—"Your will be done"?

....
....
....
....
....

No Ultimate Conflict

Forever, O LORD, Your word is settled in heaven.
Psalm 119:89

No book has been attacked over the past 200 years like the Bible. Many scholars have joined the savage attack, which continues in our day unabated. Yet the Bible is correct, and critical scholars are proven wrong again and again. (If there are certain unanswered questions about the Scriptures, give it time—the Bible will be vindicated eventually).

Just because someone is a scholar doesn't mean he or she is correct. Often they are not. When it comes to scholars, I always remember the admonition of Dr. William Childs Robinson that I heard in seminary. We were discussing some controversial theological issue in one of his classes. One student said to him, "But professor, all of the scholars say...."

Robinson said, "Hold it. Hold it right there, young man. You never want to forget that we choose our scholars. We choose our experts."

And what do the scholars say? Ah, my friend, I think it is vitally important that you know right now, and never forget, what the scholars say. The scholars say anything at all. They say everything—they express every imaginable point of view.

When you see scholars expressing anti-Christian opinions on television or read them in magazines or the newspapers, just remember, somebody chose those experts, and they didn't choose them by chance. They often stack the experts in such a way as to promote unbelief.

Question to ponder: Do you have any doubts about the Word of God that you need to get answered? What are they and what faithful source will you seek for the correct answers?

SEPTEMBER **25** ═══ *The Blessings of Giving*

It is more blessed to given than to receive.
Acts 20:35

There are in the Scripture some 72 different passages which deal with giving, and of those, some 48 passages describe the distinct and open promises of the special blessings of God upon those who give.

I believe that the motive for giving should be gratitude to God for what He has already given to us. We should give for the purpose of advancing His glory and His kingdom in the world. The additional blessings He pours out upon us are simply super-abounding blessings that He gives above everything else He has given.

Those who tithe find that they are no worse off than they were before, but rather that God has blessed them, as He said, and opened the windows of Heaven to them. They are amazed to discover that God has provided all of their needs out of His abundance, and that the nine-tenths goes farther than the ten-tenths.

To live a generous life is to imitate God. As we give much, God blesses us even more.

Question to ponder: Can you think of a time when your giving became a blessing to yourself?

....
....
....
....
....
....
....

"Everlasting Splendors"

*So also is the resurrection of the dead. The body
is sown in corruption, it is raised in incorruption.
It is sown in dishonor, it is raised in glory. It is
sown in weakness, it is raised in power.*
1 Corinthians 15:42-43

These verses from Paul describe what we have to look forward to when we die—a glorious new body. This body will be more ours than the one we have now, because it will be the perfect body we were always meant to have. We will finally be as God envisioned us in creation before the fall.

C. S. Lewis noted, "You have never talked to a mere mortal. Nations, cultures, arts, civilizations—these are mortal, and their life is to ours as the life of a gnat. But it is immortals whom we joke with, work with, marry, snub, and exploit—immortal horrors or everlasting splendours."

This has strong implications for how we treat one another, in and out of the church. We cannot fail if we show love to everyone as much as possible. Think of all people as "in disguise." We are not as we seem. Our true nature and our true self is what we will be eternally.

Question to ponder: What do you look most forward to when you think of personal glorification?

....

....

....

....

....

....

....

The Honor of God's Name

To God our Savior, who alone is wise be glory and majesty, dominion and power, both now and forevermore.
Jude 24-25

Have you ever walked into a great cathedral and been overwhelmed by the glory and majesty of God? Have you felt His beauty and power in the lofty arches and in the stained glass windows? These mighty buildings were made to the glory of Jesus Christ, and they are among the finest examples of art in the history of the world.

No doubt you have heard of Sir Christopher Wren, who was perhaps the greatest architect who ever lived. He designed many marvelous buildings, including St. Paul's Cathedral in London. He was a devout Christian who was concerned about the honor and glory of God. Not only did he design St. Paul's Cathedral, but he superintended the building of it. Wren had a sign placed in a number of different locations on the construction site that read: "Due to the heinous custom of laborers to take the name of God in vain, each person is hereby placed on notice that it shall be sufficient cause for immediate dismissal if the name of God is heard taken in vain in this place."

May we live with such a zeal for the glory of God's name.

Question to ponder: How can you glorify God in your life today?

....

....

....

....

....

Why is the Church so Weak? ≡ SEPTEMBER 28

For they have even taken some of the accursed things,
and have both stolen and deceived; and they have also
put it among their own stuff. Therefore the children of
Israel could not stand before their enemies.
Joshua 7:11-12

Israel's defeat at Ai in Joshua 7 reminds us that one of the reasons the army of God is oft defeated and does not make the progress it should is because of sin within. In this case it was Achan who, having gone into the city of Jericho to help destroy it, saw there a goodly Babylonian garment, two hundred shekels of silver, and a wedge of gold. He wrapped them up and put them under his robe and hastened back to his tent. He buried them in the earth in the center of the tent and no doubt put a carpet over it, cleaned it all up nicely, and nobody was the wiser. He had committed the perfect crime—except that the all-seeing God knew it was there.

Unhappily, the 3,000 men who made their way up the hill toward Ai did not know what Achan had done and suffered defeat as a consequence.

Why does the Church not make the progress it ought to be making? Could it be because of sin in the camp? Maybe you subscribe to it on television, or maybe it's a magazine that comes every month into your home. It is that which He has forbidden and lies buried right in the center of your tent. God knows all about it and so the people of God are defeated.

Question to ponder: Is there anything in your house which God wants you to get rid of?

....

....

....

....

....

SEPTEMBER 29 — *The Removal of the Lampstands*

*Remember therefore from where you have fallen; repent
and do the first works, or else I will come to you quickly and
remove your lampstand from its place—unless you repent.*
Revelation 2:5

The letters to the seven churches in the first three chapters of Revelation tell us what Jesus thinks of the church. Because of the sin of certain members of the church, God said he would take away their lampstands.

I have been to many of the places mentioned in this passage and those churches are no longer there. I wonder how many there are in church who, in secret sin, are impeding the progress of the church in the world.

I think back many years ago and recall a man in my own church who was engaged in adultery—a man who had been a minister and had left the ministry, but a man who seemed to be a godly man, a man who seemed to be a Christian. Only God knows the heart.

He became involved with a married woman. He was going to have her divorce her husband and marry him. I admonished him and urged him to repent. He was brought before the discipline committee and they admonished him to repent. He was suspended from the sacraments, but he did not repent. Finally, the Session (the governing body of our church) determined that since he remained impenitent, they would have to excommunicate this man from the church. Just before that took place, suddenly that young man died.

God sees all, and we should not take His mercy for granted.

Question to ponder: What is the difference between living with open unconfessed sin and falling into sin?

All Things New

Behold, I make all things new.
Revelation 1:5

Have you noticed that nothing stays new in our world? A new house, a new car, a new pair of pants—it doesn't take long before they become old, broken, and worn out.

Jesus Christ came to take things that were old, dying, and dead and make them new. Is it any wonder, then, that those who are to be a part of the new kingdom of this great King who makes things new must be "new creatures."

From the very moment He was born of a virgin, until He was laid in a new tomb, He constantly made things new, even up until now, and will continue to do so through that great climactic day when He says, "Behold I make all things new" (Revelation 21:5). That is the very essence of Jesus Christ.

The message of Jesus is Good News. He has established a *new* kingdom into which He introduces only *new* men who are *new* creatures—a kingdom which is entered by a *new* and living way, a kingdom which has *new* laws, *new* customs, *new* riches, a *new* charter, and a *new* King as well as *new* citizens.

Question to ponder: How does our glorious future of "newness" start already here on earth?

OCTOBER 1

The Face of God

*The Son is the radiance of God's glory and
the exact representation of his being....*
Hebrews 1:3 (NIV)

Many people want to know what God is like. He is like Jesus, for Jesus is like God. Jesus is God. And what was Jesus like? Is He concerned for you? He said, "Suffer the little children to come unto me." He took them up in His arms and He blessed them.

You say you feel unworthy. Jesus reached out His hands and touched the leper and made him clean. You say, "I feel guilty, I have sinned." So had the woman taken in the very act of adultery, as recorded in John 8. But Jesus said, "Neither do I condemn thee. Go and sin no more."

This is what God is like, yet only in part, because from these same gracious lips we also hear such words as: "I never knew you: depart from me, ye that work iniquity" (Matthew 7:23): "Woe unto you, scribes and Pharisees, hypocrites!" (Matthew 23:14); "Woe unto thee, Chorazin! woe unto thee, Bethsaida!... And thou, Capernaum, which art exalted to heaven, shalt be thrust down to hell" (Luke 10:13, 15).

The three cities upon which Christ pronounced His woes have disappeared into black charred remains. All other cities where Christ ministered and did not pronounce His woes have remained until this day.

God is both loving and gracious but He is also holy and just. And we do not know God apart from Jesus Christ.

Question to ponder: What attributes of God do we also find in Jesus Christ?

....

....

....

....

A Big God

*Do you not know? Have you not heard? The LORD
is the everlasting God, the Creator of the ends of the
earth. He will not grow tired or weary, and his
understanding no one can fathom.*
Isaiah 40:8 (NIV)

Your God Is Too Small proclaimed the title of a book some years ago by J. B. Phillips. I am sure that many would say, "Now just a minute. That may be true of some, but I worship the great triune Jehovah who is infinite in His wisdom, being and power." That is all very good in theory. It makes great theology, but how about in practice?

Is it not true that many Christians go about their daily lives as if they worshiped an emaciated midget? Their chief concern seems to be not to over-tax His strength and bring about a complete physical breakdown. They pray something like this: "O God, if it is not too much trouble, if you can handle this, if this is not too much to ask, would you please grant this little request?"

Maybe their God is not small in size but instead small in heart. He is some sort of a withered, shriveled miser. They anxiously pray: "O God, I know I have bugged you often before, but just one more little favor if you don't mind too much?"

We are told to come boldly before His throne. We are His dear children, and He delights in helping and in giving.

Question to ponder: What big and difficult request do you have for God?

OCTOBER 3 — *God Will Settle All Accounts*

For the LORD is a God of justice;
blessed are all those who wait for Him.
Isaiah 30:18

One time an atheistic farmer in New England tried to rob God of His glory. He wrote this letter to the newspaper in the Fall: "I bought my seed on the Sabbath, I sowed it on the Sabbath, I watered it on the Sabbath, I fertilized it on the Sabbath, and I harvested it on the Sabbath. Now it's October and I have the largest crop in the valley."

The editor printed his letter and simply added one sentence: "God does not settle all of His accounts in October."

It might seem as if the ungodly and the wicked prosper and grow, and that all goes well for them—even if they thumb their noses at God and directly defy His commandments.

Asaph wrote the 73rd Psalm, which is a classic example in the Bible of dealing with this issue. He is grieved and deeply troubled by the haughty boastfulness of the ungodly until he remembers their end: "Surely thou didst set them in slippery places: thou castedst them down into destruction" (v.18).

We can trust God to make all wrongs right. We can wait upon Him to bring justice to His children. All accounts will be settled, whether it is in this life or the next. Indeed, He does not settle accounts in October.

Question to ponder: Is there a situation in your life where you are waiting for God's justice?

....

....

....

....

....

Joy and Gladness

These things I have spoken to you, that My joy
may remain in you, and that your joy may be full.
John 15:11

The Christian message is a message of joy. God gives us joy and gladness. The singing may sometimes switch to a minor key, but we still sing. Even though there are many sorrows in this world, the Gospel message still provides the most uplifting and joyful words found anywhere. Countless people have attested to this over the centuries, including those who were killed for the sake of its message.

William Tyndale, one of the very first translators of the Bible into English in the 1500s was persecuted and martyred. Nonetheless, he wrote in his *Prologue to the New Testament* these words: "Christianity is Good, merry, glad and joyful tidings, that makes a man's heart glad, and makes him sing, dance and leap for joy."

A man who accepted Christ after a woman from our church shared the Gospel with him, told me of his great joy. "You certainly cannot know," he said, "you cannot imagine the indescribable joy I have known for the last year since I came to know Christ. I never would have believed it."

Joy is what Christ brings to the human heart. Christ is no cosmic killjoy, a wet blanket on the party of the world, as some people think He is. Rather, He is the source and fountain of all real joy.

Question to ponder: How is your joy linked to your faith?

....

....

....

....

....

OCTOBER 5 *The Folly of Ungodly Rulers*

He who rules over men must be just,
ruling in the fear of God.
2 Samuel 23:3

At a time when some nations are realizing the folly of unbelief and the fatal results in the lives of people, America continues apace down the foolish pathway—toward godlessness and secularism.

Today, having banished the Bible and having attempted to banish God from all spheres of public life, we have found that our Congress cannot even produce a budget, and that it is becoming increasingly impossible to govern this nation.

Robert C. Winthrop, a descendant of Puritan John Winthrop, served as U.S. House Speaker in the early 1800s. He said: "It may do for other countries, and other governments to talk about the state support-ing religion. Here, under our own free institutions, it is religion which must support the State."

The founders of this country believed we should inculcate in the minds of youth the fear and love of Deity. But because of our stupidity and unbelief, we have now banned God from the classrooms. We have taken away prayer, the Bible, and the Ten Commandments from our schools and have replaced them with police dogs in the halls, policemen at the doors, and metal detectors. Crime is absolutely epidemic, and teachers are retiring early from battle fatigue. This is the folly of modern America.

Question to ponder: How can godly people support the state?

Worshiping God Alone
— OCTOBER 6

You shall not make for yourself a carved image...
you shall not bow down to them nor serve them.
Exodus 20:4

I imagine that most people would consider the prohibition to worship any graven images the most out-of-date commandment of the Decalogue—the Ten Words. A commandment that may have been important a few thousand years ago in the midst of all of the pagan image worshipers. Before the words written in the tables of stone by the finger of the Almighty had even cooled, the people had made a graven image of a golden calf and had risen up to worship it right beneath the face of Jehovah.

Because we in the Western world have lived so long with the Christian culture we would not think of worshiping a statue of any sort. As Christianity wanes in the Western lands, in come the foreign gods, from Allah to Hindu gods, from crystals and horoscopes to tarot cards. We are not immune to the love of foreign gods. Perhaps this should give us pause the next time we see a statue of Buddha in a Chinese restaurant.

Question to ponder: Have you come in contact with people who worship another god?

....

....

....

....

....

....

....

OCTOBER 7 ═══ *The Constant Desire for More*

You shall not covet....
Exodus 20:17

Covetousness is a great evil in the eyes of God. Paul tells us, "Put to death, therefore, whatever belongs to your earthly nature: sexual immorality, impurity, lust, evil desires and greed, which is idolatry" (Colossians 3:5 NIV).

Jesus said, "Beware of covetousness" (Luke 12:15). We live in a society that glorifies covetousness, a society that talks about grasping all that you can get, a society which is predicated on getting and hoarding. Therefore, we have all of these forces coming to bear on our lives, militating against the teaching of Christ.

Greed is like an octopus in the soul, wrapping its tentacles around every part of our spiritual life until it squeezes all the life out of us. That is why the Bible says that the "covetous man is an idolater," and has no place in the kingdom of God.

Greed and covetousness are the same thing. It is the desire for more, and it cannot co-exist with the worship of the true God. Greed makes possessions our security and hope. It is a root sin, and the underlying reason for many other sins.

Question to ponder: What do you think is the most common motive for murder? How does greed take hold of a person?

....

....

....

....

....

....

....

Divinely Discontented

*...Grow in the grace and knowledge of
our Lord and Savior Jesus Christ.*
2 Peter 3:18

It is sad that most Christians, by the time they have been a Christian five or ten years, already feel they know enough to get by. They are not embarrassed in Sunday School trying to find a book in the Bible they are studying. They read a little bit, pray a little bit, do a little bit, give a little bit, and that should suffice. But not the Apostle Paul. He was divinely discontented.

Let us be content with what we have and discontent with what we are. That is the opposite of the world. The people of this world are often discontented with what they have, yet quite happy about who they are.

Let us pray for a new growth in our hearts, a growth in grace, and in knowledge. As we set our affections on "things above," the Holy Spirit will delight in our spiritual ambition, and God will answer a prayer for more holiness because it is His will for us.

Question to ponder: How can we grow in grace and knowledge?

....

....

....

....

....

....

....

....

OCTOBER 9

God's Guidance

This is what the LORD says—your Redeemer, the Holy One of Israel: "I am the LORD your God, who teaches you what is best for you, who directs you in the way you should go."
Isaiah 48:17 (NIV)

How does your day begin? Do you seek the guidance of our blessed God, who loves us infinitely and who is infinitely wise and all-powerful? If not, you are missing out.

When I was in graduate school at New York University, I had a speaking engagement in San Francisco. When I got there, my wife called me and said that my father was very ill and in the hospital in St. Petersburg, Florida. I had a dilemma. Should I fly there from San Francisco, or just give him a call? I didn't know which to do, but there was that still small voice whispering to me, "Go and see your father." "Go to your father."

I traded my airline ticket to New York for one to Tampa. When I arrived there, I had the opportunity of spending that afternoon and evening with him. I left for New York the next morning and got a call from my mother that day that my father had lapsed into a coma and died. If I had not listened to that still small voice, I would be regretting it to this day.

How many blessings have you missed because you have not learned to listen to that still small voice? When we learn to listen to it, it is amazing how frequently we can hear the sound of the voice of the Holy Spirit.

Question to ponder: How do you seek and find God's guidance?

....

....

....

....

....

The State—Part of Common Grace 〰 OCTOBER 10

And Jesus answered and said to them,
"Render to Caesar the things that are Caesar's,
and to God the things that are God's."
Mark 12:17

The authority of the state comes from God, and the state is answerable to God. Whenever that truth is lost sight of, totalitarianism will eventually be the result. The state, then, is an agency of God's common grace (not His special grace which deals with our salvation). It is a means by which He restrains wickedness and does not allow it to run its greatest course. In the realm of God's common grace, He has given us the state. Its purpose is to enact and to execute the laws God has given in His Word, the moral laws He has written upon the hearts of men.

It is, therefore, our responsibility to honor the state, for Scripture says the powers that be are from God. We are to yield obedience to it, we are to pay tribute, and we are to pray for those in authority over us.

What is the purpose of the state, then? It has been instituted by God to restrain the wicked and to grant justice, so that God may be glorified as citizens are free to go about their tasks and live for Him.

Question to ponder: What does godly government look like to you?

....

....

....

....

....

....

....

OCTOBER 11 — *Temptations that Rise from Prosperity*

Beware that you do not forget the LORD your God...
when you have eaten and are full, and have built
beautiful houses and dwell in them.
Deuteronomy 8:11-12

King David fell victim to what might be called "the middle-aged syndrome" of success and sex. How many people I have known who have followed in his train—individuals who once walked well. Like David, they had endured all of the temptations that arise out of adversity with reasonable success, but now a whole new set of temptations come—the temptations that arise from prosperity.

Flush with success, the devil breathes his deceitful whispers in our ears and we begin to tell ourselves, "I've done well. I have succeeded in my business. I have worked hard and I have arrived. And I deserve something better out of life now than what I have been getting."

The tempter whispers, "Why not trade in your wife too, as you did the house and car for a new model? After all, she's been giving you a lot of trouble at home anyway. Just think how other people treat you. You are well-respected, but not at home." And you go on to tell yourself, "Yeah, criticism, nagging, that's all I get. She doesn't know how great I am; how successful I've been; how hard I've worked. Others appreciate it—especially that young secretary down the hall."

The middle-aged syndrome: success, sex, and sin. May God grant us grace to resist the temptations that arise from success.

Question to ponder: Do you find your temptations tend to keep up with your circumstances?

Columbus Day

Surely you shall call a nation you do not know, and
nations who do not know you shall run to you, because
of the LORD your God, and the Holy One of Israel; for
He has glorified you. Seek the LORD while He may be
found, call upon Him while He is near.
Isaiah 55:5-6

Christopher Columbus is a somewhat unappreciated hero today. Nonetheless, his accomplishment in history was huge. He himself said, "It was the Lord who put it into my mind to sail to the Indies. The fact that the Gospel must be preached to so many lands—that is what convinced me. Charting the seas is but a necessary requisite for the fulfillment of the Great Commission of our glorious Savior."

He attempted great things for God, and he led the path for others to follow into the New World. Columbus also led daily devotions on his ship. This was the prayer they said daily during that historic voyage:

Blessed be the light of day,
And the holy cross we say;
And the Lord of verity,
And the Holy Trinity.

When he arrived on land in the western hemisphere, those were his very first words after which he planted a Cross—the Cross of Jesus Christ. Christopher, means "Christ-bearer" and Columbus believed all of his life that it was his calling by God to carry Christ to the New World, to the far isles of the sea.

Question to ponder: Have you ever felt that God put something special on your heart that you should do?

....

....

....

....

OCTOBER 13 ===

Sinning with Impunity?

...And be sure your sin will find you out.
Numbers 32:23

Sometimes Christians mistakenly think that if we sin, we can some-how escape the penalty for sin because of the forgiveness Christ purchased for us on the Cross. We may be forgiven, but we may also still face the consequences of those sins.

David's sin with Bathsheba negatively impacted his family. His son Absalom rebelled and attempted to stage a coup against David. In that rebellion, Absalom was killed.

When news was brought to the king of his son's death, David uttered what are without question, the most poignant words in all of Scripture. He said, "Oh, my son Absalom, oh, my son, my son, oh, Absalom, my son." For David knew what no parent can stand to know and that is that Absalom, his heart's desire, was a rebel not only against himself, but against God—that Absalom is in Hell. And it was because of the example of his life, and because of the sin of his life, that his own son now had perished. "Oh, Absalom, my son."

Does the Christian sin with impunity? Dear friend, ask King David.

Question to ponder: Although we may bear the scars of sin for a lifetime, doesn't it touch you deeply to know that in Christ your sins are forgiven?

The Mighty Word of God ═══ OCTOBER 14

For the word of God is living and powerful, and sharper than any two-edged sword, piercing even to the division of soul and spirit, and of joints and marrow, and is a discerner of the thoughts and intents of the heart.
Hebrews 4:12

One of the canons of multicultural America is that no culture is better or worse than any other. That is why there is very little acknowledgement of the unspeakable horrors, cannibalism among them, practiced by pagan peoples.

This raises the question: how have formerly barbarous cultures been raised to civilization? Well, there is nothing in the annals of history that compares to what the Word of God has done to civilize barbaric peoples. Even Charles Darwin confessed this after returning from his memorable voyage to the South Seas on the *Beagle*.

There was a great attack upon foreign missionaries in the *London Times*. Darwin wrote a letter to the editor in which he criticized those who attack missionaries and said that such an attitude on the part of a voyager was particularly inexcusable, for should he happen to be cast ashore on some uncharted island he will devoutly pray that the lesson of the missionary has preceded him.

God's Word changes people and nations and cultures. His Word changed the Celtic people. It changed the Vikings. The Lord uses His word to work His will. It is only God's Word and the Gospel of Jesus Christ that truly changes people.

Question to ponder: How does God's Word continue to bring changes in your life?

⌐ㅣ⌐ ....

....

....

OCTOBER 15 ═══ *Is God Jealous?*

*...For you shall worship no other god, for the
Lord, whose name is Jealous, is a jealous God.*
Exodus 34:14

What does it mean that God is a jealous God? When we use the word "jealous" in reference to other people, it almost always has a negative connotation, but not so with God. God is not jealous of us, He is not jealous of some other god, because there is no other god—merely figments of somebody's imagination.

He is jealous *for* our good in the same way that every father and mother here is jealous for their children. Hopefully no one is jealous of them, but jealous *for* them, that they might have the best education, that they might eat the best food, that they might have the best care, that they might grow up to be the best people they possibly can be. And you are angry with anything that threatens the best for your children, anything that threatens to harm them.

That is why He commands us to "have no other gods before me." He knows that if we worship anything less than the true God, we will become like that which we worship and will therefore become far less than we could be.

Question to ponder: What is the difference between jealousy and envy?

....

....

....

....

....

....

....

....

Predestination

...Having predestined us to adoption as sons by Jesus Christ to Himself, according to the good pleasure of His will.
Ephesians 1:5

God sovereignly controls and ordains all things that come to pass, from the greatest star to the smallest atom. He has done this in such a way as to leave a certain natural liberty to men. They are free to do as they please, and yet they always do that which God has eternally ordained. We find that we cannot understand this, for there are some things that are beyond our feeble comprehension—e.g., man's free will and God's eternal purpose.

He created man with a power to do good or evil. Man chose to do evil thus plunging the world into sin and bringing him into a state of bondage, into a state of condemnation and wrath.

We find that God determined not to leave him there, but from all eternity selected out of this mass of fallen mankind a people for Himself: His elect, His chosen ones—a multitude of every tongue and kindred, nation and tribe under the sun; a multitude that no man can number—and these, God determined to save. These are His sheep. These are His chosen ones, for the Father has chosen them. He has sent His Son to die for them and procure for them eternal life.

Question to ponder: What does it mean that He chose you before the foundation of the world?

OCTOBER 17 — *Satisfying the Human Heart*

One thing I have desired of the Lord, That will I seek: That I may dwell in the house of the Lord all the days of my life, to behold the beauty of the Lord, and to inquire in His temple.
Psalm 27:4

Every one of us longs for something. Every one of us has something that he desires, dreams about, hungers after, and thirsts for. I don't know what that might be in your life. Perhaps it is fame, fortune, wealth, ease, recreation. But I know this: no unbeliever pants after God. His soul does not thirst for the living God.

It is God, and nothing else, who will fill the emptiness in the human heart. This hunger for God alone is like a little child in the street who has lost her mother and is crying, "Mommy, mommy."

You may take the child into your home, offer her some ice cream and some toys. You may try everything, but she will not be all right until she can rush into the arms and bosom of her mother. So, the soul reborn will not be satisfied with anything but the living God.

The intimate knowledge of the living God is the great purpose of our lives. If you do not have that in your life, then pray that God would grant it to you, that He would give you that panting and thirsting spirit. And if, with all your heart, you truly seek Him you shall surely find Him. That is His promise.

Question to ponder: What does it mean to seek God, to seek first His Kingdom and His righteousness?

....

....

....

....

....

The Existence of God ═══ OCTOBER 18

*Although they knew God, they did not glorify Him as
God, nor were thankful, but became futile in their
thoughts, and their foolish hearts were darkened.*
Romans 1:21

Is there a God or is there not? That question eclipses all other questions that men might ask. Should you feel that this statement is merely the opinion of a theologian or minister, let me give it to you from another source. Dr. Mortimer Adler, former professor at the University of Chicago and the associate editor of that massive set of volumes entitled, *The Great Books of the Western World*—60 volumes of the greatest writings of the greatest minds of the Western world—says that with the exception of certain mathematicians and physicists, all the authors included in the Great Books are represented in the chapter on God.

In the *Syntopicon* of *The Great Books*, the two-volumes that deals with all of the subjects covered by all of the various authors, Dr. Adler says that the subject of God is the one that is handled by more authors than any other. "The reason is obvious," said Dr. Adler. "More consequences for thought and action follow the affirmation or denial of God than the answering of any other basic question."

Question to ponder: What consequences flow from belief or unbelief in God?

OCTOBER 19 ══ *The Test of John the Baptist*

He must increase, but I must decrease.
John the Baptist on Jesus (John 3:30)

Jesus said about John the Baptist that he was the greatest among men. What was so great about him? He had understood who Christ Jesus was. He is the one who proclaimed, "Behold, the Lamb of God who takes away the sin of the world" (John 1:29). He also said, "He who believes in the Son has everlasting life" (John 3:36).

But it was neither his eloquence nor his theological understanding which impressed Christ. It was his humility—his humble acceptance of his own role. John the Baptist knew that Jesus was God's Messiah, and that he himself was only the forerunner, the messenger, crying out: "Prepare the way of the Lord."

When Christ came, John's ministry was essentially over. And John the Baptist could say these famous words: "He must increase, but I must decrease."

Question to ponder: Have you ever seen a work or a ministry you helped build up taken over by another?

The Least of These

But whoever has this world's goods, and sees
his brother in need, and shuts up his heart from
him, how does the love of God abide in him?
1 John 3:17

Let me tell you a story. I was a brand new Christian and I decided to read the Bible, so I just opened it up at random (not a recommended procedure), and I looked down and read a verse that said, "Depart from Me, you cursed, into the everlasting fire prepared for the devil and his angels" (Matthew 25:41). I thought to myself, "Good heavens, what horrible things did these people do?" I discovered they had done nothing.

Jesus said, "For I was hungry and you gave Me no food; I was thirsty and you gave Me no drink; I was a stranger and you did not take Me in, naked and you did not clothe Me, sick and in prison and you did not visit Me.... Inasmuch as you did not do it to one of the least of these, you did it not to Me" (Matthew 25:42-43, 45).

God didn't create us to not do something. He created us to do something. He told us to "Do this," and "Do that," and "Do the other." And one of those things is to feed the hungry and visit the sick in His name. If we fail to do those things, we are guilty of sins of omission, which can be just as devastating in their consequences as the sins of commission.

Question to ponder: Are you involved in any acts of mercy?

....

....

....

....

....

OCTOBER 21 — Choose Your Friends Wisely

Do not be misled: "Bad company corrupts good character."
1 Corinthians 15:33

Bad companions ruin good character. How true that is for people of all ages, perhaps especially young people. Take heed whom you select as friends. One of the wisest bits of advice that you could possibly have is: choose friends that are more godly than you are.

If you want to know how spiritual or how holy you are, take a look at your friends, because they are a very good reflection of your spiritual growth. Birds of a feather, you know, flock together. How spiritual are your friends? I can tell you this: they are probably about as spiritual as you are. Jesus went among sinners, you say. Yes, but he went to give them the Gospel, not to get fellowship and companionship from them.

In Psalm 1, David contrasts the godly with the ungodly. The godly man not only spends time meditating and reflecting on the Word of God, he shuns the corruption that comes from the company of mockers. We need to choose our friends wisely, so that we can build each other up, not bring each other down.

Question to ponder: Are there any friendships that you may need to terminate, for the sake of your soul? Any friendships you should cultivate?

....

....

....

....

....

....

....

Conflict Over Worldviews

For the devil has come down to you, having great
wrath, because he knows that he has a short time.
Revelation 12:12

There's an age-old conflict between two world-and-life-views. A world-and-life-view is a set of assumptions or presuppositions that determine the way that we look at the world and our place in it. These largely determine how we consider everything.

One worldview sees God at the center, ruling over all things under His dominion that operate according to His laws. The other worldview sees a mechanistic universe in which there is no God, no reason, no purpose, with only man at the center operating according to the dictatorship of the latest tyrant. The worlds which issue forth from those two views are vastly different worlds.

It is important that we understand that it is ultimately a spiritual battle in which we are engaged—not a battle between mere economic outlooks or various political philosophies. It is a battle between Christ and Antichrist; between Jesus Christ and His followers and the Antichrist and his. Therefore, ultimately, it is a battle that will be won not by bullets, but by beliefs. You cannot change ideas with bombs.

It's very reassuring to know that when we read the end of the Bible, we know Who wins.

Question to ponder: Do you see worldviews in conflict on a daily basis?

....

....

....

....

....

OCTOBER 23 — *The Challenge of Worldliness*

Do not love the world or the things in the world. If anyone loves the world, the love of the Father is not in him. For all that is in the world—the lust of the flesh, the lust of the eyes, and the pride of life—is not of the Father but is of the world. And the world is passing away, and the lust of it; but he who does the will of God abides forever.
1 John 2:15-17

The average worldling, like a mole in its dark hole, walks in the darkness of this world without the slightest inkling of God's love and mercy or of the gracious and free atonement and salvation that God offers to those who acknowledge that they are sinners.

We have seen many times that the world in its "wisdom" has flown right into the face of God's wisdom. For decades they follow the attractions of the world, only to find that they have created yet another disaster.

There was a great preacher by the name of Bud Robinson who proclaimed the Gospel in various parts of the world. Then he visited New York City for the first time, and his friends took him on the grand tour of the city. He saw New York in all of its glory. That night he knelt to pray, and this is what he said: "Lord, I thank you that once in my life I had the opportunity of seeing the great city of New York. And Lord, I thank you even more that I didn't see one thing that I wanted."

Question to ponder: Does any form of worldliness hold any temptation to you?

....
....
....
....
....

A Sobering Letter

Nevertheless I have this against you,
that you have left your first love.
Revelation 2:4

Recently, we received a letter addressed to you and me that said, "Your everlasting happiness and well-being depends upon your reading and heeding this letter." Then on the over side it said, "From Him whose eyes are like a flame of fire, who holds the seven stars in his right hand, who walks in the midst of the seven golden candlesticks" (Revelation 2:1 paraphrased).

Now you are saying, "Did you really get a letter like that?" Well, actually, not in the mail, but such as letter was sent to the Church at Ephesus personally by the Son of God. So, since this is applicable to every church, we did receive such a letter. It came to us right out of the Scripture. It was addressed originally to the Church at Ephesus, but it applies to us as well.

The gist of what He said to this church is that He knows their works, which are relatively sound, but they have lost their first love. Jesus is no longer first in their hearts, and He tells then to repent and do the things they did at first. If you ever find your love growing cold, there is one place where it will be rekindled and that is the foot of the Cross.

Question to ponder: Is Jesus your first love?

....

....

....

....

....

....

....

OCTOBER 25 ≡ *Works for the Lord*

*So Jacob served seven years for Rachel, and they seemed only
a few days to him because of the love he had for her.*
Genesis 29:20

Christ said to the church in Ephesus that He knows their works.
Interestingly, many of us are willing to do works. If, that is, they are not too
strenuous and it won't be too inconvenient—if it is not too early, or too late,
or too far, or too heavy, or too much, or too often. So, if all those conditions
are met, well then you can count on me...once in awhile.

But I thank God there are some whose labors God knows. I even know
some who are faithful and diligent, and it doesn't matter how hard or how
often or how long or how far. I thank God for that. Christ knows your labors.
If your work is done for Him, you may be certain that He will reward you.

When we do works out of love for Christ, it makes all the difference
in the world. How powerful is the "first love" that we have for the Lord.
There is nothing that "first love" cannot do. There may be streams or rivers
to cross, and first love says, "I can swim." There may be mountains to climb,
and first love says, "I can fly." It doesn't matter what the task, "More love for
Thee, O Christ" should be our continuous prayer.

Question to ponder: Is your service to the Lord
what you want it to be?

It's All About Love

Therefore the Lord said: "Inasmuch as these people draw near with their mouths and honor Me with their lips, but have removed their hearts far from Me...."
Isaiah 29:13

First love: God asks for our hearts. We can give no more. He can accept no less. He has loved us even unto the pit of Hell. How can we not love Him back? Ah, my friends, all of those good works, all of those labors, all of those industries exercised for Christ mean nothing if that first love is not there. Without love they are only "sounding brass or a clanging cymbal" (1 Corinthians 13:1 NKJV).

Is there any husband anywhere in the world, who would be satisfied if he discovers that his wife's heart is now far from him, that she no longer loves him? Does it make any difference how diligent she is in the affairs of the home, in the tasks of keeping house? All of these things are worse than ashes if her heart is far from him.

God speaks of those who draw nigh unto Him with their lips, but their hearts are far from Him. God made us to love Him, for He loves us, and we must love Him too.

We love Him because He first loved us. As the hymn reminds us, "Lord, let me never, never outlive my love for Thee."

Question to ponder: How is the love life of your heart to the great Lover of Your Soul?

....

....

....

....

....

Christianity and Women

*...And certain women who had been healed of evil
spirits and infirmities—Mary called Magdalene, out
of whom had come seven demons, and Joanna the wife
of Chuza, Herod's steward, and Susanna, and many
others who provided for Him from their substance.*
Luke 8:2-3

A few years ago, I was in a land where the Gospel of Christ has had little impact at all. As I was passing by, I saw an ox pulling a plow and as I reached a certain angle where I could see the other beast yoked to the oxen, I saw that it was a woman. The men were all playing checkers out in front of the house.

This exemplifies the world without the Bible. This is why so many women have loved and followed Christ—because He has lifted them up and given them a nobility. Today there are more women in American colleges than men. What would Plato say about that?

In ancient times, a woman was simply the property of her husband. And then, Christ was born of the Virgin Mary. And Christ called unto Himself woman to be his fellow-laborers and friends in His ministry. And it was a woman that was first given to see the resurrected Christ and to announce it to the world. And it was His Gospel that said there is neither male nor female. And this utterly changed the view of women.

Question to ponder: Do you see the difference Jesus has made in how women are treated?

....

....

....

....

....

....

Great and Mighty Things

*Call to Me, and I will answer you, and show you
great and mighty things, which you do not know.*
Jeremiah 33:3

Do we not have a God in whom are hidden all the treasures of wisdom? Do we not have a God who has at His disposal all power in Heaven and in earth? A God whose purposes none can disannul? Who has stretched forth His hand and there is none that can stay it nor say unto Him, "What doest thou?" Do we not have a God who does according to His will among the armies of Heaven and among the inhabitants of the earth, who created the world and the heavens? There is nothing too hard for Him.

So, what do we ask Him to do? Too often our requests amount to piddling little things that do not amount to a hill of beans.

No, we can ask of Him anything. There is nothing too hard for Him. He can reach down into our souls and stretch our faith. He can open our eyes to see His awesome power and His willingness to reveal it. He can yet again bring to pass great and mighty things whereby His Kingdom may come and His name will be glorified in the earth.

Question to ponder: What great and mighty things do you want to ask God for?

....

....

....

....

....

....

....

The Fear of Death

...Without hope and without God in the world.
Ephesians 2:12

Millions of people have studied Edgar Allan Poe's most famous poem, "The Raven," and yet I doubt that one-half of one percent of them have the faintest idea what it means.

"The Raven" is the personification of the unbelief that plagued Poe's life. He was terrified by the grisly specter of death. In this poem he is seeking to find some surcease of sorrow for his lost Lenore. As he lost his wife in real life, so in this poem he loses Lenore, a beautiful, radiant maiden who has been snatched from his arms.

He can find no relief for the suffering and the heartache that grips him. He wants what everyone wants: some ease to the pain of this life. He wants to know that there is a balm in Gilead—a biblical phrase for Jesus Christ. In other words, Poe is asking, "Will I see Lenore again?" And unbelief answers, "Nevermore."

How different is Christ's answer to this question. On that glorious Easter morn He rose again from the dead and stepped forth into the light saying, "I am He that liveth, and was dead; and, behold, I am alive for evermore" (Revelation 1:18).

Unbelief says: "Nevermore." Faith says: "Forevermore." He conquered our fears and fulfills our hopes now and forevermore.

Question to ponder: Do you know people who live in fear of death, without hope and ruled by unbelief?

....

....

....

....

....

The Keeper of Wisdom

Get wisdom! Get understanding! Do not forget,
nor turn away from the words of my mouth.
Proverbs 4:5

There is a vast difference between the approach of the Hebrew and the Greek minds toward understanding wisdom. For the Greek, it was entirely a matter of the mind—a matter of putting things together and understanding the way the universe was made. It did not necessarily have much to do with the way one lived. Many renowned pagan writers of antiquity not only practiced, but also taught some of the most heinous of sins. In spite of their vast knowledge in some areas, their knowledge of holy and godly living was deficient, to say the least.

In Proverbs we find the door of wisdom open to everyone. But for the Greeks wisdom was reserved for a very select few. Over the gates to the school of Plato were inscribed the words: "Let no one enter herein who is not a geometrician." Unless you were an expert in the study of geometry, you were not even invited to school.

Proverbs is quite the contrary. Here are invited the ignorant and simple, the foolish and the young—all are warmly invited to come and learn wisdom. In addition, we are told in Proverbs 1 that the wise will also hear and increase in their learning. We are repeatedly admonished that the wise, indeed, are those who hear the Word of God.

Question to ponder: How do we become wise?

OCTOBER 31 ⸻

Reformation Day

The just shall live by faith.
Romans 1:17

If you asked the average American what October 31 is, the response would be instantaneous: "It's Halloween." Yes, but it is also something far more important. It is Reformation Day, the birthday of the Protestant Reformation. It is the day when we celebrate the reclaiming of the Gospel of grace from out of the mist and darkness of the Dark Ages.

Beginning in Germany with Martin Luther, the Reformation transformed many of the nations of Europe, spread over to Great Britain and sailed across the Atlantic. The Pilgrims and the Puritans were all followers of John Calvin, who was a follower of Martin Luther. Interestingly, those nations that have accepted the Reformation have been blessed by God, and those that have rejected it have become a part of the backwash of history. It is true not only of every nation, but of every soul as well.

The Reformation was simply a rediscovery of the apostolic message—the truth that we can't work our way to heaven. Eternal life is a free gift that we are to receive. It is faith alone that saves us, but that faith never stands alone. That faith produces good fruit in our lives.

Question to ponder: What does it mean in your life that "the just shall live by faith"?

Dealing With the Inexplicable ═══ NOVEMBER 1

If any of you lacks wisdom, let him ask of God, who gives to all liberally and without reproach, and it will be given to him.
James 1:5

In Jesus Christ we find that wisdom has become incarnate. We read that Jesus Christ "has become for us wisdom from God" (1 Corinthians 1:30 NIV). The fear of the Lord can grow into a complete love and adoration of God who now has come to live in our midst.

We need wisdom. Our world is full of the inexplicable, the inscrutable, the unfathomable, the impossible, and the insurmountable. We cannot, in fact, go three steps in any direction without running into the hard wall of mysteries, riddles, paradoxes, profundities and labyrinths—problems that we cannot solve; labyrinths that we cannot make our way out of; hiero-glyphics that we cannot decipher; anagrams that we cannot spell out and sphinxes that just will not speak. Life is full of puzzles.

God gave Solomon great wisdom and he has been regarded as the wis-est man who ever lived. But Jesus is the one "greater than Solomon" (Matthew 12:42) and in Him "are hid all the treasures of wisdom and knowledge." That wealth of wisdom from God is ours if we simply ask Him for it.

Question to ponder: With God's wisdom, what mystery would you like to solve?

....

....

....

....

....

....

Christian Citizenship

> *But now they desire a better, that is, a heavenly country. Therefore God is not ashamed to be called their God, for He has prepared a city for them.*
> Hebrews 11:16

Christianity has always been part of American life, since the time of the Pilgrims until now.

Today, people seem to think that in some way religion in general and Christianity in particular are inimical to good government and that the purpose of the government is to keep religion away from the civic arena. This is a very different view than that held by George Washington, who said, "True religion offers to government its surest support."

Why are people so against Christianity? What is it about Christ that they so abhor? They declare, "We will not have this man to reign over us" (Luke 19:14 NKJV). People do not want anybody—especially not Jesus Christ—to have power or control over their lives. Perhaps it gets back to what Jesus said in John 3:19: "light has come into the world, and men loved darkness rather than light, because their deeds were evil."

We Christians have a dual citizenship. We should do all we can to make our country the best it can be. We should seek godly values and vote for men and women of integrity and wisdom. Even as we work to make our country a good place to live, we know that there is a city, which God has prepared for us; a country where He rules. That is, and always will be, our true homeland.

Question to ponder: What are your thoughts on our dual citizenship?

....

....

....

....

Excellence in All Things

*...And know His will, and approve
the things that are excellent...*
Romans 2:18

We serve a most excellent God.

When we realize the greatness, glory, and majesty of our God, we should react with praise. Truly, our hearts should rejoice and the greatness of our God should cause us to sing of His glory and should also move us to reverential awe. When we see how great and glorious God is, when we grasp how His righteousness, holiness, and justice never change, and that He is infinite and eternal, we should be moved to awe. We should be moved to peace and comfort to know that if we have been reconciled to God through Jesus Christ, we are in the hands of a Being Who can never fail—One Who can never die.

Lastly, we should also be moved to excellence. Always, we should strive to give God our best: our best in worship, our best in work. It should be our standard as children of Him who is most excellent in power and beauty.

That is why I have always tried to employ the best musicians, the best organists, the best pastors and staff. No Christian should be content to imitate in thought, word, or deed what one has called "the Patron Saint of Mediocrity."

Question to ponder: How do you offer your best to God?

NOVEMBER 4 ——

Walking in the Light

*Then Jesus spoke to them again, saying, "I am
the light of the world. He who follows Me shall
not walk in darkness, but have the light of life."*
John 8:12

How do we continue in the communion God has called us to? John
says in the first chapter of his first letter, "If we walk in the light, as He is in
the light, we have fellowship one with another...." So we must continue to
walk in the light of God, which means we continue to repent of our sins,
continue to seek to walk honestly and purely before the Lord.

If we claim to have fellowship with God and yet walk in the darkness,
we lie, John says. We have no fellowship with Him. But if we walk with Jesus
Christ, we walk in the light. Just as physical light makes all things visible, so
spiritual light makes all things clear and visible in the spiritual realm.

The Lord wants us to keep short accounts with Him. What that means
is that when we sin, we should immediately ask for forgiveness. He promises us, "If we confess our sins, He is faithful and just to forgive us our sins
and to cleanse us from all unrighteousness" (1 John 1:9).

Question to ponder: Are you keeping short accounts with God?

....

....

....

....

....

....

....

Violation of the Conscience ══ NOVEMBER 5

The heart is deceitful above all things,
and desperately wicked; who can know it?
Jeremiah 17:9

The Scriptures clearly teach the sinfulness of man. Many violate their consciences. We know not what we are capable of doing.

At the Academy at Lyon, a thesis was written on the dangers of ambition, its author was young Napoleon. Nero declared, "Would this hand had never learned to write," when he signed the first death warrant. And Robespierre, who sent thousands to the bloody guillotine during the reign of terror in Paris, in an earlier day resigned as municipal judge in a small town when he was confronted with the task of signing a death warrant for a guilty criminal.

Sin is a very slippery slope. When we take one step down that slope, God withdraws the restraining power of His Spirit. We slide farther down, and again He withdraws His Spirit. Ah, how dangerous a thing is sin. Like the great whirlpool, Charybdis, to be caught in the outer rim of that swirling water is the kiss of death. Soon you are drawn ever closer, ever inward, ever farther down until you disappear forever into the watery chasm beneath. What a terrible, dangerous, deceitful, slippery thing is sin.

Thankfully, Jesus Christ came to break the power of sin in our lives.

Question to ponder: Have you ever violated your conscience? How did it make you feel?

....

....

....

....

....

....

NOVEMBER 6 — *All Authority Belongs to Christ*

All authority has been given to Me in heaven and on earth.
Matthew 28:18

All power is given unto Jesus Christ. After His ascension, He sat down at the right hand of God until His enemies be made His footstool (Psalm 110:1 and Hebrews 1:13). Through these last 2,000 years, Jesus Christ has been continually gaining the victory, a victory which began at the time of His death and resurrection, and which continues on through the ages.

In 363 A.D., Julian the Apostate, that emperor of Rome who tried to relight the fires on pagan altars and to overthrow the newly established Christian faith, was marching against the Persians. One of his soldiers, a Christian, was being sorely derided and persecuted by some of the heathen soldiers. They mocked him, beat him, threw him to the ground, and said, "Tell us, where is your carpenter now?"

He responded "He is busy constructing a coffin for your emperor." A few months later, a mortal wound in his side, Julian the Apostate took his hands, grasped a handful of his own blood, flung it against the sky, and said, "Thou hast conquered, O Galilean." The Carpenter of Galilee is busy constructing coffins for all the ungodly kings and kingdoms of this earth.

Christ is Lord of all.

Question to ponder: All authority—what does it mean?

He Sets the Captives Free

Therefore if the Son makes you free, you shall be free indeed.
John 8:36

For those who repent and believe, Christ removes the guilt of the past, but He can also give us victory over sin in the present and in the future. Christ breaks the shackles of sin; Christ sets the prisoner free. What hope of freedom does the drunkard, the alcoholic, the dope addict, or the immoral person—that individual who is chained to the chariot wheels of some ignoble passion—have, except in Christ?

Christ gives us victory over sin when nothing else can. All the education, all the culture in the world cannot do it. Germany in 1941 was the most highly educated nation in the world. It produced a Goering and a Goebbels; it produced a hell on earth. No, only Christ can give victory over sin.

St. Augustine was one of the most brilliant intellects in the first thousand years of this era. Though he was a rhetorician, a logistician, a philosopher; though he had all the learning of the ancient world, he wrote that before he knew Christ, he envied the simple Christians who had control of their passions. They had the reins of their lives in some unseen hands that he knew not of, whereas, he was a slave to his passions.

Christ can set you free.

Question to ponder: Are you experiencing victory in Jesus? If not, ask Him now to set you free.

....

....

....

....

....

....

NOVEMBER 8 — Existentialist Spectacles

Professing to be wise, they became fools.
Romans 1:22

Many on our university campuses today see the world through the lens of existentialism, the prevailing philosophy of modern man. And what is the modern man? He is *Irrational Man.* This is the title of a scholarly work that details how man has reached a point of total irrationality where the world has no rhyme or meaning, where there is no significance, where there is no purpose, where there is no teleology, where there is no end, and where there is no beginning. All things have been reduced to a primeval chaos in human thinking.

It is a tragic pilgrimage to meander through *Irrational Man.* We see that man without God, without divine revelation, and with only his unaided reason, has not produced a rational, enlightened, intelligent view of the universe. He has not grasped nor comprehended and understood all things, but rather, he has been led into the miry slough of despond. Pessimism is to be found everywhere among the existentialists. That is why suicide is a leading cause of death among college students today.

But God has shone His light into our world by revealing the truth through His Word—both the Bible and Jesus Christ, the Word of God. In Him we find true wisdom.

Question to ponder: Can a faithful Christian with a true Christian worldview be a pessimist?

....

....

....

....

....

....

The Burden of Guilt ⟫ NOVEMBER 9

*Come to me all you who are weary
and burdened, and I will give you rest.*
Matthew 11:28

Guilt breaks lives down like a caustic acid. Our mental institutions are filled with individuals who are utterly destroyed by guilt. One psychiatrist has said that every person in every mental institution in the country is there because of feelings of guilt.

I shared the Good News of Christ with a man, and then I asked him if he would like to receive Christ as Lord and Savior of his life. I shall never forget the way he phrased his answer. He said: "Yes, I would like to get rid of this burden of guilt."

Are you carrying such a burden? The sojourner in Bunyan's *Pilgrim's Progress* begins the story with a great, heavy burden on his shoulders—a burden of guilt that he cannot get rid of or unleash. Finally, he is pointed to a Cross on top of a hill. He climbs that hill and kneels before that Cross. Suddenly the burden breaks loose and rolls down the hill into a dark tomb, never to be seen again.

God completely removes our burden of guilt. As far as the east is from the west, so far is the punishment for our transgression removed from us.

Question to ponder: Are you still carrying the burden of guilt that you could leave at the foot of the Cross?

NOVEMBER **10** *Courage Born of Faith*

...Be of good cheer, I have overcome the world.
John 16:33

I like the story about a man who walked to the drug store from his home. When he entered the store, he found himself in the middle of a holdup. The robber, gun in hand said to him, "Give me your wallet and your keys, or I'll shoot."

This man said, "I just finished reading the Scriptures and I just finished my prayers, so go ahead, shoot." The robber was astonished. He didn't know what to do, so he turned and ran out the door.

Now there was a courage born out of faith. All that robber could do to him was simply send him on a first class ticket to Heaven—no cancer, no stroke, no lingering disease, no debilitating old age—but a first class ticket to heaven. Of course, what that robber probably realized is that if he pulled that trigger, what he could do for himself was get a ticket straight to the electric chair and then to hell. So he ran.

Obviously, we are not called to a foolish presumptuous life that takes needless risks. That is not wisdom. But, as Christians, we need not live our lives in cowering fear. Jesus Christ has overcome the world, and this life is but a second compared to all eternity.

Question to ponder: In which area of your life, do you need more courage?

....

....

....

....

....

....

In Honor of Veterans

Likewise the soldiers asked [John the Baptist], saying, "And what shall we do?" So he said to them, "Do not intimidate anyone or accuse falsely, and be content with your wages."
Luke 3:14

War is a great evil. It is a tragedy. Every Christian should abhor it and do what he can to prevent it. We are to live at peace with all men as much as lies within us. But there are times when we must fight. So the greatest of Christian theologians and Reformers down through the centuries have believed, and so too believed the founders of this nation.

Jesus did say that we are to "resist not evil" and to turn the other cheek (Matthew 5:39). This, however, is a personal ethic, and not a directive toward the state. That is why nations have police forces and armies. Romans 13 and I Peter 2 teach how the civil ruler is to bear the sword and punish evildoers. "For he [the state] is the minister of God to thee for good. But if thou do that which is evil, be afraid; for he beareth not the sword in vain: for he is the minister of God, a revenger to execute wrath upon him that doeth evil" (Romans 13:4).

Today we honor those brave men and women who have served their country faithfully. We honor these brave men and women because they have secured the freedom that we enjoy in this nation under God. Peace is precious, and it is not cheap.

Thank a veteran today.

Question to ponder: What can you do today to honor our veterans?

NOVEMBER **12** *Ultimate Home*

*...I will come again and receive you to Myself;
that where I am, there you may be also.*
John 14:3

We are constantly looking for a place to belong. We all want a home. Even here on earth, a good home is a great blessing, and it can be a little bit of heaven. But our true home is in heaven.

Jesus said, "In my Father's house are many mansions" (John 14:2). Jesus is the only one in the New Testament who refers to Heaven as a house—indeed, His Father's house. Heaven is called in Scripture a country, a city, a garden, and paradise. But it is also a home, and this speaks to the depths of the concerns of our hearts. Home used to mean, and still does for some, a retreat from the problems of this world, a place of solace, a place where loved ones gather and have the deepest of fellowship.

But Heaven is our ultimate home—a home prepared for us by our Savior. Interestingly, He didn't send angels to prepare it. He said, "I go to prepare a place for you" (v. 2). The pronouns are filled with meaning. Jesus is the architect of those mansions. He is the builder of those rooms. He is the decorator, the provider of everything needful. Jesus has provided it, and not only that, but He went to Calvary's Cross to pay for it. It is paid in full.

Question to ponder: How do you picture your home in heaven?

Homecoming

To God's elect, strangers in the world...
1 Peter 1:1

A Dr. Morrison went on a great preaching mission and spent two years preaching the Gospel in scores of different countries. About the time he got back, Teddy Roosevelt returned from big game hunting in Africa. The nation honored him with a ticker-tape parade and tens of thousands of people turned out to celebrate his return.

When Dr. Morrison arrived in his small hometown late at night, there was no one at the train station to greet him. There was one light bulb hanging from a cord, swaying and swinging in the breeze, but not a single person was there.

As he picked up his bags and started up a long hill to the little town, his heart was heavy. He said, "O Lord, Teddy Roosevelt went to shoot animals and he came back and they gave him a ticker-tape parade. I've been all over the world. I was almost killed in Borneo, and I was almost eaten in New Guinea, and several times I almost lost my life to preach the Gospel for the glory of your Son. I come home and there's nobody here to greet me. Lord, I just don't understand it." He said that it seemed there in the darkness, as the breeze blew across his face, he could almost hear a voice coming out of Heaven that said, *"You're not home, yet."*

Question to ponder: When you think of your homecoming, what do you think you will say to Jesus?

....

....

....

....

....

Living Serenely

You will keep him in perfect peace, whose mind
is stayed on You, because he trusts in You.
Isaiah 26:3

Anxiety. Fear. Worry. We live in a time of "men's hearts failing them for fear" (Luke 21:26). If you are like most Americans, you have to confess that you are often troubled by many things. People are anxious and worried; peace is elusive and never lasts.

How much serenity do we have? The word "serenity" is not found in the Bible, but it conveys the concept in words that mean the same thing. The Bible talks about "peace" and "rest" and "quiet"—something most people experience very little of. Shalom is the word in the Bible for the peace that includes security and wholeness.

How tragic that millions who have never found the solution to the sin problem are trying to find serenity in some other way. It can never, ever be done, my friends. It just will not work. You have to have the forgiveness of God before you can have serenity and peace of mind. Christ Jesus is the Prince of Peace, and He offers us the peace of God.

This is perhaps one of the reasons Paul greets his readers with "Grace and peace." Without grace, there is no peace.

Question to ponder: How can a person be serene in the midst of chaos?

....

....

....

....

....

Coping with Suffering

How long, O Lord, holy and true...?
Revelation 6:10

Some years ago, I went through a trial worse than anything I'd ever known. In the midst of that ordeal, many cries went up from my heart: "How long, O God?" In all of that, there was the belief that God is the sovereign Lord, that He is the infinite, all-powerful One who holds the reins of the world in His hand. Even beyond that, He is a loving and merciful God and therefore there was a purpose and a reason for all that happened. Furthermore, I believed that ultimately He would work all things together for my good.

One of the greatest books on suffering from a Christian perspective was first published in 1856 and retranslated into English in 2002. The book is by a Calvinistic French pastor, Adolphe Monod. His book is a series of sermons, which he delivered as he was dying of cancer. The book is *Living in The Hope of Glory* (translated recently by Constance K. Walker).

Monod said that whatever we need, we have in Christ, even if we're suffering the pangs of death: "He will never deprive me of any good except to give me some other, better one." He also noted, "Having Christ we have all things...."

Question to ponder: God is good, and God is sovereign. How do these two truths comfort us?

NOVEMBER 16 === *A Spiritual Inheritance*

A good man leaves an inheritance
to his children's children....
Proverbs 13:22

What kind of spiritual heritage are you leaving or have you left your chlidren? If you look back through the great names of God's people, you will find that in many cases their testimony is that whatever they are, they owe it to the prayers of their parents in family devotion times around the family altar when they were children.

The saintly Matthew Henry says in his own testimony that whatever there may be of good about him, he contributes it in a large part to his godly home and praying parents who gathered the children together each day for the worship of God.

I think of Patrick Henry, who wrote in his Last Will and Testament:

I have now disposed of all my property to my family; there is one thing more I wish I could give them, and that is the Christian religion. If they had that, and I had not given them one shilling, they would be rich, and if they had not that, and I had given them all the world, they would be poor.

Question to ponder: What would you like to leave to your children?

....

....

....

....

....

....

....

....

....

Holy of Holies

And every priest stands ministering daily and offering repeatedly the same sacrifices, which can never take away sins. But this Man, after He had offered one sacrifice for sins forever, sat down at the right hand of God.
Hebrews 10:11-12

Only the High Priest could enter into the Holy of Holies, and that but once a year, and then not without the blood of the sacrifice that was to be sprinkled onto the mercy seat.

What was in that Holy of Holies? There was the Ark of the Covenant. Within it were found the two tables of the Law written by the very hand of Jehovah. Those laws, looking upward, cried out against the transgressions of men against the commandments. On the top of the Ark was the mercy seat, covered in pure gold. Once a year, on Yom Kippur, the Day of Atonement, the High Priest entered into the Holy of Holies and sprinkled blood on the mercy seat of the atonement.

On either end of that Ark, gold-covered cherubim faced inward. Between those cherubim there dwelt the presence of the Almighty God. There the broken law cried out for vengeance upon the transgressors, and it was only the blood of the atonement that blocked it out. That is a great picture of Christ who entered the Holy of Holies in Heaven itself with His own blood to make atonement for our sins. There is the secret place of the most High God, where mercy is meted out through the death of the Sacrifice.

Question to ponder: How is Jesus Christ both our High Priest and sacrifice?

....

....

....

....

....

NOVEMBER **18** ⟺   *Whose Reality?*

To the pure all things are pure, but to those
who are defiled and unbelieving nothing is pure;
but even their mind and conscience are defiled.
Titus 1:15

Hollywood producers may tell you, "Well, you see, we are just a reflection of reality. We're just revealing what the country is like."

The truth of the matter is that they do reflect a portion of reality. They reflect what is going on in the gutter, what is going on in the sewer and a few of the other worst places in the country. Then they spread that vileness over the entire nation. They are not just reflecting reality. They are pushing their favorite kind of reality–the reality that appeals to their depraved minds.

We do not have to accept their version of reality. Yes, there is evil, and yes, there is ugliness. But we as Christians know that purity, innocence, goodness, and kindness exist too.

Just recently there has been a trend of good and moral movies coming and generally doing well, to the surprise of the Hollywood elite. Let us support what is good and decent and avoid what is not.

Question to ponder: What good movie have you seen recently (if any)? What made it good?

....

....

....

....

....

....

....

Impact

*These who have turned the world
upside down have come here too...*
ACTS 17:6

In many places in the world, Christians have made a tremendous impact for good. A handful of people can help ignite a city. Now a city full of Christians seems to have little impact.

Why is the Church so seemingly impotent in today's society, whereas in the early centuries, it transformed the pagan Roman Empire? One of the reasons could be that these people took the lordship of Jesus Christ seriously. They committed themselves to Him as Lord. They knew what a lord was. In the Roman world, to be a servant, doulos, meant that you gave up your will completely; you had no preferences of what you would like yourself. You were the servant of a master, the kurios.

Where are the Christians in our society? It just so happens that evangelical Christianity is generally not making the laws in the Senate or in the Congress; they are not sitting on the Supreme Court; they are not generally the ones making motion pictures in Hollywood; they are not the ones running our television networks.

This is something very obvious. Though Christianity is growing in this country, it is still far from being the controlling force or even that influential.

The question is not a matter of numbers, but the level of commitment.

Question to ponder: Can you think of a new way to serve God?

....

....

....

....

....

Heirs with Christ

...An inheritance incorruptible and undefiled and that does not fade away, reserved in heaven for you....
1 Peter 1:4

I was talking recently in my office to a young lady who had just accepted Christ. I told her that she was now the child of God and that she was, furthermore, the heir of God. I said, "Do you realize that you have just become an heiress?"

She looked very puzzled, so I opened my Bible to the New Testament and showed her the front page which had the heading on it, "The New Testament of our Lord and Savior, Jesus Christ." I said, "Did you notice the word? This is the last will and testament of Almighty God, and you have become His heir. You are written into God's will. The Bible says that we are the heirs of God, and joint heirs with Jesus Christ."

Well, it would be, I suppose, a great thing to be written into the will of some fabulously wealthy man. However, my friends, we have something more marvelous than that. We are written into the will of God, if we have received Jesus Christ and we belong to Him. We are the heirs of God and joint heirs with Jesus Christ. All things are ours; whether in this life or the world to come (see I Corinthians 3:21-23), and we know that, "My God shall supply all of your needs out of His riches in glory" (Philippians 4:19).

Question to ponder: What is the inheritance kept for you in heaven?

Living in God's Presence

He who dwells in the secret place of the Most High
shall abide under the shadow of the Almighty.
Psalm 91:1

Brother Lawrence, who wrote the famous little booklet, *The Practice of the Presence of God,* made that marvelous discovery to such a degree that he became the wonder of Europe. Kings and princes, cardinals and popes visited him to learn his secret. Was he a philosopher? A count? A theologian? No, he was a dishwasher. That's right. A dishwasher and a waiter.

Kings visited him because his reputation had spread all over the world. A reputation for what? For peace—for an almost miraculous serenity in the midst of the clamoring of the people who were crying for his services and complaining about this and that and the other. In spite of all of the demands on him, he seemed to float through life in a bubble of peace.

In his marvelous booklet, Brother Lawrence tells how through much trial, effort, and labor, he learned how to stay his mind upon God. Then, when he was turned away from whatever might demand his immediate attention, his mind automatically seemed to turn to its resting place and his thoughts to God. His mind was stayed on God, and God kept him in perfect peace.

Question to ponder: How can we practice God's presence?

....

....

....

....

....

....

NOVEMBER 22 === *Comfort My People*

For You are with me; Your rod and
Your staff, they comfort me.
Psalm 23:4

Some people are amazed to find out that the great and the mighty of the world often are in need of comfort and consolation. Handel began his *Messiah* with the words, "Comfort ye, comfort ye my people" because this verse of Scripture was dear to his heart. Luther pondered Isaiah 40 over and over again when he was in hiding at the castle in Wartburg. Oliver Cromwell also went to it for help in time of storm. The great Daniel Webster was so mighty in debate, and yet his heart was often grieved, and he read the passage again and again. Tennyson called it one of the five great classics in the Old Testament record.

We all need comfort. High and low, prince and pauper, none of us can live life to the full without this solace from Him who is the God of all comfort (2 Corinthians 1:3).

One young seminarian was filled with vim and vigor. He was coming like Daniel to the judgment and was ready to let his flock have it. He told an elderly minister who replied, "But don't forget to preach comfort. Remember that those people in the pews have heartaches and problems and fears. Always preach comfort." Indeed, in this day how great is that need for comfort.

Question to ponder: What Scripture do you read when you need comfort?

....

....

....

....

....

Idolatry

From their silver and gold they made idols for themselves.
Hosea 8:4

There are more denunciations of idolatry than any other sin in the Bible. Though this sin runs deep in the human psyche, and there is a great tendency to idolatry in the human heart, and though this dark stream seems to flow dangerously in the cold subterranean caverns of the fallen soul, it is something that has been followed by a continual stream of condemnation and denunciation by poets and prophets, by preachers and apostles, down through the centuries.

Not only did they worship idols in Moses' day, but we read further on that Jeroboam doubled the sin by creating a golden calf in Dan and another in Bethel for the people to worship. All over Israel there arose on the high places—on every hill, in every clump of trees—an altar so people could rush up the hills and worship their gods and bring down upon themselves the increasing wrath of almighty God until at length the patience of God was exhausted.

The hordes of Babylon under Nebuchadnezzar swept across the plains of Israel, broke down the walls of Jerusalem, and led the people off into captivity. It was in that burning furnace of slavery in Babylon that the last dredges of idolatry were largely burned away.

Question to ponder: John Calvin said our hearts are idol-making factories. Why is that?

....

....

....

....

....

If God is Sovereign...

Let all the earth fear the LORD; let all the inhabitants of the world stand in awe of Him.
—Psalm 33:8

God in His sovereign care is able to make all things work together for our good as believers. We cannot look at any particular singular event and say, "How is this working for my good?" We may not know. It is not a singular event, but all things working together that God is using for our spiritual well being.

Spurgeon tells about a man, who was captured for preaching the Gospel during the reign of Queen Mary. He was sentenced to be burned alive at the stake in London. When he heard the sentence, he said, "Well, never mind, for all things work together for good."

People asked, "Well, how is that going to work together for your good?"

He replied, "I do not know, but I know that it will."

On the way back to London, the guards treated him so roughly that they cast him down and broke his leg. Unsympathetically, they mocked him saying, "Well, tell us how this is going to work together for your good?"

He said, "I do not know, but I know that God will work it together for my good."

His leg was splinted so he could continue the trip. They made it to London a day late because of the accident. Queen Mary had just died. Elizabeth was now on the throne and the man was pardoned.

Question to ponder: If God is sovereign and good, then is anything He allows into the lives of His children truly and ultimately bad?

Thanksgiving

*You are the light of the world. A city
that is set on a hill cannot be hidden.*
Matthew 5:14

Thanksgiving is an annual reminder of America's Christian roots. It goes back to the Pilgrims, who gave thanks to God. Were they thankful for the abundance of their crops? No. There *was no* abundance. The average meal that winter consisted of five hard kernels of corn on the plate. Period. Just about 50 percent of all of the Pilgrims died in that first winter of 1621.

They had landed in early December of 1620, and it was the fall of 1621. Half of them are gone. There was virtually not a family left who had not lost a husband or a wife or a child. They had little food. Many were still sick. But they were men and women of the Book. They believed the Word of God.

There is nothing Americans cherish more than their freedom; and the origins of that freedom can he traced directly back to the Pilgrims. Religious freedom (the right of a people to own and read the Bible, to worship according to conscience, to form their own church); political freedom (the right of a people to frame their own constitution and form their own government); even economic freedom (the right to own one's own property and keep the fruit of one's labors)—all these freedoms in America began with the Pilgrims.

Question to ponder: Can you make a list today of 100 things you are thankful to God for? (You might have to use an additional paper.)

....

....

....

....

....

NOVEMBER **26** ≡ *Pilgrims and Socialism*

...Let him labor, working with his hands what is good, that he may have something to give him who has need.
Ephesians 4:28

In the earliest days of the Pilgrims, a type of communism was forced on them by the London company, which financed their adventure to the New World. (By the way, the Pilgrims were charged an interest of 45 per-cent interest, and they paid off every nickel.) This company required that the Pilgrims have a communal or socialistic government in which every-thing was to be brought into a common barn. Nobody owned any prop-erty. It would be from each according to his ability to each according to his need—long before Karl Marx wrote similar words.

The result: unhappy colonists and poor harvests. Gov. William Brad-ford wrote that the imposed socialism "was found to breed much confusion and discontent, and retard much employment which would have been to the general benefit and comfort."

So he changed the system. Now it was each man for himself. A piece of ground was given to every family, and the increase was astonishing. Bradford wrote that "It made all hands very industrious, so that much more corn was planted than otherwise would have been by any means the Gov-ernor or any other could devise." That led to thanksgiving celebrations filled with abundance—once free enterprise replaced communism.

Question to ponder: Do you see any tendencies toward communism in our society today?

....

....

....

....

....

No Other Gods

And in every single city of Judah he made
high places to burn incense to other gods, and
provoked to anger the LORD God of his fathers.
2 Chronicles 28:25

The first of the Ten Commandments, "Thou shalt have no other gods before me" (Exodus 20:2), requires us to worship God exclusively. Christianity, like Judaism, is an exclusive religion. It is not pluralistic; it is not tolerant.

Certainly the Old Testament and New Testament writers were not tolerant of other gods. God Almighty is not tolerant of other gods. He says with absolute clarity: "Thou shalt have no other gods before me." All of the other gods, said the apostle Paul, and all of their images are simply demons, and God would not have us to have fellowship with demons.

Even when people try to worship the true God through an idol, it becomes idolatry, as with the golden calf. What Aaron said is, "Tomorrow is a feast to the Lord. And they rose up early on the morrow, and offered burnt offerings, and brought peace offerings; and the people sat down to eat and to drink, and rose up to play" (Exodus 32:5–6).

They were worshiping Jehovah *through* the calf; they weren't worshiping the calf. And so the Bible makes it abundantly clear that idolatry is either the worshiping of images or pictures or statues—or the worship of the true God through or by means of images. Either one of them is equally idolatry.

Question to ponder: Why has the Western world been largely free from ***direct*** idolatry?

Indirect Idolatry

You shall love the LORD your God with all your heart,
with all your soul, and with all your strength.
Deuteronomy 6:5

Our gods today are usually what we regard as important, such as financial success or fame. What is it that is most important to your life? There are some people for whom their house is their god or even their car— all of their time, energy and labor centers around what they love best. There is nothing wrong with keeping a house, but when you make a house a god, there is something very wrong with that.

For some people their family is their god. Now families are wonderful. But I would not think of making my family my god. God has a way of throwing images and idols down on their faces in the dirt. That is why we must guard our hearts.

The gods of our age are materialism, self-love, hedonism, and all other "isms." An idol is anything we set before us that is more important than God and anything we love more than Him.

Question to ponder: Is there anything in your life that you love more than God?

....

....

....

....

....

....

....

The Light of the World

...The darkness is passing away,
and the true light is already shining.
1 John 2:8

Jesus did not say "I am one of many lights of the world;" He did not even say, "I am the light of the Jews;" or yet, "I am the light of the Gentiles;" nor did He declare "I bring unto you light." But rather, He said without apology, "I am the Light of the World." What a tremendous and bold statement.

The occasion that brought it forth was the Feast of the Tabernacles. Jesus took every opportunity to use that which was about Him to illustrate and make clear His teaching. One of the purposes of this ceremony was to remind the Jewish people of the pillar of fire, which had gone before them throughout those desert wanderings. They had set up in the outer court-yard (the Court of Women) of the Temple two giant candelabra. Maimonides tells us that they were fifty cubits high, which is seventy-five feet. There, thousands of women carrying torches formed a procession into that court from Jerusalem and around this they enacted this pageant to remind them of the presence of God in that pillar of fire centuries before.

God's presence is not only symbolized by light, He is the "Father of Lights," and into our dark world comes Jesus who declares: "I am the light of the world" (John 8:12).

Question to ponder: As the children of light, how do we walk in His light?

⚜ ....

....

....

....

....

....

The Name of Jesus

Therefore God also has highly exalted Him and given Him the name which is above every name.
Philippians 2:9

When the angel Gabriel appeared to Mary, he told specifically what the child to come was to be named: "And [thou] shalt call his name JESUS" (Luke 1:31). The angel was but a messenger of God, who Himself chose the name of His one and only Son.

His name was Jesus. But why Jesus? Of course, to understand that, we would have to understand that Jesus is an English word. The New Testament and the Old Testament were not written originally in English, but in Hebrew and Greek, respectively. We get the name from the Greek.

His name was Jehoshua, or as we would say it, Joshua, meaning savior. That was the name of a great champion, a great hero of the Old Testament Hebrew people. It was the name of the great conqueror, the captain of the Lord's hosts, who led the people of God into the promised land.

And so our Savior will lead us into the promised land.

At the name of Jesus, sorrow and sadness flees. At the name of Jesus, sinners are cleansed and converted. At the name of Jesus, saints are gladdened and strengthened. At the name of Jesus, evil is banished and fear must flee. At the name of Jesus, the wounded are made whole.

Question to ponder: Can you think of anything else that the name of Jesus accomplishes?

....

....

....

....

....

The First and Second Advents — DECEMBER 1

*...That at the name of Jesus every knee should bow,
of those in heaven, and of those on earth, and of those
under the earth, and that every tongue should confess
that Jesus Christ is Lord, to the glory of God the Father.*
Philippians 2:10-11

During the Advent season—Christmas time—we remember the Advent of the Son of God. The term advent is taken from the Latin, ad ventre, which mean "to come to." We remember that over 2,000 years ago, the eternal and uncreated Son of God came to this world which He had fashioned with His own hands.

At Advent, we are reminded that there is another Advent of which the Scriptures speak. He who came once will come again. He who came as a tiny and weak babe in a manger will come as a conquering king with clouds of glory. He who came in humility, seen only by a few shepherds, will one day come in great splendor and majesty and every eye shall see Him. This is a great truth of the Scripture.

We live between the first and second comings of Jesus Christ. Note how He impacts history. We count time according to how many years ago He was born, and history is marching toward His return—the climax of all history.

At the first coming, we saw His humility. At the second coming, we will see His glory. As we go through the Advent season, which calls to mind His first coming, let us also remember to prepare ourselves for His second coming.

Question to ponder: How does His second coming add meaning to Christ's first coming?

....

....

....

....

DECEMBER 2 ══ *Looking Unto Jesus*

When you pass through the waters, I will be with you;
and through the rivers, they shall not overflow you.
Isaiah 43:2

In Matthew 14, the disciples were in the boat on the Sea of Galilee, and they saw Jesus walking on water. They were terrified. They thought they had seen a spirit and they cried aloud. Jesus said, "Be of good cheer; it is I; be not afraid." Impetuous Peter said, "Lord, if it be thou, bid me come unto thee on the water."

And Jesus said, "Come."

Peter slipped first one foot and then the other out of the boat and found that he was walking on the surface of the waves. His eyes were full on the eyes of Jesus. Step after step he took on top of the water. Suddenly, a blast of wind stirred the waves into a frenzy. Looking down at the waves and the water that threatened to swallow him up, Peter began to sink. He cried out in terror, "Lord, save me."

Instantly, Jesus reached out His hand and set Peter again on the surface of the water saying, "O thou of little faith, wherefore didst thou doubt?" (Matthew 14:31).

As long as Peter kept his eyes on Christ, he walked above the problems created by the waves and the water beneath. As soon as he took his eyes off of Jesus and looked at the boisterous waves, he immediately began to sink.

Question to ponder: How can keeping our eyes on Jesus affect all our problems and troubles?

....

....

....

....

....

Noble Things

*Finally, brethren, whatever things are true, whatever
things are noble, whatever things are just, whatever things
are pure, whatever things are lovely, whatever things are
of good report, if there is any virtue and if there is
anything praiseworthy—meditate on these things.*
Philippians 4:8

In Philippians 4:8, Paul tells us that we must focus our thoughts on
positive things. He tells us that human life is forwarded by thinking on
things which are noble.

One of the great tragedies now seen in modern times is that
through their separation from God, most in the media continually fill
our minds with the very antithesis of all of these things. What we see
on television and in most movies and novels today, is not that which is
lovely. We see that which is unjust, unfair, and, ungodly; that which is
unkind, untrue; that which is unlovely, crass, and ghastly; that which is
horrible and unclean and vile all set forth constantly before our minds
and poured into our brains through the gates of the eyes and ears *in the
name of realism.*

It is true that the gutter is real. It is equally true that the gutter is neither the only reality nor the highest reality. Life is ennobled by thinking on
things that are above. Set your thoughts on those things that are above, on
things that are lovely, and true, of good report and praise.

Life is made ignoble by fixing our minds on that which is crass and
unclean and impure. If we would know real mental health and happiness, it
is going to involve our thinking on the things that are above.

Question to ponder: How do we keep our minds focused as
much as possible on the things of God?

DECEMBER 4 ═══ *One in Being with the Father*

He is the image of the invisible God,
the firstborn over all creation.
Colossians 1:15

Having demanded that no images of God be made, God, at length, in obscurity, in the little village in Judea, brought forth One who, when He was grown, was revealed as the Son of God. Jesus is not made after the image of God. Jesus is not made *in* the image of God. The Bible says that Jesus Christ *is* the image of the invisible God.

Jesus Christ is the only babe that was ever born who was older than his mother when he was born.

This little baby was "God from God, Light from Light, true God from true God."

I talked to a man one time and asked him who Jesus was and he said, "Oh, He's the greatest man that ever lived."

I said, "Anything more?"

He said, "Not that I can think of."

I said, "Let me tell you this. He is the almighty eternal Creator of the galaxies; He is the everlasting omniscient God almighty."

Immediately his eyes half-filled with tears, and he said to me, "I've never heard that before in my life, but I always thought that is the way it ought to be."

Question to ponder: The divinity of Christ makes Him Savior. What does His humanity mean for us?

....

....

....

....

....

Born of a Virgin

*Then the angel said to her, "Do not be afraid, Mary,
for you have found favor with God. And behold, you
will conceive in your womb and bring forth a Son,
and shall call His name JESUS."*
Luke 1:30-32

The Bible tells us the miraculous birth of Jesus, of how He was born
of a virgin. There are many modern, liberal theologians who deny the reality
of the Virgin Birth. Does this theological debate matter?

We believe in the Virgin Birth of Christ because it is essential for the
atonement and the redemption of mankind. It's necessary because of the
sin of Adam, our first parent, which descended down through the whole
human race, corrupting all of mankind. And it's necessary since the atonement for sin had to be accomplished by a sacrifice that was pure and without corruption—one without guilt which did not partake of the sin of all of
men. And so someone separate from sin, someone pure and perfect, was
needed to offer an atoning sacrifice that could be accepted by God.

Jesus was both the Son of Man and the Son of God. He was the infinite God-man, born of a virgin.

Question to ponder: Do you think it matters that Jesus was
born of a virgin?

....

....

....

....

....

....

....

....

DECEMBER 6 ═══   *Born in Our Hearts*

Jesus answered, "Most assuredly, I say to you, unless one is born of water and the Spirit, he cannot enter the kingdom of God."
John 3:5

Jesus came to the Jewish people, as their long-awaited Messiah. He came to the world as the Savior of humankind. But it is Him coming into our individual hearts that makes all the difference. To be included into those He came to save we have to receive Him and entrust our lives to Him as we humbly open our heart to Him, whether it is the first time or something we have done repeatedly. This Christmas season, let us surrender our lives anew to the Babe of Bethlehem.

Bethlehem is Hebrew for "House of Bread." How appropriate that Jesus, the Bread of Life who came from heaven, was born in the House of Bread.

We see masses of people crowding into the malls and even our churches this season, and for those who have not received Him into their hearts, it is as if He did not come at all. It is a tragedy that so many people celebrate Christmas without Christ Himself.

I am reminded again of a little couplet which reflects this thought so eloquently and so unforgettably:

Though Christ a thousand times in Bethlehem be born,
If He be not born in thee, thy soul is still forlorn.

Question to ponder: What does it mean to open our hearts to Jesus?

....

....

....

....

....

No One Like Jesus

And the angel answered and said to her, "The Holy
Spirit will come upon you, and the power of the Highest
will overshadow you; therefore, also, that Holy One
who is to be born will be called the Son of God."
Luke 1:35

The Virgin Birth is clearly taught repeatedly throughout the Old Testament *and* the New Testament in many different kinds of ways. Once there was a newly minted young minister in a rural area. And there was a man in the neighborhood, an old farmer who didn't attend church. One Christmas season he invited him to come. And the man agreed. The sermon was on the Virgin Birth.

As they were discussing the sermon afterwards, the minister asked the farmer what he thought. (I have learned the hard way that is a big mistake for a pastor to make.) The farmer hemmed and hawed. Finally he said, "Well, now, my boy," he said, "Let me ask you a question. If you heard about a girl today that got herself pregnant and then claimed that it was a virgin birth, would you believe that?"

Another silence. And the young man said, "Well, if he grew up to live a life like Jesus and to die and rise from the dead, why yes, I would."

Question to ponder: How was Christ different than anybody else?

DECEMBER 8 ≡

Godly Friends

*Ointment and perfume delight the heart, and the sweetness
of a man's friend gives delight by hearty counsel.*
Proverbs 27:9

I have been blessed in my life by the counsel of godly friends. Perhaps there is nothing more satisfying in this world than the close companionship of fellow Christians. God did not mean for us to walk the "straight and nar-row" by ourselves. Some have been blessed by a faithful and wise spouse. I can attest that this makes life rich and beautiful. It doubles the joy and halves our burdens.

If you are in need of godly friends, pray that God Himself will supply some. He who supplies all our needs will also honor this prayer.

I remember once I gave a sermon, and I wasn't particularly happy with it. I walked out the door, and the first person I met said, with a smile on her face, "That was magnificent." Boy, did that lift a load off my back. There are many people who carrying a load that, as a "good-finder" (as opposed to fault-finder), you could uplift. If you do, they will be your friends.

Question to ponder: Who are your most godly friends?

....

....

....

....

....

....

....

....

Star Gazers

*Let now the astrologers, the stargazers, and the
monthly prognosticators stand up and save you
from what shall come upon you. Behold, they
shall be as stubble, the fire shall burn them....*
Isaiah 47:13-14

The Bible very strongly condemns astrology, as we see in Isaiah 47.
While initially God gave us heavenly signs to tell the story of Christ, unbelievers have perverted His message and have taken these heavenly signs to
be deities that have an influence on our lives.

Today this is hidden from view and it is supposedly the stars themselves that are exerting some influence upon our lives. This is utterly
absurd. Some try to give credence to this claim by saying that the moon
influences the tides, and that it influences people's emotions, which is true.
But the moon is 250,000 miles, or slightly less, away from the earth; whereas, stars are six thousand light-years and more away from the earth. (A
light year is 3 ½ trillion miles. That is approximately 19½ quadrillion miles
away—a figure so vast it is beyond our comprehension.) The stars do not
exert any influence upon us and the deities that they supposedly represent
are but the figments of people's imaginations.

We should not worship the stars but the One who made the stars.

Question to ponder: Why do you think people are not
content to seek guidance in God's Word, but instead
in the stars, in tarot cards, in tea leaves, and the like?

....

....

....

....

DECEMBER 10 ═══

Hope is Born

For my eyes have seen Your salvation which You have prepared before the face of all peoples, a light to bring revelation to the Gentiles, and the glory of Your people Israel.
Luke 2:30-32

When religious hope dies, all real hope dies with it.

Without God, the aspirations, strivings, and wishes of countless hearts are weighed down by defeats and sorrows; they are broken by hopes never materialized and saddened by relationships gone sour.

We live in a time of rampant unbelief and godlessness. It is, therefore, a time of hopelessness very much like the time in which Paul wrote these words: "having no hope, and without God in the world" (Ephesians 2:12)—an age without hope.

Into such a world came Christ, the hope of the nations.

What a glorious thought to know that all of the hopes of the world were found in that cradle in Bethlehem. For centuries men had hoped that at last a deliverer would come—a redeemer would come to set man free, to deliver him from the shackles that bound him, to open the portal of everlasting life, to deliver him from the blackness of oblivion in the tomb. This hope was ushered into this world on Christmas morning, and it has spread all over the world ever since.

Question to ponder: What hopes and dreams has Christ fulfilled for you?

Angels

For He shall give His angels charge
over you, to keep you in all your ways.
Psalm 91:11

God sends his angels to minister to and to watch over His elect, even those who are about to come to conversion, lest they should perish before they are saved.

Corrie ten Boom, that brave Dutch lady who protected so many Jews during World War II, tells how, during a rebellion in the Congo, there was a school where 200 children of missionaries were being taught. Hundreds of rebel soldiers were closing in on that school. Word had come to those at the school that the soldiers were going to take the school and kill everyone inside. Students and staff prayed that God would intercede.

Finally, they saw the soldiers inching out of the jungle. There was only a small wall around the encampment and a couple of soldiers protecting it. The rebels came closer and closer. Suddenly they leaped up and fled back into the jungle. They came back the second day and did the same thing again, and again on the third, the exact same thing occurred.

One of the rebels was wounded and brought into the compound for treatment. As the doctor was treating him, he asked why they did not take the school as they had planned. He said, "We could not do it. We saw hundreds of soldiers in white uniforms and became scared." In Africa, solders never wear white uniforms.

Question to ponder: Can you think of any potential encounter you might have had with an angel?

....

....

....

....

DECEMBER 12 *Chariots of Fire*

*And Elisha prayed, and said, "LORD, I pray, open his
eyes that he may see." Then the LORD opened the eyes of
the young man, and he saw. And behold, the mountain
was full of horses and chariots of fire all around Elisha.*
2 Kings 6:17

If we had supernatural vision, we would see all around us God's
angels protecting us. That was certainly the case in biblical history. For
example, when enemy forces came against Elisha in 2 Kings 6, the prophet
could see God's heavenly army protecting him. But Elisha's servant couldn't
see that until Elisha prayed for his eyes to be opened.

Spiritual vision is something that is vitally important, as the servant
of Elisha discovered. Theologian Clarence Maclaren tells us what we can
learn from this text about God's angels (His messengers): (1) they were ever
near; (2) they were most near when needed most; and (3) they come in the
form most needed. Specifically, they are warriors when we are ringed about
by foes. They are counselors when we are perplexed. They are comforters
when we mourn. Their shapes are as varied as our needs, and ever corre-
spond to the "present distress."

Speaking of angels, God said, "Are they not all ministering spirits, sent
forth to minister for them who shall be heirs of salvation?" (Hebrews 1:14).
We should be thankful for God's angels, but we should never worship them,
nor talk directly to them. They are God's servants, not ours.

Question to ponder: What role do angels play in the
salvation story?

Right from Wrong

≡ DECEMBER **13**

Woe to those who call evil good, and good evil;
who put darkness for light, and light for darkness;
who put bitter for sweet, and sweet for bitter!
Isaiah 5:20

Many times, we find that our modern society has things exactly backwards. They do what Isaiah decried—they call evil good, and they call good evil.

Let me indulge in a bit of sarcasm to illustrate this phenomenon. We have a problem today in sexual matters. The problem is that we have so many of you who are "homophobes." Ah, that is the problem. No doubt homophobes have caused the plague of AIDS. Our problem is not perversion. Our problem is not homosexuality. Our problem is you, the homophobes.

"Art thou he that troubleth Israel?" asked the wicked King Ahab of the righteous Elijah. But Elijah will have none of this, and armed with the power of God, he says, "I have not troubled Israel; but thou, and thy father's house, in that ye have forsaken the commandments of the Lord" (I Kings 18:18).

We have people who won't take responsibility for their sins, but, instead, redefine illicit behavior so that they're no longer sinning. For example, there was a politician who was pulled over for a DUI. He said that it wasn't his fault: "I was overserved."

Despite the attempts of Hollywood or a sinful world to redefine good and evil, God's Word stands firm. As President Lincoln once said when he received a copy of the Bible. "But for it, we could not know right from wrong."

Question to ponder: Can you think of a few examples where someone has called evil good and good evil?

⑊ . . . .

. . . .

. . . .

DECEMBER 14 — *Valley of Indecision*

...Choose for yourself this day whom you will serve...
Joshua 24:15

One of the great problems in the Church today is that people just can't make up their minds. One minute they determine they are going to serve God and Christ. The next minute they are afraid they are going to miss out on some goodies of this world. They don't want to become too religious, and so they have just enough religion to make themselves miserable, but certainly not enough to get them into heaven. However, their indecisiveness will one day be solved for them at the final Judgment, when heart and mind and soul and body will be cast into hell. No more indecision then.

The present problem with indecision is that it causes people to do nothing. That is the great problem of the Church. That was the great problem of Joshua's day. That is why so little progress is made in the kingdom—why it is so difficult to get people to volunteer to serve.

Let us decide to follow the Lord wholeheartedly and to serve Him all the days of our lives.

Question to ponder: Can you truly say, "As for me and my house we will serve the Lord"?

The Need to Belong

*The body is a unit, though it is made up of
many parts; and though all its parts are many,
they form one body. So it is with Christ.*
1 Corinthians 12:12 (NIV)

At a national convention, sociologists came to a conclusion that I think you will find fascinating. They said most of the problems, the troubles, the anxieties and the turmoil that plague our society today are due to...to what? Now, this is not an assembly of Christians; these are secular sociologists meeting in national convention, and they said most of the turmoil, troubles, anxieties and problems that plague our society are due to.... I have a sneaking suspicion that few would guess what they said. But here it is. These problems are due to...*a lack of communion.*

They didn't say "communication," because surely we have an abundance of that.

Communication is the transfer of ideas and facts, but communion is something much deeper. It is a mutual sharing of values, emotions, and the deepest purposes of our lives. And this is what we have too little of in our society.

The lack of communion found in the home, in the school, in society, in the Church, is what is causing many people to have such aberrant and deviant behavior resulting in so many of today's problems.

We have a need to belong. The Body of Christ, the Church, helps meet this deep-seated need.

Question to ponder: Where do you belong?

The Incarnation

*"Behold, the virgin shall be with child, and bear
a Son, and they shall call His name Immanuel,"
which is translated, "God with us."*
Matthew 1:23

At Christmastime we celebrate the fact that the infinite, incomprehensible, ineffable God descended to dwell among us in human flesh—a fact so astonishing that there is no need for chipmunks or reindeer, with or without red noses.

Christmas is an incredible event. The almighty Creator of the universe with its hundreds of billions of galaxies, this glorious One has visited this planet. This small planet has been visited by the almighty God. Even more astonishing than that is the fact that this God has come for the purpose of dying for creatures such as ourselves.

The miracle of Christmas is the incarnation. According to C. S. Lewis, this supernatural act of God becoming a human being is the Grand miracle. Upon this miracle all the others stand or fall. When someone denies the virgin birth and incarnation, they deny the foundation of Christianity and the joy of the season.

Christmas is still the time for miracles.

Question to ponder: Think of how the natural and the supernatural meet in Christmas. How has it touched your life?

....

....

....

....

....

....

The Magic of Christmas === DECEMBER 17

*Sing, O heavens! Be joyful, O earth! And break out
in singing, O mountains! For the LORD has comforted
His people, and will have mercy on His afflicted.*
Isaiah 49:13

Tragically, so many today miss the real meaning of Christmas. A
little boy attended Sunday School infrequently and on Christmas, when
the teacher showed him a picture of the manger scene, the little boy said,
"What's a camel doing there? Don't they know that camels don't have anything to do with Christmas? Santa Claus uses reindeers." Sadly, many Americans, like that boy, don't even know whose birthday Christmas celebrates.

Behind all of the frenetic rushing about and the man-made glitter
of this season, I believe there is something strangely poignant, tender and
touching about Christmastime. Perhaps it is felt in the music, in carols
such as "Silent Night Holy Night," "Joy to the World," "I Heard the Bells on
Christmas Day," and "O Holy Night." There is something about the season
that seems to just reach out and tug at the human heart.

What is it that we sense? Some deep and ancient joy calls to us from
heaven above, our ultimate true home. In Christmas, God is reaching out
with His mercy for us afflicted humans. He is showing us a little glimpse
of heaven. Earth and heaven are a little closer at Christmas than any other
time of the year.

Question to ponder: Why do we long to be home for
Christmas? What is this intense longing that we feel?

....
....
....
....
....

DECEMBER 18 — *The Music of Christmas*

Glory to God in the highest.
Luke 2:14

In praise and honor of His Son, God has reserved some of the most beautiful music on earth for the celebration of Christmas. Music, this heavenly language, has been lent to us express what words can not. It has enriched our hearts when no words would do.

I recall many years ago, I went to a Christmas musical program that was being held at the high school I attended. Songs of Christmas were being sung and I recall that I was the only one seated in the balcony. Although I did not know Christ personally, there was something about the music that seemed to reach out and wrap its fingers around my heart and pull. There was a strange sort of mysterious wonder about it. I remember sitting there with tears streaming down my face. I didn't know why. There is something about Christmas.

Why not take time this Christmas season to go to a concert—Handel's *Messiah* if possible—and let the music minister to your soul?

Question to ponder: What piece of Christmas music is especially meaningful to you?

....

....

....

....

....

....

....

....

Faith and Fear

*Fear not, for I am with you; be not dismayed, for I am
your God. I will strengthen you, yes, I will help you,
I will uphold you with My righteous right hand.*
Isaiah 41:10

In *Julius Caesar,* Shakespeare puts these famous words into the mouth of Caesar as he is talking to his wife, Calpurnia: "Cowards die many times before their deaths; the valiant never taste of death but once."

It would seem that our land is filled with many who are not valiant, many who are tasting the fear of death, which for most in our secular society is the fear of the ultimate loss of all things. When faith in God and in Christ disappears, that faith is replaced not with a vacuum, but with fear. People's hearts, generally, are filled either with faith or with fear.

The deepest fears of men are these: is my life to end in a pile of ashes and a skull? Am I to occupy naught but six feet of space beneath the ground? Is there no meaning to my existence? Is there no one who really loves me or cares for me? What about my loved ones whom I have lost? Will I meet them again?

These are the deepest fears and cares of human beings throughout the years and they are met in Christ for those who believe.

Question to ponder: How does Christ Jesus conquer our fears?

DECEMBER 20 — *A Love for the Lost*

*For I have not shunned to declare to
you the whole counsel of God.*
Acts 20:27

I remember talking to ministers, older and supposedly much wiser than I. I particularly recall one who was the editor of one of the country's leading Christian magazines. I said to him, "How can we possibly do anything else? There are men and women dying and going off into everlasting condemnation and perdition without Christ. We must get the message to them."

He looked at me as if I had come from Mars and said, "You will come to understand."

What I came to understand was that he had lost his first love. Ah, dear friend, how is it with your heart? Is that first love still there? Do you remember that time when you were at church every time the doors opened? Was there a time when you spent more time in His Word? I can remember when it was nothing to me to memorize a chapter of Scripture every day. "A verse a week? Isn't he asking too much of us?"

May God open our eyes to see the precarious state of the lost. May He grant us a greater love and concern for them.

Question to ponder: Do you have a passion to win the lost? If not, could you ask God to give you one?

....

....

....

....

....

....

....

The Greatest Sermon in History — DECEMBER 21

And seeing the multitudes, He went up on a mountain,
and when He was seated His disciples came to Him.
Then He opened His mouth and taught them.
Matthew 5:1-2

The Sermon on the Mount is incontestably the greatest sermon ever preached. We can, of course, find the Sermon on the Mount in Matthew chapters 5-7.

Listen to what psychiatrist J. T. Fisher and co-author L. S. Hawley, say about the Sermon on the Mount in their book, *A Few Buttons Missing*:

> If you were to take the sum total of all authoritative articles ever written by the most qualified of psychologists and psychiatrists on the subject of mental hygiene—if you were to combine them and refine them and cleave out the excess verbiage—if you were to take the whole of the meat and none of the parsley, and if you were to have these unadulterated bits of pure scientific knowledge concisely expressed by the most capable of living poets, you would have an awkward and incomplete summation of the Sermon on the Mount. And it would suffer immeasurably through comparison. For nearly two thousand years, the Christian world has been holding in its hands the complete answer to its restless and fruitless yearnings. Here...rests the blueprints for successful human life with optimum mental health and contentment.

The Sermon on the Mount gives us great wisdom concerning how to live a life that is pleasing to our heavenly father. It gives us the Lord's prayer. Above all, like the law of God, it shows us our need for the Savior's redemption.

Question to ponder: Can you think of some of your favorite teachings in the Sermon on the Mount?

....

....

....

....

DECEMBER 22 ══ *One Little Poem*

*For there is born to you this day in the city
of David a Savior, who is Christ the Lord.*
Luke 2:11

Though his sermons were masterpieces, today they gather dust, moldering on the shelves of antiquarians like myself. Yet he still lives and has a revival every year about Christmastime. He is not known for the erudition of his sermons, for the eloquence of his speaking, but rather for the simplicity of one little poem he wrote.

I am talking about the Reverend Phillips Brooks, author of "O Little Town of Bethlehem." On Christmas Eve, in the year 1865, he arrived at the little town of Bethlehem and was struck by the sublimity, the beauty, the simplicity, the quietness, the darkness of that little town in whose streets there shone the Light of the World. Of that town and of that time, he wrote, "The hopes and fears of all the years are met in thee tonight"—that night, when the Light of the World came into the darkness of Bethlehem.

As long as the Church shall last, Phillips Brooks and his little poem will be remembered. And as "God imparts to human hearts the blessings of His heaven," so this Christmas hymn captures the stillness, the wonder, and the awe of Christmas. It happens every year it is sung: "where meek hearts will receive him still, the dear Christ enters in."

Question to ponder: Will you take the time to quietly read through the lyrics of this and other great Christmas carols?

╫ ....

....

....

....

....

God With Man

I dwell in the high and holy place, with him
who has a contrite and humble spirit....
Isaiah 57:15

"The Word was made flesh" (John 1:14). The Greek word used here means He "tabernacled" among us, even as the tabernacle was among the Jews. God dwelt in the visible presence of the Shekinah Glory between the cherubim over the Mercy Seat. In Jesus Christ, God has come and we beheld His glory—the glory as of the only begotten of the Father.

John says, "In the beginning was the Word, and the Word was with God, and the Word was God" (John 1:1). And that Word which was God, became flesh. "All things were made by him, and without him was not anything made that was made" (John 1:3). He was the Great Creator.

Jesus Christ, the Eternal Word of God, stepped out one morning onto the balcony of eternity and dipped His fingers in a chalice of light and sprinkled the vast blackness of space with scintillating, coruscating stars. He swirled with His finger and set into motion the spinning, swirling nebulae that now glows so gloriously in the night sky.

J. B. Phillips once described earth in a special way—not as "the green planet" or "the blue planet," but as "the visited planet"—that planet which had received special visitation from the Almighty. He, the Almighty, is pleased to dwell with the lowly.

Question to ponder: Can you wrap your mind around this concept: God wants to be with you?

DECEMBER 24 — *Christmas According to Mary*

Then Mary said, "Behold the maidservant of the Lord!
Let it be to me according to your word."
Luke 1:38

There are many things about Mary that I think we could well emulate. The first is her humility. She was a "lowly handmaiden of the Lord," as she described herself. The Scripture says, "And in the sixth month [of the conception of Elisabeth, her relative] the angel Gabriel was sent from God unto a city of Galilee, named Nazareth, to a virgin espoused to a man whose name was Joseph...the virgin's name was Mary. And the angel came in unto her, and said, Hail, thou that art highly favoured, the Lord is with thee: blessed art thou among women" (Luke 1:26-28).

When Mary heard this, what did she say? Did she say, "Well at last I'm getting the recognition I deserve"? No, not at all. Rather, the Scripture says "She was troubled at his saying, and cast in her mind what manner of salutation this should be" (v. 29) [That thou art highly favored and blessed among women (v. 28)]. She described herself as simply the handmaiden of the Lord; that she was of lowly estate, and could not possibly imagine what the angel intended by that saying.

God chose Mary as a humble servant through whom the world would be blessed, by her Son. We should imitate Mary, in the same way we should imitate Peter, Paul, or John.

Question to ponder: If you were in Mary's shoes, how do you think you would have reacted to the angel's news of the virgin birth?

....

....

....

....

The Wondrous Gift ═══ DECEMBER 25

For God so loved the world that He gave His only begotten Son, that whoever believes in Him should not perish but have everlasting life.
John 3:16

Christmas is all about giving. God gives. Therefore, we give.

For years spiritual analysts have lamented the secularization and commercialization of Christmas, but I think there is something perhaps even worse: the trivialization of Christmas. Stop to think about it. Santa Claus, Rudolph the red nosed reindeer, a chattering Christmas chipmunk—that trio is like "Three Blind Mice" compared to the *Hallelujah Chorus.*

Or, when asked the meaning of Christmas, a six-year-old child replied: "Santa Claus' birthday." I think this is symbolic of the spiritual blindness of the world as it gropes in its darkness for some meaning to Christmas.

The good news is that at Christmas, we are reminded annually of God's indescribable gift in Christ. The wondrous gift is given, God's Son for our salvationthat is what Christmas is about. The most important gift will not be found under any tree on Christmas morning; rather, it was purchased on a tree outside a city wall long ago.

At Christmas, "God imparts to human hearts the blessings of His heaven." This Christmas, let God rain down His blessings on you and yours. Let us receive Him who has come to make all things well.

Question to ponder: As you enjoy all the trimmings of Christmas, what do you consider the greatest blessing?

⋔ ....

....

....

....

....

DECEMBER 26 ≡   *Farsighted Vision*

> *By faith [Moses] left Egypt, not fearing the king's anger;*
> *he persevered because he saw him who is invisible.*
> Hebrews 11:27 (NIV)

The Bible gives us examples of both shortsightedness and farsighted vision. Certainly it was shortsighted for Eve and Adam to contemplate only the immediate delight and satisfaction that would come from eating the forbidden fruit. They didn't take the long look at the consequences that would come.

Abraham, on the other hand, was a man of great vision. We are told that he sought a city whose builder and maker was God, though he passed through many of the cities of this world. He was looking for something that had foundations, something permanent, something that would last—a city whose builder and maker was God.

Moses is a prime example of a man with farsighted vision. We are told that he endured, seeing Him who is invisible. That is what we are called upon to do. We are not to look merely upon the things that are seen, things that are temporal, but upon the things that are unseen and eternal.

Yet most people spend more time planning for a two-week vacation than for where they are going to spend eternity. How many people have told me that they are ready to die, because they have made out their will and they have bought a plot. That is not adequate preparation. Let us look beyond this world and see things from an eternal perspective.

Question to ponder: How is your present affected by the eternal?

⸕ ....

....

....

....

....

The Peace of God === DECEMBER 27

*And let the peace of God rule in your hearts, to which
also you were called in one body; and be thankful.*
Colossians 3:15

A young lady told me that all her life at Christmas time she always
felt very sad, because no matter whether she was in the church or out, she
always felt she was standing outside the candy store looking through the
window. Now that she knows Christ, however, she said, she is on the inside,
and her heart is filled with joy.

Joy is to be shared, and we need to keep busy helping others, praying for others, witnessing to others, and sharing our joy. Joy is increased by
sharing. The more we give to other people as we encourage and uplift them,
the more our joy is increased. The result: "The peace of God, which passeth
all understanding, shall keep your hearts and minds through Christ Jesus"
(Philippians 4:7). It is true joy which leads to peace, and the two are closely
linked to each other.

The term used here for "keep" is an interesting one. It is a military
term. Paul brings the idea of peacefulness, serenity, into close accompani-
ment to a military term. The word means "to garrison, to set up as a for-
tress, to guard with armed soldiers." The peace of God will garrison our
hearts from all of the buffetings of this life, if we will do these things.

Question to ponder: How does the peace of God
rule in the human heart?

DECEMBER 28

Numb to the Cold

...Continue in the faith, grounded and steadfast, and
are not moved away from the hope of the gospel...
Colossians 1:23

In his book *To Light a Fire*, Jack London describes a man walking through the freezing, frigid cold of Alaska, where the temperature had dropped down to 40 degrees below zero. The biting cold was searing his lungs and throat, freezing his breath and his hands and feet. He was utterly exhausted. He felt, at length, that if only he could sit down for a few minutes and regain his strength, perhaps he could go on and make it to his home.

Having sat down and leaned back against the snow, he began to feel the burning pain assuage, until he felt a warmth that surged through his body. He began to relax. He thought, "If I could just lean my head against the bank of snow and perhaps catch a few minutes sleep, then I would be refreshed and able to go on." And so he closed his eyelids and soon slept the sleep of death.

So Satan would have us to be comfortable in our apostasy. The one thing he doesn't want us to do is come back to God and rejoice in His presence and His love. Sometimes we need to be startled awake and realize that we have slidden back. We need to realize we are far from that comfortable relationship of joy and intimacy that once we knew—that comfort that only Christ can give—and be drawn back to Him.

Question to ponder: How can you watch your walk so that you draw closer to the Lord and not away from Him?

Spectator Christians or Active Christians? — DECEMBER 29

For whoever gives you a cup of water to drink in
My name, because you belong to Christ, assuredly,
I say to you, he will by no means lose his reward.
Mark 9:41

Christianity is not a spectator sport. Christ does not call us to be "spectator Christians." There are some people in our churches, however, who, to my knowledge, have never done any work at all. They have merely seen themselves as spectators. They come to watch on Sunday morning, and that is the extent of what they do. They never put their shoulder to the wheel. They never dirty their hands. They never exert themselves in any work.

But Christ says in His letter to the church in Thyatria in Revelation 2:19, "I know thy works, and charity, and service, and faith, and thy patience, and thy works." Christ had not forgotten their good works.

I am so glad that many Christians are always working and serving the Lord with love and patience. Christ calls us to get into the arena and glorify Him by our good works. Any deed done in Jesus' name is precious to Him and has its reward, whether in this life or the next.

Question to ponder: Saved, not by works, but saved unto good works—how do these truths connect?

DECEMBER 30 — The Reality of Hell

*And if your eye causes you to sin, pluck it out and cast it
from you. It is better for you to enter into life with one eye,
rather than having two eyes, to be cast into hell fire.*
Matthew 18:9

Jesus took hell very seriously. He spoke about it as a real place to
avoid at all costs.

The most awful thing imaginable would be to die and go into eternity
without Christ; to stand before the judgment bar of Almighty God, who
knows your every thought and word and deed, and to have all of your sins
brought out before the universe and be justly condemned unto eternal perdition and cast out into a lake of fire.

There are some people who have tried every conceivable way to deny
the reality of impending judgment for unrepentant sinners. This ranges from
denying that there is a God who could possibly punish them; to denying that
there is a Hell where they could be punished; to denying that a loving God
would ever send anyone there (even such a reprobate as themselves); to claim-
ing that God must, at least, give everyone the opportunity to hear the Gospel.

Not that this would help them, because they have been doing what
people constantly try to do, which is to justify themselves by condemning
God and end up proving that God is unjust and unfair and unloving, and
they themselves must be, by comparison, pretty decent sort of folks.

Since Jesus took hell so seriously, so should we.

Question to ponder: Is there anything in your life that you
should get rid off, anything that hinders your Christian walk?

In God's Dwelling Place ━━ DECEMBER **31**

The Lord shall preserve your going out and your
coming in from this time forth, and even forevermore.
Psalm 121:8

As we come to the close of another year, we see that the Lord has been with us. He has watched over and protected us. Yes, there has been trouble and pain, but He has been with us every step of the way.

The Lord is the One who helps us through it all. As the psalmist said, "I will lift up my eyes to the hills—From whence comes my help? My help comes from the Lord, Who made heaven and earth" (Psalm 121:1-2).

In all the hurry and hustle and bustle of modern life, we need to give God time to heal us and cure us, to build us up and strengthen us in Him. We need to trust in Christ and find that place of quiet rest. As one poet put it:

Slow me down Lord.
Ease the pounding of my heart by the quieting of my mind.
Steady my hurried pace with a vision of the eternal reach of time.
Give me, amid the confusion of the day, the calmness of the everlasting hills.
Break the tensions of my nerves and muscles with the soothing music of the
   singing streams that live in my memory. . . .
Let me look upward to the towering oak and know that it grew great and
   strong because it grew slowly and well.

Question to ponder: How have you grown in the Lord this year?

A plan for Bible reading to take readers through the New Testament and Psalms twice a year, and through the rest of the Bible once each year.

January

1st	Genesis	1	Matthew	1	Ezra	1	Acts	1
2nd	Genesis	2	Matthew	2	Ezra	2	Acts	2
3rd	Genesis	3	Matthew	3	Ezra	3	Acts	3
4th	Genesis	4	Matthew	4	Ezra	4	Acts	4
5th	Genesis	5	Matthew	5	Ezra	5	Acts	5
6th	Genesis	6	Matthew	6	Ezra	6	Acts	6
7th	Genesis	7	Matthew	7	Ezra	7	Acts	7
8th	Genesis	8	Matthew	8	Ezra	8	Acts	8
9th	Genesis	9–10	Matthew	9	Ezra	9	Acts	9
10th	Genesis	11	Matthew	10	Ezra	10	Acts	10
11th	Genesis	12	Matthew	11	Nehemiah	1	Acts	11
12th	Genesis	13	Matthew	12	Nehemiah	2	Acts	12
13th	Genesis	14	Matthew	13	Nehemiah	3	Acts	13
14th	Genesis	15	Matthew	14	Nehemiah	4	Acts	14
15th	Genesis	16	Matthew	15	Nehemiah	5	Acts	15
16th	Genesis	17	Matthew	16	Nehemiah	6	Acts	16
17th	Genesis	18	Matthew	17	Nehemiah	7	Acts	17
18th	Genesis	19	Matthew	18	Nehemiah	8	Acts	18
19th	Genesis	20	Matthew	19	Nehemiah	9	Acts	19
20th	Genesis	21	Matthew	20	Nehemiah	10	Acts	20
21st	Genesis	22	Matthew	21	Nehemiah	11	Acts	21
22nd	Genesis	23	Matthew	22	Nehemiah	12	Acts	22
23rd	Genesis	24	Matthew	23	Nehemiah	13	Acts	23
24th	Genesis	25	Matthew	24	Esther	1	Acts	24
25th	Genesis	26	Matthew	25	Esther	2	Acts	25
26th	Genesis	27	Matthew	26	Esther	3	Acts	26
27th	Genesis	28	Matthew	27	Esther	4	Acts	27
28th	Genesis	29	Matthew	28	Esther	5	Acts	28
29th	Genesis	30	Mark	1	Esther	6	Romans	1
30th	Genesis	31	Mark	2	Esther	7	Romans	2
31st	Genesis	32	Mark	3	Esther	8	Romans	3

February

1st	Genesis	33	Mark	4	Esther	9–10	Romans	4
2nd	Genesis	34	Mark	5	Job	1	Romans	5
3rd	Genesis	35–36	Mark	6	Job	2	Romans	6
4th	Genesis	37	Mark	7	Job	3	Romans	7
5th	Genesis	38	Mark	8	Job	4	Romans	8
6th	Genesis	39	Mark	9	Job	5	Romans	9
7th	Genesis	40	Mark	10	Job	6	Romans	10
8th	Genesis	41	Mark	11	Job	7	Romans	11
9th	Genesis	42	Mark	12	Job	8	Romans	12
10th	Genesis	43	Mark	13	Job	9	Romans	13
11th	Genesis	44	Mark	14	Job	10	Romans	14
12th	Genesis	45	Mark	15	Job	11	Romans	15
13th	Genesis	46	Mark	16	Job	12	Romans	16
14th	Genesis	47	Luke	1:1–38	Job	13	1 Corinthians	1
15th	Genesis	48	Luke	1:39ff	Job	14	1 Corinthians	2
16th	Genesis	49	Luke	2	Job	15	1 Corinthians	3
17th	Genesis	50	Luke	3	Job	16–17	1 Corinthians	4
18th	Exodus	1	Luke	4	Job	18	1 Corinthians	5
19th	Exodus	2	Luke	5	Job	19	1 Corinthians	6
20th	Exodus	3	Luke	6	Job	20	1 Corinthians	7
21st	Exodus	4	Luke	7	Job	21	1 Corinthians	8
22nd	Exodus	5	Luke	8	Job	22	1 Corinthians	9
23rd	Exodus	6	Luke	9	Job	23	1 Corinthians	10
24th	Exodus	7	Luke	10	Job	24	1 Corinthians	11
25th	Exodus	8	Luke	11	Job	25–26	1 Corinthians	12
26th	Exodus	9	Luke	12	Job	27	1 Corinthians	13
27th	Exodus	10	Luke	13	Job	28	1 Corinthians	14
28th	Exodus	11–12:21	Luke	14	Job	29	1 Corinthians	15

March

1st	Exodus	12:22ff	Luke	15	Job	30	1 Corinthians	16
2nd	Exodus	13	Luke	16	Job	31	2 Corinthians	1
3rd	Exodus	14	Luke	17	Job	32	2 Corinthians	2
4th	Exodus	15	Luke	18	Job	33	2 Corinthians	3
5th	Exodus	16	Luke	19	Job	34	2 Corinthians	4
6th	Exodus	17	Luke	20	Job	35	2 Corinthians	5
7th	Exodus	18	Luke	21	Job	36	2 Corinthians	6
8th	Exodus	19	Luke	22	Job	37	2 Corinthians	7
9th	Exodus	20	Luke	23	Job	38	2 Corinthians	8
10th	Exodus	21	Luke	24	Job	39	2 Corinthians	9
11th	Exodus	22	John	1	Job	40	2 Corinthians	10
12th	Exodus	23	John	2	Job	41	2 Corinthians	11
13th	Exodus	24	John	3	Job	42	2 Corinthians	12
14th	Exodus	25	John	4	Proverbs	1	2 Corinthians	13
15th	Exodus	26	John	5	Proverbs	2	Galatians	1
16th	Exodus	27	John	6	Proverbs	3	Galatians	2
17th	Exodus	28	John	7	Proverbs	4	Galatians	3
18th	Exodus	29	John	8	Proverbs	5	Galatians	4
19th	Exodus	30	John	9	Proverbs	6	Galatians	5
20th	Exodus	31	John	10	Proverbs	7	Galatians	6
21st	Exodus	32	John	11	Proverbs	8	Ephesians	1
22nd	Exodus	33	John	12	Proverbs	9	Ephesians	2
23rd	Exodus	34	John	13	Proverbs	10	Ephesians	3
24th	Exodus	35	John	14	Proverbs	11	Ephesians	4
25th	Exodus	36	John	15	Proverbs	12	Ephesians	5
26th	Exodus	37	John	16	Proverbs	13	Ephesians	6
27th	Exodus	38	John	17	Proverbs	14	Philippians	1
28th	Exodus	39	John	18	Proverbs	15	Philippians	2
29th	Exodus	40	John	19	Proverbs	16	Philippians	3
30th	Leviticus	1	John	20	Proverbs	17	Philippians	4
31st	Leviticus	2–3	John	21	Proverbs	18	Colossians	1

April

1st	Leviticus	4	Psalms	1–2	Proverbs	19	Colossians	2
2nd	Leviticus	5	Psalms	3–4	Proverbs	20	Colossians	3
3rd	Leviticus	6	Psalms	5–6	Proverbs	21	Colossians	4
4th	Leviticus	7	Psalms	7–8	Proverbs	22	1 Thessalonians	1
5th	Leviticus	8	Psalms	9	Proverbs	23	1 Thessalonians	2
6th	Leviticus	9	Psalms	10	Proverbs	24	1 Thessalonians	3
7th	Leviticus	10	Psalms	11–12	Proverbs	25	1 Thessalonians	4
8th	Leviticus	11–12	Psalms	13–14	Proverbs	26	1 Thessalonians	5
9th	Leviticus	13	Psalms	15–16	Proverbs	27	2 Thessalonians	1
10th	Leviticus	14	Psalms	17	Proverbs	28	2 Thessalonians	2
11th	Leviticus	15	Psalms	18	Proverbs	29	2 Thessalonians	3
12th	Leviticus	16	Psalms	19	Proverbs	30	1 Timothy	1
13th	Leviticus	17	Psalms	20–21	Proverbs	31	1 Timothy	2
14th	Leviticus	18	Psalms	22	Ecclesiastes	1	1 Timothy	3
15th	Leviticus	19	Psalms	23–24	Ecclesiastes	2	1 Timothy	4
16th	Leviticus	20	Psalms	25	Ecclesiastes	3	1 Timothy	5
17th	Leviticus	21	Psalms	26–27	Ecclesiastes	4	1 Timothy	6
18th	Leviticus	22	Psalms	28–29	Ecclesiastes	5	2 Timothy	1
19th	Leviticus	23	Psalms	30	Ecclesiastes	6	2 Timothy	2
20th	Leviticus	24	Psalms	31	Ecclesiastes	7	2 Timothy	3
21st	Leviticus	25	Psalms	32	Ecclesiastes	8	2 Timothy	4
22nd	Leviticus	26	Psalms	33	Ecclesiastes	9	Titus	1
23rd	Leviticus	27	Psalms	34	Ecclesiastes	10	Titus	2
24th	Numbers	1	Psalms	35	Ecclesiastes	11	Titus	3
25th	Numbers	2	Psalms	36	Ecclesiastes	12	Philemon	1
26th	Numbers	3	Psalms	37	Song of Songs	1	Hebrews	1
27th	Numbers	4	Psalms	38	Song of Songs	2	Hebrews	2
28th	Numbers	5	Psalms	39	Song of Songs	3	Hebrews	3
29th	Numbers	6	Psalms	40–41	Song of Songs	4	Hebrews	4
30th	Numbers	7	Psalms	42–43	Song of Songs	5	Hebrews	5

May

1st	Numbers	8	Psalms	44	Song of Songs	6	Hebrews	6
2nd	Numbers	9	Psalms	45	Song of Songs	7	Hebrews	7
3rd	Numbers	10	Psalms	46–47	Song of Songs	8	Hebrews	8
4th	Numbers	11	Psalms	48	Isaiah	1	Hebrews	9
5th	Numbers	12–13	Psalms	49	Isaiah	2	Hebrews	10
6th	Numbers	14	Psalms	50	Isaiah	3–4	Hebrews	11
7th	Numbers	15	Psalms	51	Isaiah	5	Hebrews	12
8th	Numbers	16	Psalms	52–54	Isaiah	6	Hebrews	13
9th	Numbers	17–18	Psalms	55	Isaiah	7	James	1
10th	Numbers	19	Psalms	56–57	Isaiah	8–9:7	James	2
11th	Numbers	20	Psalms	58–59	Isaiah	9:8–10:4	James	3
12th	Numbers	21	Psalms	60–61	Isaiah	10:5ff	James	4
13th	Numbers	22	Psalms	62–63	Isaiah	11–12	James	5
14th	Numbers	23	Psalms	64–65	Isaiah	13	1 Peter	1
15th	Numbers	24	Psalms	66–67	Isaiah	14	1 Peter	2
16th	Numbers	25	Psalms	68	Isaiah	15	1 Peter	3
17th	Numbers	26	Psalms	69	Isaiah	16	1 Peter	4
18th	Numbers	27	Psalms	70–71	Isaiah	17–18	1 Peter	5
19th	Numbers	28	Psalms	72	Isaiah	19–20	2 Peter	1
20th	Numbers	29	Psalms	73	Isaiah	21	2 Peter	2
21st	Numbers	30	Psalms	74	Isaiah	22	2 Peter	3
22nd	Numbers	31	Psalms	75–76	Isaiah	23	1 John	1
23rd	Numbers	32	Psalms	77	Isaiah	24	1 John	2
24th	Numbers	33	Psalms	78:1–37	Isaiah	25	1 John	3
25th	Numbers	34	Psalms	78:38ff	Isaiah	26	1 John	4
26th	Numbers	35	Psalms	79	Isaiah	27	1 John	5
27th	Numbers	36	Psalms	80	Isaiah	28	2 John	1
28th	Deuteronomy	1	Psalms	81–82	Isaiah	29	3 John	1
29th	Deuteronomy	2	Psalms	83–84	Isaiah	30	Jude	1
30th	Deuteronomy	3	Psalms	85	Isaiah	31	Revelation	1
31st	Deuteronomy	4	Psalms	86–87	Isaiah	32	Revelation	2

June

1st	Deuteronomy	5	Psalms	88	Isaiah	33	Revelation	3
2nd	Deuteronomy	6	Psalms	89	Isaiah	34	Revelation	4
3rd	Deuteronomy	7	Psalms	90	Isaiah	35	Revelation	5
4th	Deuteronomy	8	Psalms	91	Isaiah	36	Revelation	6
5th	Deuteronomy	9	Psalms	92–93	Isaiah	37	Revelation	7
6th	Deuteronomy	10	Psalms	94	Isaiah	38	Revelation	8
7th	Deuteronomy	11	Psalms	95–96	Isaiah	39	Revelation	9
8th	Deuteronomy	12	Psalms	97–98	Isaiah	40	Revelation	10
9th	Deuteronomy	13–14	Psalms	99–101	Isaiah	41	Revelation	11
10th	Deuteronomy	15	Psalms	102	Isaiah	42	Revelation	12
11th	Deuteronomy	16	Psalms	103	Isaiah	43	Revelation	13
12th	Deuteronomy	17	Psalms	104	Isaiah	44	Revelation	14
13th	Deuteronomy	18	Psalms	105	Isaiah	45	Revelation	15
14th	Deuteronomy	19	Psalms	106	Isaiah	46	Revelation	16
15th	Deuteronomy	20	Psalms	107	Isaiah	47	Revelation	17
16th	Deuteronomy	21	Psalms	108–109	Isaiah	48	Revelation	18
17th	Deuteronomy	22	Psalms	110–111	Isaiah	49	Revelation	19
18th	Deuteronomy	23	Psalms	112–113	Isaiah	50	Revelation	20
19th	Deuteronomy	24	Psalms	114–115	Isaiah	51	Revelation	21
20th	Deuteronomy	25	Psalms	116	Isaiah	52	Revelation	22
21st	Deuteronomy	26	Psalms	117–118	Isaiah	53	Matthew	1
22nd	Deuteronomy	27–28:19	Psalms	119:1–24	Isaiah	54	Matthew	2
23rd	Deuteronomy	28:20ff	Psalms	119:25–48	Isaiah	55	Matthew	3
24th	Deuteronomy	29	Psalms	119:49–72	Isaiah	56	Matthew	4
25th	Deuteronomy	30	Psalms	119:73–96	Isaiah	57	Matthew	5
26th	Deuteronomy	31	Psalms	119:97–120	Isaiah	58	Matthew	6
27th	Deuteronomy	32	Psalms	119:121–144	Isaiah	59	Matthew	7
28th	Deuteronomy	33–34	Psalms	119:145–176	Isaiah	60	Matthew	8
29th	Joshua	1	Psalms	120–122	Isaiah	61	Matthew	9
30th	Joshua	2	Psalms	123–125	Isaiah	62	Matthew	10

July

1st	Joshua	3	Psalms	126–128	Isaiah	63	Matthew	11
2nd	Joshua	4	Psalms	129–131	Isaiah	64	Matthew	12
3rd	Joshua	5–6:5	Psalms	132–134	Isaiah	65	Matthew	13
4th	Joshua	6:6ff	Psalms	135–136	Isaiah	66	Matthew	14
5th	Joshua	7	Psalms	137–138	Jeremiah	1	Matthew	15
6th	Joshua	8	Psalms	139	Jeremiah	2	Matthew	16
7th	Joshua	9	Psalms	140–141	Jeremiah	3	Matthew	17
8th	Joshua	10	Psalms	142–143	Jeremiah	4	Matthew	18
9th	Joshua	11	Psalms	144	Jeremiah	5	Matthew	19
10th	Joshua	12–13	Psalms	145	Jeremiah	6	Matthew	20
11th	Joshua	14–15	Psalms	146–147	Jeremiah	7	Matthew	21
12th	Joshua	16–17	Psalms	148	Jeremiah	8	Matthew	22
13th	Joshua	18–19	Psalms	149–150	Jeremiah	9	Matthew	23
14th	Joshua	20–21	Acts	1	Jeremiah	10	Matthew	24
15th	Joshua	22	Acts	2	Jeremiah	11	Matthew	25
16th	Joshua	23	Acts	3	Jeremiah	12	Matthew	26
17th	Joshua	24	Acts	4	Jeremiah	13	Matthew	27
18th	Judges	1	Acts	5	Jeremiah	14	Matthew	28
19th	Judges	2	Acts	6	Jeremiah	15	Mark	1
20th	Judges	3	Acts	7	Jeremiah	16	Mark	2
21st	Judges	4	Acts	8	Jeremiah	17	Mark	3
22nd	Judges	5	Acts	9	Jeremiah	18	Mark	4
23rd	Judges	6	Acts	10	Jeremiah	19	Mark	5
24th	Judges	7	Acts	11	Jeremiah	20	Mark	6
25th	Judges	8	Acts	12	Jeremiah	21	Mark	7
26th	Judges	9	Acts	13	Jeremiah	22	Mark	8
27th	Judges	10–11:11	Acts	14	Jeremiah	23	Mark	9
28th	Judges	11:12ff	Acts	15	Jeremiah	24	Mark	10
29th	Judges	12	Acts	16	Jeremiah	25	Mark	11
30th	Judges	13	Acts	17	Jeremiah	26	Mark	12
31st	Judges	14	Acts	18	Jeremiah	27	Mark	13

August

1st	Judges	15	Acts	19	Jeremiah	28	Mark	14
2nd	Judges	16	Acts	20	Jeremiah	29	Mark	15
3rd	Judges	17	Acts	21	Jeremiah	30–31	Mark	16
4th	Judges	18	Acts	22	Jeremiah	32	Psalms	1–2
5th	Judges	19	Acts	23	Jeremiah	33	Psalms	3–4
6th	Judges	20	Acts	24	Jeremiah	34	Psalms	5–6
7th	Judges	21	Acts	25	Jeremiah	35	Psalms	7–8
8th	Ruth	1	Acts	26	Jeremiah	36 & 45	Psalms	9
9th	Ruth	2	Acts	27	Jeremiah	37	Psalms	10
10th	Ruth	3–4	Acts	28	Jeremiah	38	Psalms	11–12
11th	1 Samuel	1	Romans	1	Jeremiah	39	Psalms	13–14
12th	1 Samuel	2	Romans	2	Jeremiah	40	Psalms	15–16
13th	1 Samuel	3	Romans	3	Jeremiah	41	Psalms	17
14th	1 Samuel	4	Romans	4	Jeremiah	42	Psalms	18
15th	1 Samuel	5–6	Romans	5	Jeremiah	43	Psalms	19
16th	1 Samuel	7–8	Romans	6	Jeremiah	44	Psalms	20–21
17th	1 Samuel	9	Romans	7	Jeremiah	46	Psalms	22
18th	1 Samuel	10	Romans	8	Jeremiah	47	Psalms	23–24
19th	1 Samuel	11	Romans	9	Jeremiah	48	Psalms	25
20th	1 Samuel	12	Romans	10	Jeremiah	49	Psalms	26–27
21st	1 Samuel	13	Romans	11	Jeremiah	50	Psalms	28–29
22nd	1 Samuel	14	Romans	12	Jeremiah	51	Psalms	30
23rd	1 Samuel	15	Romans	13	Jeremiah	52	Psalms	31
24th	1 Samuel	16	Romans	14	Lamentations	1	Psalms	32
25th	1 Samuel	17	Romans	15	Lamentations	2	Psalms	33
26th	1 Samuel	18	Romans	16	Lamentations	3	Psalms	34
27th	1 Samuel	19	1 Corinthians	1	Lamentations	4	Psalms	35
28th	1 Samuel	20	1 Corinthians	2	Lamentations	5	Psalms	36
29th	1 Samuel	21–22	1 Corinthians	3	Ezekiel	1	Psalms	37
30th	1 Samuel	23	1 Corinthians	4	Ezekiel	2	Psalms	38
31st	1 Samuel	24	1 Corinthians	5	Ezekiel	3	Psalms	39

September

1st	1 Samuel	25	1 Corinthians	6	Ezekiel	4	Psalms	40–41
2nd	1 Samuel	26	1 Corinthians	7	Ezekiel	5	Psalms	42–43
3rd	1 Samuel	27	1 Corinthians	8	Ezekiel	6	Psalms	44
4th	1 Samuel	28	1 Corinthians	9	Ezekiel	7	Psalms	45
5th	1 Samuel	29–30	1 Corinthians	10	Ezekiel	8	Psalms	46–47
6th	1 Samuel	31	1 Corinthians	11	Ezekiel	9	Psalms	48
7th	2 Samuel	1	1 Corinthians	12	Ezekiel	10	Psalms	49
8th	2 Samuel	2	1 Corinthians	13	Ezekiel	11	Psalms	50
9th	2 Samuel	3	1 Corinthians	14	Ezekiel	12	Psalms	51
10th	2 Samuel	4–5	1 Corinthians	15	Ezekiel	13	Psalms	52–54
11th	2 Samuel	6	1 Corinthians	16	Ezekiel	14	Psalms	55
12th	2 Samuel	7	2 Corinthians	1	Ezekiel	15	Psalms	56–57
13th	2 Samuel	8–9	2 Corinthians	2	Ezekiel	16	Psalms	58–59
14th	2 Samuel	10	2 Corinthians	3	Ezekiel	17	Psalms	60–61
15th	2 Samuel	11	2 Corinthians	4	Ezekiel	18	Psalms	62–63
16th	2 Samuel	12	2 Corinthians	5	Ezekiel	19	Psalms	64–65
17th	2 Samuel	13	2 Corinthians	6	Ezekiel	20	Psalms	66–67
18th	2 Samuel	14	2 Corinthians	7	Ezekiel	21	Psalms	68
19th	2 Samuel	15	2 Corinthians	8	Ezekiel	22	Psalms	69
20th	2 Samuel	16	2 Corinthians	9	Ezekiel	23	Psalms	70–71
21st	2 Samuel	17	2 Corinthians	10	Ezekiel	24	Psalms	72
22nd	2 Samuel	18	2 Corinthians	11	Ezekiel	25	Psalms	73
23rd	2 Samuel	19	2 Corinthians	12	Ezekiel	26	Psalms	74
24th	2 Samuel	20	2 Corinthians	13	Ezekiel	27	Psalms	75–76
25th	2 Samuel	21	Galatians	1	Ezekiel	28	Psalms	77
26th	2 Samuel	22	Galatians	2	Ezekiel	29	Psalms	78:1–37
27th	2 Samuel	23	Galatians	3	Ezekiel	30	Psalms	78:38ff
28th	2 Samuel	24	Galatians	4	Ezekiel	31	Psalms	79
29th	1 Kings	1	Galatians	5	Ezekiel	32	Psalms	80
30th	1 Kings	2	Galatians	6	Ezekiel	33	Psalms	81–82

October

1st	1 Kings	3	Ephesians	1	Ezekiel	34	Psalms	83–84
2nd	1 Kings	4–5	Ephesians	2	Ezekiel	35	Psalms	85
3rd	1 Kings	6	Ephesians	3	Ezekiel	36	Psalms	86
4th	1 Kings	7	Ephesians	4	Ezekiel	37	Psalms	87–88
5th	1 Kings	8	Ephesians	5	Ezekiel	38	Psalms	89
6th	1 Kings	9	Ephesians	6	Ezekiel	39	Psalms	90
7th	1 Kings	10	Philippians	1	Ezekiel	40	Psalms	91
8th	1 Kings	11	Philippians	2	Ezekiel	41	Psalms	92–93
9th	1 Kings	12	Philippians	3	Ezekiel	42	Psalms	94
10th	1 Kings	13	Philippians	4	Ezekiel	43	Psalms	95–96
11th	1 Kings	14	Colossians	1	Ezekiel	44	Psalms	97–98
12th	1 Kings	15	Colossians	2	Ezekiel	45	Psalms	99–101
13th	1 Kings	16	Colossians	3	Ezekiel	46	Psalms	102
14th	1 Kings	17	Colossians	4	Ezekiel	47	Psalms	103
15th	1 Kings	18	1 Thessalonians	1	Ezekiel	48	Psalms	104
16th	1 Kings	19	1 Thessalonians	2	Daniel	1	Psalms	105
17th	1 Kings	20	1 Thessalonians	3	Daniel	2	Psalms	106
18th	1 Kings	21	1 Thessalonians	4	Daniel	3	Psalms	107
19th	1 Kings	22	1 Thessalonians	5	Daniel	4	Psalms	108–109
20th	2 Kings	1	2 Thessalonians	1	Daniel	5	Psalms	110–111
21st	2 Kings	2	2 Thessalonians	2	Daniel	6	Psalms	112–113
22nd	2 Kings	3	2 Thessalonians	3	Daniel	7	Psalms	114–115
23rd	2 Kings	4	1 Timothy	1	Daniel	8	Psalms	116
24th	2 Kings	5	1 Timothy	2	Daniel	9	Psalms	117–118
25th	2 Kings	6	1 Timothy	3	Daniel	10	Psalms	119:1–24
26th	2 Kings	7	1 Timothy	4	Daniel	11	Psalms	119:25–48
27th	2 Kings	8	1 Timothy	5	Daniel	12	Psalms	119:49–72
28th	2 Kings	9	1 Timothy	6	Hosea	1	Psalms	119:73–96
29th	2 Kings	10	2 Timothy	1	Hosea	2	Psalms	119:97–120
30th	2 Kings	11–12	2 Timothy	2	Hosea	3–4	Psalms	119:121–144
31st	2 Kings	13	2 Timothy	3	Hosea	5–6	Psalms	119:145–176

November

1st	2 Kings	14	2 Timothy	4	Hosea	7	Psalms	120–122
2nd	2 Kings	15	Titus	1	Hosea	8	Psalms	123–125
3rd	2 Kings	16	Titus	2	Hosea	9	Psalms	126–128
4th	2 Kings	17	Titus	3	Hosea	10	Psalms	129–131
5th	2 Kings	18	Philemon	1	Hosea	11	Psalms	132–134
6th	2 Kings	19	Hebrews	1	Hosea	12	Psalms	135–136
7th	2 Kings	20	Hebrews	2	Hosea	13	Psalms	137–138
8th	2 Kings	21	Hebrews	3	Hosea	14	Psalms	139
9th	2 Kings	22	Hebrews	4	Joel	1	Psalms	140–141
10th	2 Kings	23	Hebrews	5	Joel	2	Psalms	142
11th	2 Kings	24	Hebrews	6	Joel	3	Psalms	143
12th	2 Kings	25	Hebrews	7	Amos	1	Psalms	144
13th	1 Chronicles	1–2	Hebrews	8	Amos	2	Psalms	145
14th	1 Chronicles	3–4	Hebrews	9	Amos	3	Psalms	146–147
15th	1 Chronicles	5–6	Hebrews	10	Amos	4	Psalms	148–150
16th	1 Chronicles	7–8	Hebrews	11	Amos	5	Luke	1:1–38
17th	1 Chronicles	9–10	Hebrews	12	Amos	6	Luke	1:39ff
18th	1 Chronicles	11–12	Hebrews	13	Amos	7	Luke	2
19th	1 Chronicles	13–14	James	1	Amos	8	Luke	3
20th	1 Chronicles	15	James	2	Amos	9	Luke	4
21st	1 Chronicles	16	James	3	Obadiah	1	Luke	5
22nd	1 Chronicles	17	James	4	Jonah	1	Luke	6
23rd	1 Chronicles	18	James	5	Jonah	2	Luke	7
24th	1 Chronicles	19–20	1 Peter	1	Jonah	3	Luke	8
25th	1 Chronicles	21	1 Peter	2	Jonah	4	Luke	9
26th	1 Chronicles	22	1 Peter	3	Micah	1	Luke	10
27th	1 Chronicles	23	1 Peter	4	Micah	2	Luke	11
28th	1 Chronicles	24–25	1 Peter	5	Micah	3	Luke	12
29th	1 Chronicles	26–27	2 Peter	1	Micah	4	Luke	13
30th	1 Chronicles	28	2 Peter	2	Micah	5	Luke	14

December

1st	1 Chronicles	29	2 Peter	3	Micah	6	Luke	15
2nd	2 Chronicles	1	1 John	1	Micah	7	Luke	16
3rd	2 Chronicles	2	1 John	2	Nahum	1	Luke	17
4th	2 Chronicles	3–4	1 John	3	Nahum	2	Luke	18
5th	2 Chronicles	5–6:11	1 John	4	Nahum	3	Luke	19
6th	2 Chronicles	6:12ff	1 John	5	Habakkuk	1	Luke	20
7th	2 Chronicles	7	2 John	1	Habakkuk	2	Luke	21
8th	2 Chronicles	8	3 John	1	Habakkuk	3	Luke	22
9th	2 Chronicles	9	Jude	1	Zephaniah	1	Luke	23
10th	2 Chronicles	10	Revelation	1	Zephaniah	2	Luke	24
11th	2 Chronicles	11–12	Revelation	2	Zephaniah	3	John	1
12th	2 Chronicles	13	Revelation	3	Haggai	1	John	2
13th	2 Chronicles	14–15	Revelation	4	Haggai	2	John	3
14th	2 Chronicles	16	Revelation	5	Zechariah	1	John	4
15th	2 Chronicles	17	Revelation	6	Zechariah	2	John	5
16th	2 Chronicles	18	Revelation	7	Zechariah	3	John	6
17th	2 Chronicles	19–20	Revelation	8	Zechariah	4	John	7
18th	2 Chronicles	21	Revelation	9	Zechariah	5	John	8
19th	2 Chronicles	22–23	Revelation	10	Zechariah	6	John	9
20th	2 Chronicles	24	Revelation	11	Zechariah	7	John	10
21st	2 Chronicles	25	Revelation	12	Zechariah	8	John	11
22nd	2 Chronicles	26	Revelation	13	Zechariah	9	John	12
23rd	2 Chronicles	27–28	Revelation	14	Zechariah	10	John	13
24th	2 Chronicles	29	Revelation	15	Zechariah	11	John	14
25th	2 Chronicles	30	Revelation	16	Zechariah	12–13:1	John	15
26th	2 Chronicles	31	Revelation	17	Zechariah	13:2ff	John	16
27th	2 Chronicles	32	Revelation	18	Zechariah	14	John	17
28th	2 Chronicles	33	Revelation	19	Malachi	1	John	18
29th	2 Chronicles	34	Revelation	20	Malachi	2	John	19
30th	2 Chronicles	35	Revelation	21	Malachi	3	John	20
31st	2 Chronicles	36	Revelation	22	Malachi	4	John	21